Against Democracy and Equality

Against Democracy and Equality

The European New Right

Dr. Tomislav Sunic

ARKTOS
MMXI

Third English edition published in 2011 by Arktos Media Ltd.

First edition published in 1990 by Peter Lang Publishing, New York.

Second edition published in 2004 by Noontide Press, California.

Printed in the United Kingdom

ISBN 978-1-907166-25-9

BIC classification: Social & political philosophy (HPS)
Political structures: democracy (JPHV)

Editor: John B. Morgan
Cover Design: Andreas Nilsson
Layout: Daniel Friberg

ARKTOS MEDIA LTD.

www.arktos.com

TABLE OF CONTENTS

EDITOR'S FOREWORD

I am extremely pleased that Arktos has been given the opportunity to produce a third edition of Dr. Sunic's book *Against Democracy and Equality*. I can still remember when I came across a copy of the first edition in the 1990s, when I was in my mid-twenties. It was a crucial experience for me. By then, I had figured out that I was *of* the Right, but I had not yet found an active segment of the Right that I felt genuinely represented my own beliefs. Back then, the Internet had yet to develop into the remarkable resource that it is today, and for someone living in the United States, there was scant information available on the European New Right (ENR) available anywhere, outside of the pages of the obscure academic journal *Telos*. What little I had heard about the ENR was intriguing, however, and I was excited to find a copy of Tom's book — courtesy of my local university library — so that I could learn something about it.

I was not disappointed. It opened up a whole new world for me, a world in which the ideas of the 'true Right', as Julius Evola called it, were still being passionately defended and discussed at a high intellectual and cultural level. I was simultaneously overjoyed that such a thing existed, and disappointed since I knew there was nothing like it in America. More than a decade later, while the situation is more hopeful, there is still no 'American New Right', although at least some efforts are being made in that direction, notably through Greg Johnson's *Counter-Currents* (www.counter-currents.com), as well as Tom's own endeavours with *The Occidental Observer* (www.theoccidentalobserver.net) and with his friend Kevin MacDonald. I can also say that the work we are doing in Arktos, at least for me, is largely a result of the inspiration I received when I first read this book. We are trying to ensure that future English-speaking readers who are sympathetic to the New Right, and related schools, will have more than just a single book with which to educate themselves. A few other books — not many — on the New Right have been published since this one first appeared, most notably Michael O'Meara's outstanding *New Culture, New Right*, but Tom's book remains an unparalleled introduction to the basic figures and themes with which the ENR is concerned.

When reading this book, it should be remembered that it was initially written while the Cold War was still going on, and when Soviet Communism remained a very real presence in the daily lives of everyone in the West. While I am certain that if Tom were to rewrite it today, he would spend a lot less space discussing Communism, it is still valuable to read his thoughts on it, and not just from a historical standpoint. While the world is no longer locked in a Manichean conflict between Communism and liberal democracy, with each side prepared to incinerate the other at a moment's notice, the worldview which informed Communism is still very much alive and well throughout the world, albeit in a much more subtle form. Just as the former Soviet *apparatchiks* managed to reinvent themselves as good capitalists, the former Marxist radicals of the West from the 1960s and '70s have traded in their bombs and their mimeographed manifestoes for the more respectable garb of academia, the media and the corridors of financial and political power. In this guise, they continue to exert influence on society, especially over misguided young idealists who, to quote Evola, 'lack proper referents' when it comes to solving the political and cultural problems of the West. One only needs to consider how completely American and Western European society have been transformed over the last half-century to realise that the danger today is not from tanks or ICBMs, but rather emanates from the mouths, the keyboards, and the bank accounts of some of the wealthiest and most influential people in the world, those who have never given up the dream of realising their peculiar form of universal equality and sameness. And even Communism in its original form has yet to give up the ghost. As I write, here in India, armed Communist insurgencies are ongoing all over Asia, and it is not at all unusual in some of the poorer parts of India to come across the hammer-and-sickle or portraits of Marx, Lenin, and Stalin. In nearby West Bengal, the Maoists regularly carry out targeted assassinations — ironically, not against the wealthy, but of their own rivals in the more established Communist

Party, which has gained power there through elections. While it has suffered many setbacks around the world, Communism is far from finished, which is not surprising since, as Tom demonstrates in this book, it will always linger in the shadows so long as the ideology of liberal democracy remains pre-eminent.

This volume is not simply a reprint of the earlier edition. The book has been completely re-edited and re-formatted. Tom has contributed a new Preface for this edition, and we have also included the Preface that Alain de Benoist wrote for the Croatian edition in 2009. Lastly, we have added de Benoist's and Charles Champetier's *Manifesto for a European Renaissance*, which was written to summarise the philosophical standpoint of the ENR at the turn of the millennium, as an Appendix.

All quotations from texts cited in other languages were translated by the author himself, unless references to existing translations are made in the accompanying footnotes. In most cases I did not feel that I had anything to add to the existing text, but in a few cases I have added explanatory notes where they were needed. They are marked to distinguish them from Tom's own footnotes.

John B. Morgan IV
Mumbai, India
31 January 2011

PREFACE TO THE THIRD EDITION

Adding an additional preface to already existing prefaces may look and read strangely. More or less everything was already said about the purpose of this book in the previous editions and previous prefaces and introductions. I would like to draw the attention of my readers, however, to Alain de Benoist's new introduction, which I have translated into English, and which sheds some light on a whole set of etymological and conceptual problems, in this third edition now published by Arktos.

This book was first written in 1988 as my doctoral dissertation. It was supposed to be a small summary and an even smaller introduction to what one could roughly describe as the enormous cultural heritage of Western Right-wing thought (whatever 'West' or 'Right-wing' may mean today), of which the philosopher Alain de Benoist is a unique modern representative. The reader must be advised, however, to subsequently read his classic, encyclopaedic and thick volume *Vu de Droite*, as well as dozens of his other books and hundreds of his essays, in order to better grasp the main thesis of my book. In short, I am only trying to summarise Alain de Benoist's ideas as well as those of similar scholars, who for some clumsy, often bizarre reasons have been dubbed by their detractors as 'Right wingers' or 'New Rightists'! Therefore, for want of a better term, I will also stick to the expression 'the New Right'. However, the ideas that stand behind this awkward, voguish, derisive, often meaningless and evocative label 'the New Right' are neither on the 'Left' nor on the 'Right'. The so-called European New Right can be more accurately described as a school of thought, a cultural group comprising a substantial number of philosophers, artists, sociobiologists, poets, writers, and scientists whose main subject of research and interest is the critique of egalitarianism and the critique of the idea of progress — including the critique of their modern, postmodern, secular and mundane offshoots.

So why is this book of mine important? It is important, in my view, because it offers its readers some clues as to how to retrieve bits and pieces of what was once known as 'conservative' or 'Right wing' thought, a current of thought which has been deliberately deemphasised, forgotten, or even worse, forbidden in higher education and in public discourse by the liberal ex-Communist ruling class and its scribes. The book is also important because it provides an intellectual countercurrent to the dominant ideas that have shaped the West for well over a thousand years, especially since the fateful year of 1945. The book may also be a valuable tool for students in the humanities insofar it tries to demolish the widespread portrayal of many important thinkers in Europe and America as stupid 'rite-wingers', toothless hicks, 'nutzies' and brainless hacks, all bent on cannibalising the minds of young, multicultural children. This point is important to stress given that the dominant ideas in modern discourse are still firmly formulated by a small caste of people who call themselves 'liberal democrats' and who never tire of decorating themselves with the verbiage of 'tolerance', 'diversity', and 'human rights'.

I must admit when I first wrote this book in America — which was on the eve of the end of the Communist experiment in Eastern Europe — I was not aware that its liberal imitators in the West would become far more insidious and far more repressive against freedom of speech and free inquiry. I was naïve. Later on, the issue of political discourse and many aspects of the dominant ideas in their political usage, and especially the interpretation of some complex political concepts, I addressed in greater detail in my book *Homo Americanus: Child of the Postmodern Age* (2007). Alain de Benoist and other New Right thinkers and scholars have also done so in their far more voluminous work.

When defining the concept of the political, a volume needs to be written on the masters of modern discourse. Democracy, totalitarianism, liberalism, Nazism, Fascism, socialism, Stalinism — all these powerful labels are subject to semantic shifting; they can be a badge of honour in a given historical epoch; they can also become frightening words meant to discredit a political or intellectual opponent. Likewise, someone may strongly object to my usage of the title *Against Democracy and Equality* — as if I am hell-bent on offering a recipe for destroying democracy. Things would have been much easier if I had instead employed the terms 'mobocracy', 'plutocracy', 'mafiocracy', 'kleptocracy', or 'democratism' in order to denounce the ex-Communist and the present liberal democratic system — both systems which have never tired, to be sure, of posing as 'the only true democracy'.

Essentially, the message of my book is that political activists, usually labelled as Right-wingers or 'White racialists', must first and foremost come to terms with the crucial importance of *cultural hegemony* if they *ever* wish to carry out any meaningful political activity or aspire to political office. This has been sorely lacking, particularly among American conservatives and White racialists. Ideas always rule the world; political actions come in their wake — however well these actions may be planned, financed or executed. The so-called Left and the New Left understood that with deadly seriousness after 1945, both in the United States and Europe. That is the reason why they still thrive politically, both in Washington and in Brussels.

In the present volume I describe, in a didactic and straightforward fashion, some major thinkers who are indispensable in understanding our modernity. Of course, I understand that some readers may object that I did not include Friedrich Nietzsche, Francis Parker Yockey, Ezra Pound, or H. L. Mencken, or for that matter that I skipped over thousands of other conservative American and European authors and scientists who deserve respect. These countless authors and their postmodern significance will be covered by others someday — I hope. I do believe, however, that the present book will open up some new vistas, and, to say the least, help in the intellectual 'arming' of younger readers and students for the upcoming cultural battle.

I may have been naïve back in the late 1980s, when I daydreamed of a better and less mendacious world order while the Communist pathology was coming to an end in Eastern Europe. This time, however, beginning in 2008, I think that my predictions concerning the West (again, whatever 'the West' may mean) may be right on target. Liberalism and its various offshoots are now in their death throes, all over the West, and it is only a matter of how many years remain before we see it crash. We must all prepare for this titanic crash, whose outcome we can barely imagine at present. Hopefully, this book, short of providing a formula on how to survive the crash, may at least help the reader to spot the right alternative.

Tomislav Sunic
Zagreb, Croatia
January 2011
www.tomsunic.info

THE NEW RIGHT: FORTY YEARS AFTER[1]

Alain de Benoist

In 1990, as a current of thought under the name 'European New Right' (ENR) had begun to celebrate its twenty-first birthday, a Croatian friend of mine, Tomislav Sunic, published the first edition of his book on the New Right in English. This was originally the text of his doctoral dissertation, defended two years earlier at the University of California in Santa Barbara. Having acquired a very good knowledge of French during his studies at the University of Zagreb, Sunic was keen to probe very early on into the ENR. Moreover, he also had the opportunity to read ENR works in the original French language. Unlike many other commentators, who spoke of the ENR on the basis of hearsay and made judgments from second-hand sources, he demonstrated the ability to go right to the core of the issue. He showed sympathy for the ENR, which further distinguished him from others.

Obviously it was not just his sympathetic treatment from which most of the interest in his book was derived. The importance of his book is due to its pioneer character. Certainly, in the late 1980s, several books (but also a number of scholarly works) had already been published on the ENR, but they were almost all published in French. Tomislav Sunic's book was one of the first to appear abroad, a privilege he shared with some Italian authors. Presenting the history and

---

1   The following was written in French as a Preface to the Croatian edition of *Against Democracy and Equality* (entitled simply *The European New Right*) which was published in 2009. It has been translated by Tomislav Sunic.-Ed.

main ideas of the ENR to a public that had never heard of it before was not an easy task. Thanks to the information he presented as well as his ability to synthesise it, as well as his familiarity with the readers he addressed, there is no doubt that Sunic greatly succeeded in his endeavour.

In hindsight what I find remarkable is that Tomislav Sunic's book was written in English, given that the author resided at that time in the United States — a country he knew from the inside out and which he examined in a very critical manner (as evidenced by one of his other books, *Homo Americanus*).

When addressing the English-speaking audience, Tomislav Sunic faced difficulties that an Italian, Spanish or a German author would have never encountered. The first of these difficulties arose due to the lack of interest shown, generally speaking, in the Anglo-Saxon world for debates based upon ideas. The English, and to a greater extent the Americans, pretend to be 'pragmatic'. In philosophy, they adhere mostly to the schools of Empiricism and Positivism, if not to a purely analytical philosophy. In their craving for 'facts' they forget that facts cannot be dissociated from hermeneutics, i.e., from a given form of interpretation. The famous distinction made by David Hume between factual judgments and value judgments (the indicative and the imperative, being and what should be) can only have relative value. As for the resulting political theory, it often boils down, especially in America (with only a few notable exceptions), to purely practical considerations that steer the projects of the ruling class. This explains why intellectuals there are looked down upon and why they have never held the role of moral arbiters as is the case in other countries, notably in France.

The expression 'New Right' presented another difficulty. There was already an English New Right and an American New Right, but such 'New Rights', far from being schools of thought related to the ENR, represented rather their very opposite. Combining religious fundamentalism and moral order, coupled with a mish-mash of Atlanticism, 'Westernisation' and with the defence of capitalism and adherence to free market ideology superimposed on it, such Anglo-American New Rights in fact represent everything of which the ENR has always been critical — and this in a very radical manner. Sympathisers of the New Right, who might have otherwise been intrigued by Tomislav Sunic's book, must surely have been disappointed.

In general, and irrespective of all the misunderstandings that may have been caused by such a label (I will come back to that later) it must have been very arduous, on the other side of the Atlantic, to attempt to grasp the meaning of the ENR. What one dubs in America 'the Right' consists in fact of two currents. One is mainstream, moderate, and based upon the middle class, corresponding to 'conservative' circles (themselves divided into numerous sects and clans) and whose main characteristic is its unwavering praise for the economic system — i.e., capitalism — and which, in fact, leads to the destruction of everything else for which it stands. The other current is spearheaded by a faction of radicals, often embodied by small extremist groups, describing themselves as 'racialists' and whose ideology boils down to a simplistic mixture of nationalism and xenophobia. For its part not only has the ENR never identified itself with any of these Anglo-Saxon New Right sects, but has consistently fought against their principles and their premises.

One must add to this another ambiguity, pertaining to vocabulary. I will only use one example. In the realm of ideas the ENR has consistently targeted liberalism as one of its chief adversaries. The word 'liberal' has a radically different meaning in Western Europe than it does in the United States. On the other side of the Atlantic, a 'liberal' is an individual leaning to the centre-Left who defends a particular form of social policy, and who also advocates a state which redistributes wealth. He is also easy-going in terms of social mores and tends to be a great proponent of the ideology of human rights. We call him in France a 'progressive'. In contrast, on this side of the Atlantic, a liberal is primarily a spokesman of individualism, a supporter of free trade, and an opponent of the state (and also a supporter of America). If one asks a Frenchman to quote the name of some well-known liberal politician, the names of Ronald Reagan and Margaret Thatcher would immediately come to his mind. In other words, what we call 'liberal' corresponds to a large extent to that what the Americans call a 'conservative' — and therefore the foe of a 'liberal'! This difference has historical origins: the Americans have retained the original meaning of the word 'liberalism' which, when it first appeared as a doctrine in the Eighteenth century, actually stood for a 'Leftist' current of thought, being the primary heir of the philosophy of the Enlightenment. In Europe, in contrast, the Liberals were gradually pushed to the Right by incoming Socialist and Communist currents of thought, to the point that the Liberals, as of the late Nineteenth century, began to identify themselves with the conservative bourgeoisie (sometimes called 'Orléanistes' in France). We can see right away what kind of scorn such a book could be subjected to in America, a book representing an 'antiliberal' current of thought, and which attracts all kinds of associations based upon misunderstanding.

Finally, there is no doubt that criticism of the United States and of the Americanisation of the world, which has resulted from the gradual assertion of American hegemony, and which has been a standard topic of the ENR discourse, could hardly seduce Americans who perceive their country, not only as the 'Promised Land' and the incarnation of the best of all possible worlds, but also, and precisely for that reason, as a model way of life that merits to be exported worldwide. It is significant that very few texts by ENR authors have been translated into English although they have been translated into fifteen other languages. This seems to be a sign that the 'old Europe' (or the so-called 'rest of the world') will never be fully understood across the Atlantic unless it becomes totally Americanised. The ENR remains *terra incognita* for the vast majority of Americans.[2]

The English edition of Tomislav Sunic' book carries the title *Against Democracy and Equality: The European New Right.* I suspect the author chose this title out of sheer provocation—a title that I have always considered inappropriate! It must be emphasised that the ENR has never held positions hostile to equality and democracy. It has been critical of egalitarianism and has highlighted the limits of liberal democracy—which is quite a different matter. Between equality and egalitarianism there is roughly the same difference as between liberty and liberalism, between the universal and universalism, or between the common good and Communism. Egalitarianism aims at

---

2   Let us mention the special issue of the journal *Telos, New Right — New Left — New Paradigm?* (issue 98-99, Autumn-Winter 1993), as well as the book by Michael O'Meara, *New Culture, New Right: Anti-Liberalism in Postmodern Europe* (Bloomington: 1stBooks, 2004). I would add that criticism of the United States by the ENR has never slid off into 'americanophobia'. Quite the contrary. The ENR has instead welcomed a number of writers and thinkers from the U.S.A., few in number, but not without importance. Let me refer to the theorists of communitarianism, such as the American Michael Sandel, the Canadian Charles Taylor, the Englishman Alasdair MacIntyre, and especially Christopher Lasch, also from America, a theorist of 'populist socialism' who calls to mind the great George Orwell. Lasch's ideas were popularised by Paul Piccone in his journal, *Telos*.

introducing equality where there is no place for it and where it does not match with reality, as for instance when somebody argues that all individuals have the same skills and the same gifts. But egalitarianism also aims at apprehending equality as a synonym for 'sameness', i.e., the opposite of diversity. Yet the opposite of equality is inequality and not diversity. Equality of men and women, for example, does not obliterate the reality of the differences between the two sexes. Similarly, equal political rights in democracy do not presuppose that all citizens must be identical or have the same talents; rather they must have the same rights based on their belonging equally to the same polity of citizens.

The ENR has always denounced what I have named the ideology of sameness, i.e., the universalist ideology, which under a religious or a profane veneer aims at reducing the diversity of the world, such as the diversity of cultures, value systems, and rooted ways of life, to one uniform model. The implementation of the ideology of sameness leads to the reduction and eradication of differences. Being fundamentally ethnocentric despite its universalistic claims, it has never stopped legitimising all forms of imperialism. In the past, it was exported by missionaries who wished to convert the entire planet to the worship of one God; later, in the same vein, by colonisers who, in the name of the 'course of history' and the cult of 'progress', wanted to impose their way of life on 'indigenous peoples'. Today it carries on under the sign of the capitalist system (*forme-capital*, i.e., capitalism as a way of life and thought) which, by subjugating the symbolic imagination to mercantile values, turns the world into a vast and homogeneous marketplace in which individuals, reduced to the role of producers and consumers (and soon to become commodities themselves), are destined to adopt the mentality of *Homo economicus*. Insofar as it seeks to reduce diversity, which is the only true wealth of mankind, the ideology of sameness is itself a caricature of equality. In fact it creates inequalities of the most unbearable kind. In contrast, equality is quite another matter, particularly when it must be defended.

As for democracy, whose primary tenet is equal political rights, the ENR, which has never had any taste for despotism, nor for dictatorship, and even less so for totalitarianism, has always considered it to be, if not the best possible, at least the regime that best meets the requirements of our times. But we must first understand its exact meaning. Democracy is the regime in which sovereignty resides in the people. But for the people, in order to be truly sovereign, it must be able to express itself freely and those whom it designates as its representatives must act in accordance with its wishes. That is why true democracy is participatory democracy, i.e., a democracy which allows people to exercise their sovereignty as often as possible and not just during elections. In this sense universal suffrage is only a technical means to assess the degree of consent between the government and the governed. As understood by the ancient Greeks, democracy, in the final analysis, is a system that allows all of its citizens to participate actively in public affairs. This means that liberty in democracy is defined as an opportunity to participate in activities that are deployed in the public sphere, and certainly not as the freedom to become oblivious to the public sphere, or to withdraw oneself into the private sphere. A purely representative democracy is, at best, an imperfect democracy. Political power must be exercised at all levels, and not only from the top. This is only feasible by means of implementing the principle of subsidiarity, which means that the people make as many decisions as possible regarding issues of concern to them, and relegate matters that concern large communities to a higher level of decision-making. In an age when political representatives are more and more cut off from the people and where the authority of the appointed and the corrupt prevails over those who were elected, and where a politician is stripped of his decision-making powers on behalf of some 'governance' whose only goal is to mould the government of the people in accordance with the wishes of business or corporate managers, the priority must be to resuscitate participatory democracy — a grass-roots democracy and a direct democracy. The active public sphere, which is the only one capable of upholding the social relationship and guarantee the exercise of common values, must also be revived.

When this book was first published in 1990, Tomislav Sunic was obviously not able to take into account what has happened since that time. Over the last eighteen years, in light of the fact that numerous works have been published in the field of social critique, the objectives of the ENR have become more focused. However brief it could be I do not intend to write a summary of it, given that this is the *raison d'être* of Sunic's present book. However, I am glad that his book contains as an appendix the full translation of the *Manifesto for a European Renaissance*, first published in 1999, which proposes a method of orientation for the ENR at the dawn of the Twenty first century and, which, to date, has been translated into Spanish, Italian, English, German,

Hungarian, and Dutch. The reader can thus keep track of everything which the ENR has written over the past two decades about social science, Europe, postmodernity, federalism, the contrast between a nation-state and an empire, the critique of the ideology of labour, the capitalist system, 'governance', the decline of the political, the crisis of democracy, the question of identity, environmental threats, criticism of 'development', new prospects opened by the theory of economic decline, and so on.

Nonetheless I would like to focus on some important issues. To start I will mention the continuity of work undertaken and implemented by the ENR since 1968. The ENR is exactly forty years old now. The main journals that are part of our current of thought have shown their longevity: *Nouvelle École* was launched in 1968, *Éléments* in 1973, and *Krisis* in 1988. Even if duration and continuity are not the only qualities that one takes into account, one must agree, however, that there are but a few schools of thought that have remained active for a such an extended period of time. Therefore, the ENR is primarily an ongoing story. But it is also a record of where we have been. Over the last forty years, the ENR has published a considerable number of books and articles; it has organised countless conferences, symposia, meetings, summer schools, etc. In doing so, it has abandoned some paths that it had wrongly judged to be promising at the beginning, while continually exploring new ones and thus remaining faithful to its 'encyclopaedic' inspiration from the very beginning of its journey.

I must also point out that, from the very beginning, the ENR has viewed itself as a school of thought and not as a political movement. This school of thought has by far exceeded the organisational structures of an association, which was first known as the Groupement de recherche et d'études pour la civilisation européenne (GRECE, or the Research Group for the Study of European Civilisation), founded in 1968. With its publications the ENR has been engaged in metapolitical work. What does metapolitics mean? Certainly not a different way of doing politics. The issue of metapolitics was born out of a consciousness of the role of ideas in history and out of the conviction that any type of intellectual, cultural, doctrinal and ideological work must be a prerequisite for any form of (political) action. This is something that activists, who constantly argue about 'urgency' (only to safeguard themselves from any in-depth type of reflection), or who simply prefer a reactive mode of action to a reflective mode — have a great difficulty in understanding. To sum it up with a simple formula: the Enlightenment was born before the French Revolution, but the French Revolution would not have been possible without the Enlightenment. Before any Lenin, there must always be some preceding Marx. This is what Antonio Gramsci understood very well when he addressed 'organic' intellectuals. He stressed that the transformation of political and socio-historical structures in a given epoch implies that this epoch must already initiate within itself a vast transformation of values.

The ENR was founded in the late 1960s by young people who, in most cases, had some experience as political activists and could therefore measure the shortcomings and limitations of such an approach. In an effort to lay the foundations for a political philosophy and in order to develop a concept for a new world, they wanted to somehow start from scratch and were ready to give up illusions about any immediate political action.

By that time, however, they had become aware of the simplistic and obsolete cleavage between Left and Right. They knew that every society is in need of conserving and changing. They were ready to critically examine the tradition in order to identify its operating and living principle, while also tackling the major problems of their time from a truly revolutionary perspective. Undoubtedly, this explains their interest in, among other things, the 'Conservative Revolution' in Weimar Germany. In general, they rejected false antitheses. They adhered to the logic of 'the inclusive third'. They did not claim, 'We are neither on the Right nor on the Left' — which means nothing. Rather, they decided to be both 'on the Right and on the Left'. They wanted to make clear that they were determined to examine the ideas they considered to be the best, regardless of the labels that those ideas had acquired. As far as they were concerned, there were no 'Rightist ideas' vs. 'Leftist ideas', but only false ideas vs. just ideas.

These convictions soon found justification in the evolution of history in recent decades. The Left-Right divide, having been born with modernity, is now in the process of fading away with the passing of modernity. This does not mean that in the past, the labels 'Right' and 'Left' were devoid of meaning, but these notions were always equivocal, given that there has never existed any 'ontological' Right and Left, but rather a large variety of different 'Lefts' and 'Rights'. The spectrum was so large that there is no doubt that some of these Lefts and some of these Rights were closer to each other than they were when taken separately from other Rights and other Lefts respectively. This also explains why certain issues — such as regionalism, ecology, federalism, the ideology of progress, and so on, have, in the course of time, drifted from the Right to the Left or vice versa. The ideology of progress, if one were to mention only one of the above issues, has clearly moved into the 'Rightist' camp, to the point that it is the liberals now who have become its avid supporters, whereas a significant part of the 'Left' remains radically critical of it as part of its fight against industrialism and its defence of the ecosystem. Notions such as Right and Left have become meaningless today. They only survive in the field of parliamentary politics, after becoming obsolete in the fields of ideas. Let us mention an important fact: all major events in recent decades, far from resurrecting the Left-Right cleavage, have, on the contrary, revealed new dividing lines, which only indicates the complete reconfiguration of the political and ideological landscape. For example, the two Gulf wars, the establishment of the European Union, and the Balkan conflicts, have all split up the traditional Left and the traditional Right, thus confirming the anachronism of this dichotomy.

The preceding lines will help us understand why I am reluctant to use the denomination 'the New Right'. It should be recalled that, when it was first coined, this expression was never used as a self-description. In fact, this label was invented by the media in 1979 to depict a school of thought and an intellectual and cultural current, born eleven years earlier and which, until then, had never described itself using this label. However, in view of the fact that this expression had become so widespread, it had to be more or less adopted thereafter. But it was never used without apprehensions, for several reasons. The first is that this label is reductive in a twofold manner: first, it suggested that the ENR was essentially a political organisation — which has never been the case. It also positioned our school of thought within a denomination (the 'Right') which our school of thought has always opposed. The second reason is that it facilitated and unjustifiably suggested links to various movements in several countries who use this label themselves. I have already given the example of the Anglo-Saxon New Right organisations. Other parallels, equally significant, could also be drawn. In Italy, our friends from the *Nuova Destra* have long ago renounced this expression. We did the same in France. I happen to define myself as a 'man of Right-Left' — i.e., as an intellectual who simultaneously refers to the ideas of the Left and the values of the Right.

What is equally important is the fact that the ENR has never claimed any predecessors. It has never claimed to be pursuing a road paved by others who came before. It has greatly benefited from numerous readings, but it has never attached itself exclusively to one single author, or a single current of thought. The eclecticism of its references has sometimes been criticised — wrongly in my opinion. Based on a hasty and fragmentary reading, some were quick to conclude that the ENR lacks coherence. The diversity of its approaches prompted many who observed the ENR, whether in a sympathetic or a hostile manner, to voice erroneous opinions about it. Quite the contrary, the approach of the ENR has always been strictly consistent. But this approach cannot be understood unless one realises that the leading figures of the ENR always utilise a dynamic perspective: their goal has never been to repeat slogans or utter preconceived ideas, or even dish out small and dogmatic catechisms written in stone once and for all time. Instead, they have always strived to move forward, in order to put their ideas into action and open up new vistas of analysis.

It is precisely for this reason that the ideas of the ENR, at the dawn of the Twenty-first century, are more apposite than ever before. Why? Because we have now entered a world different from the one that prevailed after the end of the Second World War. With the fall of the Berlin Wall, the disintegration of the Soviet system and the rise of globalisation, we are witnessing not only the end of the Twentieth century, but the end of the great historical cycle of modernity. We have entered the era of postmodernity, which is characterised by waves, flood tides and ebb tides; a time of communities and networks; but also an epoch of the rise of major blocs comprising civilisations and continents. Certainly, this mutation, which is still in process, is not over yet. We are in a period of transition, and like all periods of transition, it is especially rich in uncertainties, in new projects and new syntheses. One could characterise this epoch as *Zwischenzeit*, or an *interregnum*. In such an epoch it is indispensable, more than ever before, to be aware of the historical moment we live in. But we cannot analyse this historical moment and everything new it brings about (and a harbinger of future developments) by referring to the images of the past, and especially not by using old references and obsolete conceptual tools. It is precisely because the ENR has never shunned from evolving and renewing its discourse that it is now able to provide the necessary elements for carrying out an orderly critical assessment that matches the realities of our time.

When Soviet Communism collapsed, an American commentator, Francis Fukuyama, ventured to predict the 'end of history'. What he meant by that was that after the fall of Communism, capitalism and liberal democracy had lost their main competitor, and that from now on, all peoples on Earth were compelled to adopt, more or less in a long-term manner, the 'Western', or short of that, the American model. This thesis was subsequently criticised by Samuel Huntington, who assumed the role of a theoretician of the 'clash of civilisations'. Both visions were wrong. Instead of the end of history, we have been witnessing, in recent years, the return of history. How indeed can history ever come to a 'stop'? Human history is always open to a plurality of possibilities, and such plurality can never be defined in advance and with certainty. History is unpredictable because the characteristic of a human being — precisely because of its fundamentally historical nature — is to be always unpredictable. If history became predictable, it would no longer be human history. It would not be history at all. It is striking that none of the major events that have occurred in the world over the last decades have been predicted by specialists in futurology. Huntington, for his part, was right in his argument against Fukuyama's daydreaming, noting that humanity is not a unified whole. But his mistake was to believe that 'civilisations' can become full-fledged actors in international politics, which has never been the case. Samuel Huntington's thesis was obviously designed to legitimise Islamophobia, which is inherent in the hegemonic views of the United States of America (which quickly found a 'substitute devil' in a caricaturised Islam, badly needed after the disappearance of the Soviets' 'evil empire'). It is quite revealing that in order to perpetuate or consolidate the 'Atlanticist' mentality, Huntington does not hesitate to cut Europe in two, placing its Western part into the camp of America, while throwing its Eastern part over to Russia and the Orthodox world.

The ENR, however, has never lost sight of its main reference: Europe. Europe is conceived in its dual historical and geopolitical dimensions. First, in its historical dimension, because the nations of Europe, apart from what separates them (which is not negligible), are heirs of a common cultural matrix, which is at least five thousand years old. Then there is also the geopolitical dimension. As we enter the era of 'large spaces' (*Grossraum*), as described by Carl Schmitt, those large groups of culture and civilisations will be factors of decision-making within tomorrow's globalised world. In order to think in terms of globalisation, at a time when nation-states are too large to meet the expectations of their citizens and too small to meet the global challenges of our time and are thus becoming less powerful with each passing day, requires first and foremost to think in terms of continents.

The ENR has also been in favour of a federal Europe, because full-fledged federalism is the only way to reconcile the necessary unity of decision at the top with all due respect for the diversity and autonomy at the bottom of the pyramid. Undoubtedly, federalism follows the tradition of the Empire, rather than that of the nation-state. Europe would indeed be meaningless if it were to be built on the false model of centralisation inherent to Jacobinism, from which France has suffered for such a long period of time. Hence the need for the principle of subsidiarity mentioned above.

The construction of Europe, which we are witnessing today, is the very opposite of its principle. From the outset, this construct went against common sense. It gave priority to trade and economics instead of to politics and culture. It was built from the top — starting with the European Commission, which soon became omnipotent although devoid of any democratic legitimacy — instead of trying to gradually build itself from the bottom. It embarked on a hasty expansion into countries wishing to join the European Union solely in order to receive financial help and move closer to America and NATO, instead of having as its goal the in-depth strengthening of its political structures. Thus it has condemned itself in advance to powerlessness and paralysis. It has been built without the will of its peoples while trying to impose on them a draft of its constitution, without ever raising a question as to who constitutes the constituent power. Moreover, it has never been clear regarding the desired outcome of its own endeavours. Should one first construct a vast free trade area with unclear borders that would serve as a sidekick of America, or rather should it first lay the foundations for a genuine European power, with borders demarcated by geopolitics and which could simultaneously serve as a new model of civilisation and a pole for the better regulation of the globalisation process? These two projects are incompatible. If we were to adopt the first one, we will live tomorrow in a unipolar world subservient to American power. In contrast, in a multipolar world we can preserve the diversity of the world. This is the alternative most Europeans face: to be the architects of their own history or to become the subjects of the history of others.

When Tomislav Sunic wrote his thesis on the ENR he could not predict the tragic events that would accompany the breakup of the former Yugoslavia and the subsequent wars which caused so much horrific bloodshed in his own country, as well as in neighbouring countries. I myself witnessed those events with a broken heart. I have had Croatian and Serbian friends for a very long time, as well as Slovenian and Bosnian friends — friends who are Christians and friends who are Muslims. For me that conflict meant the failure of Europe, and especially a sign of its impoverishment. Each time European peoples fight each other, it is always to the benefit of political and ideological systems that yearn to see the disappearance of all peoples. Adding insult to injury, it was humiliating to see the U.S. air bombardment of a European capital, Belgrade, for the first time since 1945.

I know well the historical roots of all these disputes, which too often resulted in wars and massacres in Central and Eastern Europe. I know well the reasons on all sides. These disputes still feed upon ethnic nationalism, religious intolerance and irredentism of all sorts. Not wishing to take sides — since I do not wish to elevate myself to the position of supreme judge — I nevertheless believe that these disputes must be overcome. Many of these disputes hark back to the times that are definitively over. Irredentism, in particular, makes no sense at the present time. Once upon a time borders played a significant role: they guaranteed the continuation of collective identities. Today, boundaries no longer guarantee anything and do not stop or halt anything. Flows and fluxes of all kinds are the hallmark of our time, making borders obsolete. Serbs and Croats, Hungarians and Romanians, Ukrainians and Russians watch the same movies, listen to the same songs, consume the same information, use the same technology, and are subject to the same influences — and are in the same way subject to Americanisation. I know that past antagonisms are difficult to overcome. But my deepest belief is that the identity of a people will always be less threatened by the identity of another neighbouring people than by the ideology of sameness, i.e., by the homogenising juggernaut of globalisation, and by the global system for which any collective identity whatsoever is an obstacle that needs to be erased.

Once the noose was loosened, countries that were once part of the Soviet and Communist *glacis* believed they had found in the West the paradise they had so long dreamed about. In reality they exchanged one system of coercion for yet another system of coercion, different but equally fearsome. One can argue, based on our experience, that global capitalism has proved much more effective than Communism in dissolving collective identities. It proved to be much more materialistic. In a few years it managed to impose on a global scale a model of *Homo economicus*, i.e., a creature whose main reason to exist in this world is reduced to the role of production and consumption. As shown by liberal anthropology, this being is selfish and dedicated purely to the quest for his own best interest. It would be frightening to see in the countries of Central and Eastern Europe only two categories of people: on the one hand the Western liberals, and on the other, chauvinistic nationalists. There is also something fascinating in observing former *apparatchiks* making themselves virgins again by prostrating themselves in front of America — and this with the same alacrity they once used when bending over for the Communist system. The countries in which they now live were yesterday's satellites of Moscow. Today, many of them seem to be too eager to become vassals of Washington. In either case, Europe loses again.

The ENR makes a great effort to identify its real enemy. The main enemy is, on the economic level, capitalism and the market society; on the philosophical level, individualism; on the political front, universalism; on the social front, the bourgeoisie; and on the geopolitical front, America. Why capitalism? Because, contrary to what Communism preached, capitalism is not only an economic system. It is first and foremost an anthropological system, based on values that colonise the symbolic imagination and radically transform it. It is a system that reduces everything of value to its values in the market, and to exchange value. It is a system that considers secondary, transient, or non-existent everything that cannot be reduced to a number in terms of quantity, such as money. Finally, it is a dynamic system whose very structure forces it to engage in a frantic attempt to get ahead of itself. Karl Marx was not wrong when he wrote that capital considers any limitation as an obstacle. The capitalist system consists of the logic of 'always more' — more trade, more market, more goods, more profit — in the belief that 'more' means automatically better. It is the universal imposition of the axiom of interest, i.e., the idea that infinite material growth is possible in a finite world. It is domination through the 'enframing' (*l'arraisonnement*) of the whole Earth — the *Gestell* as mentioned by Heidegger — by the values of efficiency, performance and profitability. It means transforming the planet into a giant supermarket and a giant civilisation of commerce.

I first met Tomislav Sunic in Washington in June 1991, in the company of Paul Gottfried. At the end of March 1993, we participated together in a symposium organised by the journal *Telos,* which was attended by the late Paul Piccone, Thomas Molnar, Gary Ulmen, Tom Fleming, Anthony Sullivan, and so on. Since then, we have been seeing each other frequently, both in Paris (in June 1993, in January 2002, in October 2003, in March 2006, etc.), in Flanders and elsewhere. This book enables us to meet again, but this time in his homeland. I am very pleased with that.

Alain de Benoist
Paris
January 2009

INTRODUCTION AND ACKNOWLEDGMENTS TO THE SECOND EDITION (2003)

When writing a preface to the second edition of his book, the author may be tempted to be too apologetic. Aside from the lengthy list of his fellow travellers, moral supporters, nephews, wives, etc., who must figure in a book's preface, one often encounters a dose of the author's own *mea culpa*, and his refusal to admit that his original views or predictions could have been initially wrong. Who, after all, wants to be associated with his written ideas that, a decade later, may have turned out to be disproven? When I wrote this book approximately thirteen years ago, although I used a neutral and descriptive style, a reader could definitely spot that both in terms of style and substance, the book reflected not just the views of 'New Right' authors, but also my own.

A reader can therefore now call me to account on some of the subjects which I, or for that matter the 'New Right' authors themselves, discussed in the first edition of this book. Firstly, it needs to be pointed out that New Right authors, contrary to their wishful thinking, have not played a cohesive pedagogical role as they announced in their earlier voluminous writings. More than ever before, New Right intellectuals in Europe remain scattered in dozens of feuding and vanity-prone clans which, despite the enormous erudition of some of their members, have not been able to win over cultural hegemony from the Left, let alone dislodge the liberal establishment. In addition, the name 'New Right' continues to lend itself in Europe to confusing connotations, false accusations, and outright media vilification. Perhaps the denomination 'New Right' should never have been used. After all, the very antithesis and mortal enemy of the European New Right, which by the beginning of the Twenty-first century came to hold a firm cultural and political grip upon the United States, also carries the title of the New Right — better known as the 'neo-conservatives'!

An uninitiated reader can also shrug off some of my gloomy discussions concerning Communism and Alexander Zinoviev, a former Russian dissident whom I discuss in the last chapter. Communism is now dead and gone and its legal superstructure is of no interest to its erstwhile followers. But is it really?

I do think, however, and without any false sympathy, that the European New Right, despite its limited influence, has played a revolutionary role in the European and American cultural scene, whose effects will be visible in the years and decades to come. When one rereads de Benoist's early essays on liberalism, totalitarianism, and on 'soft repression' in the so-called democratic West, one can spot a man of great vision and insight. Few can dispute that despite the fact that Communism has been swept away, its soft replica under Orwellian clichés of 'human rights', 'tolerance', 'sensitivity training', and 'multiculturalism', have operated more successfully in the West — without leaving any traces of blood or homemade gulags. Those of us who had the opportunity to live under Communism had the privilege of knowing exactly who our enemy was. Masses of people in the liberal West often ignore their true enemy — whom they often cherish and adore as a friend. Therefore, I must continue to argue that Communist principles are alive and well in the United States and Europe, albeit decorating themselves with different iconography and resorting to a different language.

It could probably be argued that accepting the label 'New Right' presupposes a more distinct form of intellectual sensibility than a credo of political adherence. Given the diversity of its followers and sympathisers, both in the United States and Europe, probably the only common denominator that links them all is their non-conformism and rejection of academic fads and modern myths. Its authors and sympathisers must be credited with impeccable intellectual integrity and a refusal to sell out to the ruling liberal class at the turn of the century. Although there are few if any contacts amidst chief figures of the European New Right, all of them, however, have ventured into the dangerous territory of freedom of speech and 'political incorrectness', often risking vilification by the modern thought police and their well-paid media clerks and court historians. Whether one has in mind the challenging work of the historian Mark Weber from the Institute for Historical Review, or the evolutionary theorist Kevin MacDonald, or for that matter, of some French or German scholar trying to 'revise' the role of some literary figures dating back to the period prior to the Second World War—all of these intellectuals, researchers, and militants can be classified as being part of the European New Right.

After the end of the Cold War and following the rapid disillusionment with the liberal system, particularly in post-Communist countries in the East, it is imperative to study the views of the European New Right and its intellectual forefathers and precursors, both in the United States and Europe.

*

I would like to express my thanks to Michael Lyster, a former student of mine at California State University at Fullerton, for proofreading and typing the first edition of this monograph. I am also grateful to Eric Smith, who made valuable suggestions regarding the style and format of this book. I also need to thank Joseph Pryce and David Stennett for their help.

Parts of the book have appeared in different forms in *The World and I*, *The Journal of Social, Political, and Economic Studies*, and *CLIO: A Journal of Literature, History and the Philosophy of History*.

Tomislav Sunic
Zagreb, Croatia
May 2003

PREFACE TO THE
SECOND EDITION

David J. Stennett

In his Preface to the first edition of Dr. Sunic's book, Dr. Paul Gottfried suggests that the New Right is not a singular, cohesive intellectual movement, but represents currents of thoughts of various 'pro-European' individuals opposed to the liberal-communistic *status quo*. Therefore, there is no need to retort in an idiosyncratic manner and pitch a tent in the same camp. I shall restrict my comments to addressing the European New Right as an admirer, not as one of its members.

I do agree that if there ever was an intellectual movement which could be considered the diagnostician of cultural malignancy, then the European New Right has played this part well. Dr. Sunic, who is sympathetic to the New Right, sets before us the New Right's fundamental targets: Liberalism (social egalitarianism from its inception during The Terror of 1793), Christianity (as a religion of egalitarianism and Levantine proto-totalitarianism), Capitalism (with its transformative process of turning the sacred into the profane, and the worship of crass materialism), and finally Marxism-Communism (The Terror forged into an economic system).

The first two, Liberalism and Christianity, were dealt with at considerable length by the European New Right's intellectual forebears, the Conservative Revolutionaries of the pre-Second World War generation and their predecessors. Friedrich Nietzsche wrote that 'God is dead', that Christianity as a force was all but spent; it was the last purveyor of 'slave morality' which would eventually lead to the 'last man' in an age of 'democracy' and 'equality', with unforeseen decadence. The Overman, a being in possession of 'master morality', would eventually regain his rightful place in the world of the eternal recurrence.

Oswald Spengler, who owed his philosophy to the influence of Nietzsche and Goethe, penned his magnum opus *The Decline of the West* under the spell of both. In it, among many observations, Spengler notes that an excess of rationalism and technology will all but kill the spiritual world that is a prerequisite to make the soil in which culture develops fertile. To Spengler, decline was inevitable, but the modern European-Faustian culture was not necessarily doomed. Although Spengler believed that only the spirituality of the Slavic peoples could initiate high culture, once they threw off the yoke of Bolshevism, drastic corrective measures, if rigorously enforced, could slow down or reverse the process of decline. After the German revolution of 1933, Spengler embraced the German National Socialist doctrine, although this mutual romance did not last long.

With the defeat of National Socialism and the absolute triumph of plutocracy and Bolshevism came the turning of the tide after 1945, as Sunic and other New Right authors attest. For men on the 'Right', things turned from bad to worse. National Socialist atrocities, real or alleged, completely turned the 'right side' upside-down, even as Allied atrocities were swept under the rug. This gave the Marxist Left the moral imperative, which it has maintained ever since as a virtual monopoly, in all of the ex-Eastern and Western European establishments.

Unfazed, albeit not responsible for the events of the Second World War, the leading authors of the European New Right continued to carry, at least in part, the torch that had been lost by the Weimar-era Conservative Revolutionaries in their fight against liberalism, materialism, Christianity, and Marxism. In a similar vein as their heavyweight predecessor, Julius Evola, who called for 'pagan imperialism' in the 1920s, the New Right, by the mid-1960s, started once again to shout that a 'pagan' universe in the real world was not only possible, but necessary. Therefore, a radical cleansing of all things Levantine became mandatory.

Unfortunately, as the New Right proclaims, and as Sunic helps to clarify, this cannot happen in a world where the level of material comfort determines the *summum bonum*. When the pursuit of material comfort takes precedence over all other human affairs, the world as the sacred sanctuary of human existence becomes a profane and unbearable mess. Regardless of whether the system is called Marxism-Communism or capitalism, both of them encapsulate the history of humanity as the quest for material accumulation, forcing upon mankind the idea that the world must exist solely for economic enrichment. These two systems, as the New Right argues, are the mortal enemies of all rooted peoples. The New Right's criticism does not stop there. Sunic shows us that, once The Terror of 1793 had been unleashed, liberalism and its incipient theology of absolute equality, i.e., mass social levelling, began to gather momentum. Mobocracy and mediocrity led to the breakdown of the natural order of authority, and as Nietzsche succinctly stated, it brought about a 'transvaluation of all values'.

As each genuine authority was weakened and as abstract individualism was placed upon the pedestal of the new politically correct priesthood, equality-mongers monopolised the discourse both in Western academe and the political arena. Yet this victory cannot last long. Liberalism means equality before the law, but it cannot find a remedy to the inequality of histories, races, human biology and IQs. Accordingly, equality zealots first found an ideal terrain among professional Marxist rabble-rousers, and later, amidst their latter-day acolytes, the American academic affirmative action pontiffs. They all argue that men are not only supposed to be equal before the law, but also in the billfold.

A deeper analysis of the New Right's assault on these two systems would take volumes, and it is up to the reader to seek out and find the appropriate chapter in this book for their own critical inquiry of modern 'soft' liberal totalitarianism.

As the reader will notice, the New Right takes its enemies apart at the seams, although questions arise as to whether New Right authors have the gusto to lead European Man out of his darkness and into a new era of personal enlightenment. No doubt, their arguments are persuasive, and when studied closely from a rational and scientific viewpoint, their ideas do seem to be sound. However, the world still turns as if there were no New Right authors on the European and American intellectual and educational horizons.

What could explain this lack of influence by the New Right? This should be obvious: humans are irrational creatures, today easily manipulated by false images and powerful opinion makers. The New Right observes that 'culture is the soul of politics'. But if this is the case, why are the people of the New Right still ignored? One must admit that culture today is no longer defined by 'intellectuals' sitting behind desks, but by rootless and alien producers, writers, and directors from behind digital cameras.

The New Right, like their Conservative Revolutionary predecessors, eschews technology, and for good reasons. However, its ignorance of how to utilise technology and its failure to access an important segment of the population have weakened its effectiveness. If the New Right wishes to counter this, it must take to the airwaves and to the Internet. At no time in world history has a man had the ability to transmit his personal ideas to the entire planet as quickly as he can today. Those intellectuals who fail to embrace new technologies are destined to die out.

More importantly, cultural decay must be rooted out at its cause, not just at the symptomatic level. In the preceding century, fascist movements showed that disciplined organisations were the only viable means to victory. The New Right, as a cultural diagnostician, has shown us things that need to be avoided, but it has failed to provide educational methods needed to help achieve the 'right' cultural dominance. Intellectual battles today are waged on different fronts and they require a radically new school syllabus.

The world, as it currently stands, is controlled by money and the media. The New Right despises these two instruments of power, but unless it is willing to embrace them, it will fail. This does not mean, however, that the New Right's efforts have been in vain. Its prolific authors have influenced and gained followers in many countries in Europe and North America. Should the New Right's authors and its disciples quickly learn to master technology, including the virtually uninhibited Internet, and actively wield the power of finance capitalism, they will garner a much larger following and transfer the reins of power into their spheres of influence.

Whether or not Sunic's observations about the New Right are correct or not is beside the point. What matters are results, and results are the by-products of clear plans of action. If, after reading Sunic's work, the reader finds some appreciation for the New Right, and in addition, detects a clearer picture of what must be done to compel victory, then this book has served its purpose. At this juncture it is worthwhile quoting an icon of the New Right, Ernst Jünger: 'Again we have to substitute the sword for the pen, the blood for the ink, the deed for the word, the sacrifice for the sensibility — we must do all this, or others will kick us into the dirt.'

David J. Stennett
St. Petersburg, Russia
MMDCCLVI a.u.c.

PREFACE TO THE
FIRST EDITION (1990)

Paul Gottfried

The following book is the first in English dedicated to a culturally significant theme hitherto largely ignored by Anglo-American scholars: the Continental European Right since 1945. Tomislav Sunic does not deal with the conventional political right-of-centre in European parliamentary states. Rather, he focuses on the dominant ideas of what today in Europe is called the New Right. Clusters of editors and professors of philosophy, political theory, linguistics, and anthropology who proclaim their 'European' identity, New Right intellectuals are found today in most major Western and Central European countries. They speak of preserving Europe against military imperialism from the East but also against contamination from American democratic and commercial civilisation. In such provocative magazines as *Nouvelle École*, *The Scorpion*, *Éléments*, and *Trasgressioni*, they warn against the multiple menaces besetting the European spirit: American commercial vulgarity, Marxist levelling, and the destruction of historical identities through the propagation of abstract human rights.

New Right spokesmen trace these bedevilling problems to explicit sources that come up repeatedly for criticism in their writings. Judaeo-Christianity is seen as the *pons omnium asinorum*: the foundation for a despiritualised world without the mystery that pagans once attached to Nature; and the model for a universal order based on a deracinated mankind. New Rightists, as Sunic shows, draw heavily on Nietzsche in depicting Christianity as a slave religion and, in the

phrase of *Nouvelle École's* spirited editor Alain de Benoist, as 'the Bolshevism of Antiquity'.

The New Right also attacks the French Revolution as an extension
of the ideological intolerance aroused first by the Christian Church
as a bearer of revolutionary universalism. The French revolutionaries
continued the Christian practice of brutalising and killing in the name
of a universalist creed. They also trumped the Christians by adding to
the early Church's stress on spiritual equality the more unsettling claim
that mankind was to be politically as well as spiritually equal. In their
claim to represent humanity, the revolutionaries repudiated existing
legal and social arrangements, believing that all Europeans should be
captive to their abstract ideal of equality.

The New Right's brief against the French Revolution clearly over-
laps with the arguments of European counterrevolutionaries in the
Nineteenth century. And their publications abound in praise of Joseph
de Maistre and Juan Donoso Cortés as critics of the French Revolution, notwithstanding the fervent Catholicism expressed by such
counterrevolutionaries. New Right diatribes against Judaeo-Christianity resemble those of interwar Latin Fascists, particularly Gabriele
d'Annunzio, Henry de Montherlant, and Julius Evola, who pined for
the gods of the ancient city and for a redivinised pagan Nature. It is
therefore not surprising that anxious defenders of liberal democracy
charge the New Right with reviving Fascist ideas. Jean-Marie Benoist
in France, Jürgen Habermas in West Germany, and contributors to
Commentary and *Encounter* have all accused the New Right of the
biases that contributed to Nazism and to other anti-democratic and
racist movements of the past. Though the New Right has celebrated
some of the personalities and impulses associated with Latin Fascism,
its spokesmen have repeatedly expressed contempt for the Nazis. Nor
do they show interest in defending the clericalist politics that Admi-
ral Horthy in Hungary, General Franco in Spain, and other interwar
counterrevolutionaries incorporated into their governments. Alain de
Benoist is correct when he insists on the *sui generis* character of this
Right.

It is this unique blend of ideas that Sunic captures in his comprehensive monograph. He is tireless in pointing out the creative eclecticism that marks the developing worldview of the European New Right.
While it clings to often-eccentric views about returning Europe to pre-
Christian religion, it also turns to modern science and even ecology to

fight the claim of Christian revelation and homogenising commercialism. Despite their dislike of Marxism for its appeal to Christian universalism and equality, New Rightists enthusiastically but selectively study the Italian Marxist Antonio Gramsci. They use Gramsci to arrive at their own critique of the cultural hegemony of 'big business' and of the social engineering working to subvert what remains of rooted societies at the present time.

Sunic notes the attraction exercised by the German legal theorist Carl Schmitt and by the Italian philosopher Julius Evola on the swelling ranks of the New Right. Both were political-cultural pessimists who had little faith in modern secular liberal society. Schmitt warned against the escape from legitimacy through the emphasis on mere legality in parliamentary governments; and he believed that shifting interests were no substitute for a state built on a stable source of sovereignty coming from recognised authority. Evola, in contrast, thought less about the erosion of sovereign states than about the loss of pagan religion and civic virtue. He looked back beyond the Christian epoch for the models that might guide the West once Christianity had lost its hold. What may remain for the New Right to do is move beyond its present identity as a merely critical force. On the attack it is both inventive and flamboyant; and the shrill intolerance of its accusers often serves to bestow upon it a useful underdog image. All the same, it has still not created a coherent body of ideas or a credible political alternative to what it denounces. It has also become parasitic on other movements, mostly on the far Left, that preach anti-Americanism, environmental controls, and the demilitarisation of Western Europe. The French New Right now seems to be divided between support for the Right-wing Front National and for the Leftist Greens. Its members move back and forth, without apparent embarrassment, between extolling Catholic counterrevolutionaries and calling for the tighter enforcement in French public schools of the Laic Laws of 1905. Such intellectuals cannot decide what they hate more, the French Revolution or organised Christianity.

Such tactics betray the political immaturity of the European New Right as it struggles to define itself. But its confusion may not be fatal. As Sunic demonstrates, the New Right's strength has been its vitality more than its consistency. Its further evolution may require that it display both. As the price of growth, it will have to make a necessary choice between political gestures and becoming a stronger cultural force. If it chooses the latter, it may be around *à la longue durée* and cast a lengthening shadow on European universities and other centres of learned opinion. As a further price of growth, it will also have to move towards greater rigour and consistency in staking out its positions. It will have to eschew what is merely makeshift in its attacks on modernity, and it will have to recognise that not all who are against something are necessarily on the same side. If the European New Right can succeed in mastering these lessons, it may even survive its already mounting opposition. Otherwise Sunic's well-researched monograph will have antiquarian but not prophetic value.

Paul Gottfried
Elizabethtown College
Pennsylvania

PART ONE

INTRODUCING THE NEW RIGHT

'*Morality in Europe today is herd animal morality...* anyone who fathoms the calamity that lies concealed in the absurd guilelessness and blind confidence of "modern ideas" and even more in the whole Christian-European morality — suffers from an anxiety that is past all comparisons... The *overall degeneration of man* down to what today appears to the socialist dolts and flatheads as their "man of the future" — as their ideal — this degeneration and diminution of man into the perfect herd animal (or, as they say, to the man of the "free society"), this animalisation of man into the dwarf animal of equal rights and claims, is *possible*, there is no doubt of it. Anyone who has once thought through this possibility to the end knows one kind of nausea that other men don't know — but perhaps also a new *task*!'

— Friedrich Nietzsche, *Beyond Good and Evil*

'Modernity will not be transcended by returning to the past, but by means of certain premodern values in a decisively postmodern dimension. It is only at the price of such a radical restructuring that anomie and contemporary nihilism will be exorcised.'

— Alain de Benoist and Charles Champetier,
Manifesto for a European Renaissance

INTRODUCTION

On the ideological battlefield, the 1970s were hailed as a decade of another conservative revolution. In both America and Europe a number of intellectuals began to mount attacks not only against the purported evil of Communism, but also against the threat of egalitarianism, 'welfarism', 'the revolt of the masses', and the rising social uniformity of liberal societies. Many conservative authors went so far as to publicly denounce modern liberal society for its alleged drifting towards 'soft' totalitarianism. The ideas and theories that were relegated into intellectual semi-dormancy after the Second World War, or were thought to be on the wane, suddenly gained intellectual popularity. Since the late 1970s, labelling oneself with the tag 'Right', and expressing disapproval of liberal democracy, has no longer been viewed with scorn or worry. Indeed, in some academic circles, the ideas of those portraying themselves as 'Rightists' or conservatives have often been met with considerable respect and sympathy.

This book has a twofold purpose. The first part describes resurgent conservative movements in Europe and their intellectual heritage. More specifically, this book examines the *ideas* and *theories* of the authors and intellectuals who may roughly be characterised as the European 'revolutionary conservatives' or the New Right. Their intellectual predecessors, their theories, and their impact on the contemporary European polity will be examined in the following chapters.

First, however, one conceptual and semantic problem needs to be resolved. The term 'European New Right' is used more as a label of convenience than as an official denomination for a group of specific conservative authors. It will soon become apparent that the authors who represent or subscribe to the ideas of the so-called European

New Right are basically pursuing the intellectual and philosophical legacy of earlier European conservatives such as Vilfredo Pareto, Carl Schmitt, Oswald Spengler and many others.

Second, the authors of the New Right do not insist on being qualified as 'conservatives' or 'Rightists', let alone 'fascists'; rather, it is their ideological opponents and detractors who label them as such. I even briefly thought of rejecting the name New Right and adopting instead 'European Leftist Conservatives' in view of the fact that the authors and theories presented in this book often embrace the legacy of both the European Left and the extreme Right.

Needless to say, labels such as 'Stalinist', 'fascist', and 'Nazi' still remain emotionally charged, and very often their inappropriate use distorts sound social analyses. How many times have conservative politicians in America and Europe been labelled as 'fascist' by certain Leftist intellectuals? And have we not witnessed that some East European émigrés and anti-Communists refer to Stalin or Brezhnev as 'Red fascist leaders'? Aside from this self-serving labelling, one thing remains certain, however. The authors and the ideas presented here are critical of socialism, liberalism, and various other forms of egalitarian beliefs, including the Judaeo-Christian origins of modern democracy. Whether these authors and ideas can be termed fascist or not remains for the reader to judge.

The second part of the book lays down the New Right's criticism of equality, liberal capitalism, 'economism', and socialism in a theoretical and analytical manner. For the New Right the difference between liberalism, socialism, and Communism is almost negligible, because all of these ideologies rest on premises of universalism, egalitarianism, and the belief in economic progress. In my description of socialism and liberalism, an effort will be made to regroup a number of conservative authors who officially and 'unofficially' enter into the category of the conservative anti-egalitarian, anti-capitalist, and anti-Communist intellectual tradition, and who, in addition, unanimously share the view that modern mass society equals totalitarianism. Some readers may object to the one-sidedness of this analysis and will probably accuse me of neglecting somewhat the ideas of those conservative authors who seem to be more favourable to the classical liberal interpretation of equality. I must admit that, given the vast amount of literature that has already been written on the virtues of equality, I decided to provide a somewhat different and probably controversial view of this heated topic. In addition, I also intended to raise some questions and induce some doubt and criticism regarding the use and abuse of political concepts such as 'totalitarianism', 'freedom', and 'Communism'. Why does the New Right fear that unchecked equality leads to totalitarianism? Why does it hold the view that national rights are more important than human rights? These are just some of the questions that shall be raised in the following pages and to which the authors of the New Right present their own unique answer.

To my knowledge, there are a number of books on the New Right, although none of them deals with the European New Right and its cultural and political uniqueness.[1] As we shall presently see, there has been an incorrect assumption in the media and academe, particularly in America and England, that the European New Right is just another brand of European contemporary neo-conservatism. I hope this book will rectify this assumption, dispel some myths and concepts, clarify some misunderstandings, and in addition, contribute to a better understanding of the European conservative scene.

Although this book does not attempt to supplant the old categories of political analysis, the reader will notice that an ideological dimension has also been added to our discussion — a dimension that has been somewhat neglected in the study of political movements and parties in Europe. To a great extent, therefore, this book is also an 'abridged' ideological and cultural history of European 'revolutionary conservatives', including their contemporary followers among European conservative intellectuals.

Great ambiguities still surround the term and the concept 'Right'. Who is the man of the Right, and how does he manifest himself in various historical epochs? Would it not be more appropriate to write about many different Rights or Right-wing movements? The stereotype usually brings to mind several characteristics associated with the term 'Right', and one immediately conjures up the image of a landed proprietor, a paunchy banker from Honoré Daumier's lithographs, an ugly financier from a sketch by George Grosz, a hopelessly ignorant peasant, or a dour clergyman. On what do they agree, these different

---

1   For example, Desmond S. King, *The New Right* (Chicago: The Dorsey Press, 1987), in which the author discusses the neo-conservative approach to the welfare state in Europe. See also Alexander Yanov, *The Russian New Right* (Berkeley: University of California, 1978), in which the author examines Russian nationalism in the Soviet Union and among Russian émigrés.

categories of people? What makes them choose or vote for some Right-wing party or join some Right-wing movement? The more one tries to narrow down the stereotype of the Right-wing person, the more the stereotype blurs and its outward aspect decomposes. If Right-wing movements in Europe today appear to be so incoherent and so disconnected, it is because of the different historical experiences they had to endure. Today there is a liberal Right profoundly committed to parliamentary institutions and opposed to all Right-wing movements violating these institutions. But there is also a certain Right that has traditionally derided parliamentary systems, even when it stubbornly insisted on being admitted to parliament. Furthermore, there is also a certain Right that glorifies nationalism and opposes doctrines espousing internationalism. And finally there is the European New Right, which professes none of the above, yet remains indebted to all of them.

'In our political vocabulary', writes Jean-Christian Petitfils, 'there are few words so heavily discredited and loaded with such negative connotations as the term "Right". Inasmuch as the label "Left" seems flattering, the label Right sounds like an insult.'[2] This quotation from Petitfils' book may serve as a useful guideline in demonstrating the inadequacy of the political terminology associated with modern Right-wing movements and ideologies. Of course, the difficulty in inventing a more appropriate denominator is not accidental. For a long period of time after the war, the political arena in Europe was summarily described in terms of two competing ideological camps, 'Left' vs. 'Right'. Although this cleavage still continues to be a major factor in determining voting preferences, its social significance does not always objectively reflect the various ideological changes that have recently occurred in contemporary Europe. The line of ideological demarcation, which had earlier distinguished the Left from the Right, shifted abruptly after the war, bringing entirely new social issues to the forefront of political confrontation. And as the spirit of the times changed, so did the issue of political confrontation. Undoubtedly, for the majority of the post-war intellectuals, it was far more preferable to declare themselves to be on the Left rather than the Right. After all, who wanted to be associated with conservative ideologies, which were often, at least in the Leftist vocabulary, reminiscent of the fascist

---

2   Jean-Christian Petitfils, *La Droite en France de 1789 à nos jours* (Paris: PUF, 1973), p. 5.

past? The political dualism that prevailed during the 1940s and 1950s, sharpened by the earlier fascist experience, prompted many intellectuals to label everything that remained on the Right as the 'dark forces of reaction fighting against the enlightened principles of progress'. Of course, those who still cherished conservative ideas felt obliged to readapt themselves to new intellectual circumstances for fear of being ostracised as 'fellow travellers of fascism'. It is hard to deny that, despite the overwhelmingly conservative institutional framework of European societies, the cultural tone after the war was dictated primarily by the Left-wing intelligentsia. Moreover, this intelligentsia seldom refrained from using the same methods against their conservative adversaries that they had often themselves endured and deplored before and during the war. In the name of democracy, they argued, non-democratic movements and ideas cannot be allowed to thrive. To what extent Leftist intellectuals themselves believed in democracy, and what significance they gave to democracy, are entirely different matters that go beyond the scope of the present book.

The disgrace of the term 'Right' can thus be directly attributed to the Second World War, the period during which many prominent conservatives sided with, or at least paid tacit lip service, to fascism. Therefore, it is a small wonder that the post-war conservatives enjoyed the least influence precisely in those European countries where conservative ideas had been most influential previously. The reason that cultural conservatives, including the European Right, have the largest intellectual following in France today, instead of in Germany, is quite understandable given, on the one hand, the unique international position of France, and on the other, the enormous historical mortgage that still lies heavily on the historical consciousness of German conservatives.

For the purpose of clarity this book will also occasionally examine the differences between the European New Right and the so-called American 'new right'. Although the European New Right shares some similarities with its American counterpart, the following pages will demonstrate that their points of convergence are negligible in view of their tangible differences. Very often there is a tendency among American conservatives and liberals to analyse foreign social phenomena in accordance with American social reality and, by analogy, reduce them to American historical and intellectual experience. To portray the American new right as the American ideological equivalent of the

European New Right may obscure one of the fundamental issues with which the European New Right engages: criticism of the American new right.

The first chapter of the book sets out a general description of the European New Right: its influence, impact, and the reaction it received to its theories. The following chapters examine the intellectual predecessors of the European New Right: the 'revolutionary' conservative thinkers Oswald Spengler, Vilfredo Pareto, and Carl Schmitt. The writings of these three authors have contributed significantly to the overall intellectual formation of the European New Right, and therefore, I deemed it necessary to include them in my book. Although the intellectual legacy of the New Right stretches far beyond Spengler, Pareto, and Schmitt, these three authors are crucial in understanding the New Right's attitude towards liberalism, socialism, and the contemporary political crisis. In addition, the anti-liberal and anti-socialist theories developed by Pareto, Spengler, and Schmitt constitute important epistemological tools in the New Right's own analyses of modern politics.

The last chapter in the first part of the book explains the 'polytheistic' and the anti-Judaeo-Christian foundations of the European New Right. It is not difficult to guess that the New Right sees the origins of totalitarianism in Biblical monotheism; in contrast, it is in a return to the Indo-European pagan cosmogony that the New Right sees the only possible remedy for the ills of liberal and Communist mass societies. This chapter is also important because it sets the stage for further discussion concerning the roots of the modern crisis.

The second part of the book focuses on what the European New Right terms the 'challenge of egalitarianism'. How and why did the egalitarian mystique emerge in modern European polities, and why is the 'terror of the majority', as the New Right asserts, conducive to not just socialist totalitarianism, but to liberal totalitarianism as well? This part of the book discusses some contemporary occurrences that the New Right terms the 'egalitarian entropy' in liberal and Communist systems. Moreover, this chapter discusses not just the theoretical concepts of liberalism and socialism, but also the ways in which they manifest daily in modern societies. The last chapter deals with Communist totalitarianism as seen through the eyes of the New Right and some other prominent conservatives. The message of the New Right is simple: egalitarianism, economism, and universalism, when left unchecked, set the stage for the most horrendous form of totalitarianism — Communism.

In the closing years of this century the ideas of the European New Right and its predecessors seem to be arousing considerable interest among European conservatives. These ideas and views, which one can justifiably call both revolutionary and conservative, as well as modernist and archaic, merit our full attention and sympathetic understanding. My endeavour, which is descriptive, analytical, and theoretical, is to comprehensively present their political significance in contemporary Europe.

I

ENTER THE NEW RIGHT

The Twentieth century has not only been marked by the inflation of political movements but also by the inflation of political terminology. The term *New Right* was first used in the mid-1970s by the French media to announce, but also to warn against, a group of young French intellectuals who had, a decade earlier, proclaimed an all-out war against Communism, liberalism, and the Judaeo-Christian heritage in Europe. Although the New Right appears to be a relatively new ideological and cultural phenomenon, upon closer scrutiny there are few things on its agenda that are radically new or that were not already elaborated by earlier conservative thinkers. Over the last hundred years both liberalism and Communism have been targets of many conservative critics, and therefore one could probably argue that the New Right is basically an old 'anti-democratic' Right wearing today more respectable ideological clothes. Yet, despite similarities to former radical Rightist currents, the New Right is indeed a new movement considering that its sympathisers and members are mostly younger people facing social issues that were previously unknown in Europe. The New Right is also 'new' inasmuch as it claims to have made a complete break with all extreme Right-wing movements and parties. In addition, unlike other forms of the Right, the New Right does not claim its spiritual roots in a single European country, but instead declares its homeland to be the entire European continent.

When the New Right announced its official entry into the European cultural and political scene in the mid-1970s, the timing was not accidental. Several years earlier a tacit ideological realignment had begun in France and other parts of Europe; notably, a considerable number of former Left-wing socialist intellectuals had ceased attacking capitalism and the United States and in turn became ardent supporters of NATO and the American crusade for human rights. The former Left-wing 'romanticists'—to borrow Schmitt's term—suddenly became aware of the rigours of 'real socialism'; anti-Communist dissidents, such as Solzhenitsyn and the Sakharovs, began to be hailed as new prophets of liberty; and the American way of life became a guideline for a new political preference. About the same time, the Marxist credo started gradually losing its political and cultural grip on the post-war intellectuals after its influence had already been reduced to a handful of isolated and dwindling Communist parties in Western Europe. It may be said that the process of 'intellectual de-Marxification' in Europe was considerably accelerated by the growing awareness of the ongoing human rights violations in the Soviet Union and Eastern Europe.

It is in such a social context of apparent 'de-ideologisation' and disenchantment with Marxism that the New Right appeared. Suddenly, conservative ideas again gained in popularity, America came to be hailed as the centre of world democracy, and proclaiming oneself on the 'Right' no longer ran the risk of being met with intellectual disapproval.

The European New Right, which also calls itself GRECE (Groupement de recherche et d'études de la civilisation européenne, or the Research Group for the Study of European Civilisation), characterises itself as 'an association of thought with an intellectual vocation'. Its avowed goals are to establish an association of thinkers and scholars sharing the same ideals, as well as to organise its membership into the form of an organic and spiritually-based working community.[1] The choice of the word GRECE is not accidental: the acronym GRECE is a homonym of the French word 'Grèce' (Greece), suggesting that the New Right's long-term objective is the revival of the pre-Christian and Hellenic heritage.

In addition, the term GRECE indicates that the New Right does not limit its cultural activity to France or Germany alone, but attempts to extend its influence to all Indo-European peoples—Slavs, Celts, and Germans alike.[2]

---

1 Jean-Claude Valla in an interview with Pierre Vial, 'Une communauté de travail et de pensée', in *Pour une renaissance culturelle*, ed. by Pierre Vial (Paris: Copernic, 1979), p. 23.

2 The New Right publishes *Diorama Letterario* in Italy (Florence), *Orientations* and *Vouloir* in Belgium (Brabant), *Fundamentos* in Spain (Madrid), and *Futuro*

In many aspects, in terms of cultural strategy, the New Right shows a striking similarity to the New Left. Numerous critical analyses by the New Right regarding the danger of mass society, consumerism, and economism closely parallel those of the New Left, to the point that their ideological differences often appear blurred. The main figure of the New Right, the French philosopher Alain de Benoist, explains the ideological posture of the New Right in the following words:

> Personally, I am totally indifferent to the issue of being or not being on the Right. At the moment, the ideas that [the New Right] espouses are on the Right, but they are not necessarily *of the Right*. I can easily imagine situations where these ideas could be on the Left. The extent to which these ideas can change will solely depend on how the political landscape will have evolved.[3]

From the above lines, it appears that the New Right is opposed to being labelled with the tag 'Right'. Instead, it contends that its theories are meant to cross the ideological divide irrespective of the fact that it presently espouses ideas that are more in accordance with the conservative agenda.

There is another ambiguity regarding the role of the New Right that needs to be clarified. Is the New Right a political movement or a cultural movement, and where exactly does the difference lie between the two? In Europe in general, and in France in particular, culture and politics often seem to be interwoven and hardly discernible from each other. Great cultural figures often play quiet yet prominent roles in the political arena, and their influence sometimes has more bearing on the political process than do elected governmental representatives. From de Gaulle to Mitterrand, from Adenauer to Kohl, European leaders have frequently vied for the support of prominent intellectuals, and often the political survival of their governments has depended on the tacit support of their hand-picked intellectuals. Cultural and artistic figures, although not politically visible, use this advantage to operate in political affairs in the capacity of 'grey eminences'; they provide each decision-maker with a sense of political respectability; yet, they seldom take the blame in case a political decision goes sour.

Presente in Portugal (Lisboa).

3   Quoted by Pierre Vial in 'Nouvelle Droite ou nouvelle culture', *ibid.*, p. 9.

Drawing from the example of the New Left, New Right thinkers contend that culture is the soul of politics, and that only through cultural efforts can political movements gain lasting political legitimacy. It is worth noting that both the New Left and the New Right emerged first as cultural movements, with the New Left holding the cultural dominance in Europe until the mid-1970s and losing it to a certain extent by the beginning of the 1980s. In contrast, whereas the political influence of the New Left is today on the demise, that of the New Right is on the rise. How and to what extent the New Right can influence the political process in Europe, and what its tools will be for translating its cultural gains into the political arena, remains to be seen.

In a decade when new political movements are often viewed with apprehension and suspected of totalitarian aberrations, to portray the New Right as just another political movement can pose an additional difficulty. The concept 'movement' implies broad mass and popular support — something with which the New Right, as a rather elitist and narrow body of thinkers, cannot be compared. The term that seems more appropriate in describing the role of the New Right is as a 'cultural school of thought', particularly if one considers that the New Right's relatively small following precludes all comparison to European political parties or movements. In addition, the fact that the New Right considers the ideological cleavage of 'Left vs. Right' to be a secondary issue explains why it is impossible to place it into the category of either a Left-wing or a Right-wing movement. For instance, given the New Right's opposition to foreign immigration, one may be tempted to suspect it of having political connections to the French Front National and other extreme Right-wing parties. This assumption is not to be completely dismissed, although it must be pointed out that the New Right has not hesitated to publicly criticise all extreme Right-wing movements and parties, including the French Front National and its leader Jean-Marie Le Pen. Conversely, it has never been a secret that the New Right is sympathetic to the ideas of many French Leftist and socialist leaders and intellectuals, with whom, for example, it is in full agreement on the issue of a Europe free of occupation by the United States and the Soviet Union, as well as the dismantlement of the Western Alliance. Furthermore, on numerous occasions, the New Right has expressed great admiration for those socialist intellectuals who, in its view, have remained loyal to their socialist ideals despite the recent neo-conservative trend among their former comrades. In order to understand the New Right's ideological 'volatility', one must again refer to the general credo expressed earlier by de Benoist, in which he stresses that the ideas of the New Right are designed to undermine ideological orthodoxy and remain open to the socialist and Rightist intelligentsia alike. Can one conclude, therefore, that the New Right is using Leftist tactics of ideological deception or simply a new conservative strategy for political survival?

The European New Right vs. the American Right

The portrait of the European New Right would remain incomplete without at least a cursory description of the American conservative scene. The American 'new right' and American neo-conservatives have an agenda that is currently being associated with the rise of the 'moral majority' and some former disenchanted intellectuals from the liberal and Leftist camps who profess staunch anti-Communism and anti-welfarism, and who emphasise the necessity of the capitalist free market. Similar to the heterogeneous character of European contemporary conservatives, of which the European New Right is just the most recent and radical offshoot, an open rift exists among contemporary American conservatives. For instance, while a great majority of American conservatives and neo-conservatives agree on upholding the rights of free speech and constitutional liberty, a significant number of conservatives resort to language aimed at reasserting the liberal heritage of conservatism. Furthermore, the serious split among the American 'new right' and 'old right' adherents seems to have its roots in such issues as Jewish identity, support for Israel, and anti-Semitism. It must not come as a surprise that a number of well-known American neo-conservatives frequently find themselves at odds with those American conservatives who appear ambivalent on the issue of the Jewish question and American support for Israel. In the words of one prominent American conservative, this latent rift among American conservatives is not likely to end soon:

> These disputes grow not from the contemporary world alone, but from the historical roots of neo-conservatism and the personal journeys of the neo-conservatives themselves. Before they were neo-conservatives,

they were Jewish intellectuals and liberal cold warriors. These issues remain, despite travels across the political spectrum.[4]

Furthermore, some American conservatives view conservatism as inseparable from Roman Catholic and Protestant beliefs and contrast it with a brand of neo-conservatism identified with an 'instantiation of modernity among secularised Jewish intellectuals...'[5] As Russell Kirk asserts, 'What really animates the neo-conservatives, especially Irving Kristol, is the preservation of Israel.'[6] Similar statements can be heard from Norman Podhoretz, a conservative intellectual of Jewish ancestry, for whom the defence of Israel is a defence of American interests and ultimately of the entirety of Western civilisation.[7] Although the European New Right shares some ideas with the American 'new right' and other American conservatives, notably staunch anti-Communism, and to some extent anti-egalitarianism, it must be pointed out that, unlike its American counterpart, the European New Right opposes the free market, as well as American economic and cultural predominance in the world. The European New Right has so far not elaborated its own economic doctrine, although one may suspect it of having some sympathy for the theories of 'organic' and corporatist economics, advocated earlier in the Twentieth century by Othmar Spann and Léon Walras. As we shall see later, the main thrust of the New Right's argument is that economics must be completely subordinated to politics and culture and not the other way around.[8]

Their differences notwithstanding, in terms of social momentum, both the European New Right and the so-called American new right emerged as a result of the same intellectual stratification that occurred in the mid-1970s in both the United States and Europe. Peter Steinfels notes:

> The question of what is 'new', if anything, about neo-conservatism is not trivial. It bears on the manner in which this phenomenon is

---

4   Alexander Bloom, 'Neoconservatives in the 1980s', in *The World and I*, October 1986, p. 692.

5   *Loc. cit.*

6   John B. Judis, unnamed essay, in *The New Republic*, August 11 & 18, 1986.

7   Bloom, *loc. cit.*

8   See, for example, a book by an author of the New Right, Guillaume Faye, *Contre l'économisme: Principes d'économie politique* (Paris: Le Labyrinthe, 1983).

studied and discussed. By emphasising their continuity with traditional liberalism, by suggesting that they are only being faithful to old
struggles and eternal verities, the neo-conservatives displace the burden of examination from their own ideas to those of the supposed
innovators, their adversaries. On the other hand, many of the neo-
conservatives' critics are not at all disposed to grant the newness of
this outlook. For them it is just the same old conservatism; what is new
is its advocacy by *these* spokesmen, most of them former liberals and
even former socialists.[9]

These lines basically indicate an American echo of the same intellectual malaise that occurred earlier in Western Europe, notably when a
number of former socialist and liberal intellectuals started realigning
themselves around the conservative agenda. All these things considered, despite similarities between the European New Right and European conservatives on the one hand, and on the other, as well as with
the American new right and American conservatives, it is important to
note that their reciprocal ideological differences are by and large very
profound. It is commonly overlooked that almost *all* European conservatives, including the thinkers of the New Right, display features
that are absent from all brands of American conservatism. American
conservatives, in general, seldom question the validity of their constitutional tenets that depict America as the promised land of guaranteed
rights of free speech, freedom of contract, and the rule of law. Also,
unlike European conservatives, American conservatives are traditionally suspicious of strong government, and additionally conceive of 'organic' and European-style stratified societies as something contrary to
economic progress. In contrast, European conservatives, including the
European New Right, unanimously agree on the necessity of strong
state authority, and generally appear more willing to question the virtues of individual liberty.

Another point often overlooked by American conservatives and the
American public at large is a deeply rooted scepticism, agnosticism, and
sometimes outright nihilism among European conservatives — a trait
which stands in sharp contrast to the Judaeo-Christian religious attitude among many American conservatives. As David Gress indicates,
historically and temperamentally, conservatives in Europe (with the
partial exception of Britain) are profoundly suspicious of capitalism,

---

9   Peter Steinfels, *The Neoconservatives* (New York: Simon and Schuster, 1979), p. 2.

believe in the necessity of a strong state, and before 1945, did not like Americans at all—whom they 'regarded as threatening, disruptive, and alien, and because Americans appeared to them as politically and socially naïve'.[10] This is a point the New Right constantly brings up in its debates with European neo-conservatives, whom it also accuses of introducing the American 'moralising' tendency into politics.

In addition to its disagreement with the American new right on the matters of national and global economics, as well as differences in historical and cultural heritage, there is also a 'continental' and geopolitical cleavage between American neo-conservatives and the European New Right. It should not come as a big surprise that even in 'European' England, the influence of the European New Right is largely marginal, due to the fact that England has had a different political and intellectual development than continental Europe. In the eyes of the New Right, unlike continental Europeans, Anglo-Saxon peoples fail to perceive the importance of organic community and the primacy of political over economic factors. The excessive individualism of Anglo-Saxon society and a unique political theology of 'secularised' Protestantism resulted over a period of time in the subordination of traditional politics to unbridled economic expansion. In his essay on democracy, de Benoist explains that real and 'organic' democracy can only exist in a society in which people have developed a firm sense of historical and spiritual commitment to their community. In such an organic polity, the law must not derive from some abstract, preconceived principles, but rather from the genius of the people and its unique historical character. In such a democracy, the sense of community must invariably preside over individualistic and economic self-interest.[11] This description of an organic polity, as proposed by the New Right, stands in sharp contrast to the universalist and liberal agenda currently espoused by both American and European neo-conservatives.

From the above, it appears that neo-conservatives, be they American, English, or even European, often constitute the very antithesis of everything for which the European New Right stands. Moreover, the New Right does not hesitate to warn against the threat from the

10 David Gress, 'Conservatism in Europe and America', in *The World and I*, October 1986, p. 678.

11 Alain de Benoist, *Les Idées à l'endroit* (Paris: Libres-Hallier, 1979). (De Benoist also discusses this at length in *The Problem of Democracy* [London: Arktos Media, 2011].-Ed.)

'conservative' Anglo-Saxon order to traditional European communities. Harold T. Hewitson, an English scholar affiliated with the New Right, notes that the ultimate objective of the conservative order in liberal-democratic societies consists in the 'overtaking of community spirit by blind pursuit of self-interest, ignorance of the implication of ethnic affiliation in community values, allowing the virtues of the people to be suffocated by the meddling of intellectuals and managers.'[12] Therefore, although the name 'New Right' may suggest a different version of European neo-conservatism, it would be an error to draw even a remote parallel between the European New Right and the Western (American) neo-conservatives. The originality of the New Right lies precisely in recognising the ethnic and historical dimension of conservatism — a dimension considered negligible by the rather universalist and transnational credo of modern Western conservatives. As further chapters will demonstrate, the European New Right perceives the greatest enemy of Europe in the capitalist doctrine of individualism and economism — two factors that make up the driving force behind modern Western neo-conservatism.

So how, then, do we define the European New Right? Is it some sort of a semi-religious, semi-political sect, like those that abound today throughout the Western hemisphere? The above description has demonstrated that social categories are not neatly divided by well-defined social concepts, and that before using or abusing political terminology, each social scientist must redefine every concept in its given historical and social environment.

The New Right characterises itself as a revolt against formless politics, formless life, and formless values. The crisis of modern societies has resulted in an incessant 'uglification' whose main vectors are liberalism, Marxism and the 'American way of life'. The dominant ideologies of modernity, Marxism and liberalism, embodied by the Soviet Union and America respectively, are harmful to the social well-being of peoples because both reduce every aspect of life to the realm of economic utility and efficiency. The principle enemy of freedom, asserts the New Right, is not Marxism or liberalism *per se*, but rather their common belief in egalitarianism. Marxism, incidentally, is not the antithesis of liberalism — it is simply the most dangerous form of the

12 Harold T. Hewitson, 'G.R.E.C.E. Right Side Up', in *The Scorpion* (London), Autumn 1986, p. 28.

egalitarianism that runs rampant through all sectors of the Soviet and American polity:

> The enemy is embodied in all those doctrines, all *praxis* representing and incarnating a form of egalitarianism. Certainly, in the first place among them, is Marxism — the most extreme, the most terrorist form of egalitarianism. The considerable influence of Marxism on contemporary minds — and especially on those who will be called tomorrow to make *decisions* in society — is one of the fundamental causes of the modern crisis.[13]

The error that liberal thinkers fail to discern is that the liberal doctrine of individualism, economism, and the 'pursuit of happiness' cannot constitute a solid weapon against Marxism, since liberal intellectuals, while denouncing the consequences of Marxism, are unable to critically examine the egalitarian premises of their own doctrine. As Jean-Claude Valla writes, 'They [intellectuals] are attracted to Marxism because in front of it, beside it, and against it, there is no *alternative*. Marxism coexists with liberalism since nobody wishes to challenge it on its own terrain, and nobody is able to dispute its monopoly.'[14]

For the New Right, conservative and neo-conservative parties and movements share a great part of the historical responsibility for the almost proverbial unpopularity of conservative ideas. Victims of historical circumstances, impotent to carry out the 'battle for the brains', and entangled in the past of colonialism, racism, and Judaeo-Christian messianism, neo-conservatives and traditional conservatives have already signed their own death warrants. In short, these 'Rights' are unable to gain much intellectual credibility. As Michael Walker, the editor of the English journal, *The Scorpion*, writes:

> The baggage of the old Right, were it the nationalist Right, the Nazi Right, the Christian Right, the imperialist Right, the liberal Right, with its simplistic slick solutions to the issues of the day, left these young

---

13 Jean-Claude Valla, 'Une communauté de travail et de pensée', in *Pour une renaissance culturelle*, p. 31.

14 *Ibid.*, p. 32.

people profoundly unsatisfied. The far Right, shrill, monotonous and wholly predictable, was an insult to the intelligence. [15]

In the eyes of the New Right thinkers and writers, the traditional Christian conservatives have done more damage to the conservative cause than their ideological adversaries among the Left-wing socialist intelligentsia. Not surprisingly, after the Second World War, an intellectual or an artist could hardly reconcile himself to some ill-defined conservative doctrine that often appeared reminiscent of fascism. After 1945, the only option for somebody in search of intellectual respectability was to jump on the socialist bandwagon or accept the dominant ideology of liberalism — especially when the popularity of Marxism began to erode. In other words, in order to gain intellectual prestige, intellectuals first and foremost had to pay lip service to the dominant ideologies, irrespective of their own political beliefs.

The New Right or the Fascist Right?

Such fierce criticism from Marxists, liberals, conservatives, and neo-conservatives has made the New Right in a very short time the most disliked cultural current of thought in Europe. Soon after its appearance in the media in France, numerous attempts were made to marginalise its importance, or at the very least to discredit it as another fascist aberration. Judging by the number of articles published about it, the New Right came under a barrage of crossfire from both the Left and the Right, from both the neo-conservative and neo-liberal intelligentsia. Yet the more frequently these attacks occurred, the more intellectual curiosity the New Right managed to arouse. Pierre Vial, a thinker of the New Right, notes:

> After they had been silent about this new current of thought represented by the GRECE, its adversaries have set out — without much success until now — to *discredit* it. This effort abides by a very simple method: firstly, the opinions of the 'New Right' are presented in a very deformed and caricatured manner; secondly, the refusal to engage in any debate and dialogue is justified on the grounds of the infamous

---

15 Michael Walker, 'Spotlight on the French New Right', in *The Scorpion*, Autumn 1986, p. 8.

and odious character of the New Right — the caricature drawn by the critics themselves in the first place. The purpose is to discredit and also to incite hatred. Finally, and to top it all off, the attempt is made to prevent people from reading and referring to the texts of the New Right.[16]

And the critics of the New Right have certainly not remained mute. Jacquot Gruenewald, the editor of the French *Tribune Juive*, said, 'Let us be proud to show proofs of intolerance towards this theory [of the New Right].'[17] For its part, the French socialist daily *Le Matin*, in its issue for 31 July 1979, reported that 'Every debate is not open to the people and ideas whose expression should not even exist in a democratic society.'[18] The strongest indictment, however, came from the prestigious French news magazine *Le Nouvel Observateur*, which carried a five-page diatribe against the New Right, exhorting its readers to 'utmost vigilance'.[19] The reporter from *Le Nouvel Observateur* contended that the New Right is not just a harmless cultural movement whose battlefield is the cultural arena, but that instead the New Right constitutes a genuine *risorgimento* of the ideological laboratories and groupings of the extreme Right.[20] For *Le Nouvel Observateur*, the problem is all too simple: the old fascist Right is now clad in new clothes, and its members are none other than the well-known former students who were earlier, in the mid-1960s, active in the fascist groups in France. 'The masks fell off', continues the article, 'and the polls that were conducted demonstrate that the French Right today advances and makes progress with its face uncovered — even when it deems it necessary to decorate itself with the rags of modernism.'[21]

Some journalists and authors were less vitriolic in criticising the New Right, despite their visible concern and even profound disagreement with some of its ideas. A correspondent for *Les Nouvelles Littéraires*, amidst the campaign of defamation against the New Right, noted that 'serious debates have been skirted in favour of reductionist

16 Pierre Vial, 'Nouvelle Droite ou nouvelle culture', in *Pour une renaissance culturelle*, pp. 10-11.

17 Quoted in Vial, *Pour une renaissance culturelle*, p. 11.

18 *Loc. cit.*

19 'Les habits neufs de la droite française', in *Le Nouvel Observateur*, 8 July 1979, p. 33.

20 *Loc. cit.*

21 *Loc. cit.*

anathemas'.[22] And another bi-weekly magazine wrote in a sober, but nonetheless critical manner:

> The task undertaken by Alain de Benoist and the New Right still leaves one perplexed. His message, both modernist and archaic, mythic and scientific, remains rather ambiguous, despite clarity and an effort to provide the political (conservative) majority in search of bestsellers with its own 'negroes', as well as to disturb some journalist from *Libé-ration*. It appeals to those fascinated by the critique of mass society and the eulogy of diversity.[23]

Nor were the neo-conservatives more sympathetic to the ideas espoused by the New Right. The well-known critic and author Jean-François Revel, known for his considerable influence among American neo-conservatives, wrote quite bluntly that the New Right presents as great a threat to democracy as that represented by the New Left and Marxist intellectuals, and that the New Right is practically an 'intellectual aberration'.[24]

As the beginning of the New Right controversy started to unfold, the French, and later the whole of European media searched for every opportunity to draw the ideas professed by the New Right under fire. Thus, in the wake of its first press conference, held on 18 September 1979, the New Right was accused of advocating social Darwinism, biological materialism, and racialism. In addition, its adversaries staged several attacks against its offices and launched well-orchestrated campaigns of defamation prior to all of its meetings and conferences. Moreover, some publishing companies refused to publish the texts of the New Right.[25]

---

22 *Les Nouvelles littéraires*, 26 July 1979, as quoted by Vial in *Pour une renaissance culturelle*, p. 12.

23 'Mais qu'est-ce donc la Nouvelle droite?', in *La Quinzaine littéraire* (Paris), 15 November 1979, p. 8.

24 Jean-François Revel, *Comment les démocraties finissent* (Paris: Pluriel, 1983), pp. 37-38. (Translated into English as *How Democracies Perish* [Garden City: Doubleday, 1984].-Ed.)

25 Books by the authors of the New Right have been translated into Italian, German, Spanish, Dutch, and Greek. Except for some book reviews, articles, and reports published by the English *The Scorpion* and the American *Telos* and *Chronicles*, the European New Right has been largely ignored by American and English publishers.

By the beginning of the 1980s, the media outcry abated somewhat in France, but gained in momentum in other parts of Europe, notably Germany, where the German chapter of the New Right has become active relatively recently. The German New Right, which operates in conjunction with the conservative Thule-Seminar, soon had to endure the same procedure of intellectual ostracism and fierce criticism previously experienced by their French colleagues. In July 1986, the Tübingen home of Wigbert Grabert, the chief publisher of the Thule-Seminar, was severely damaged, apparently by Leftist extremists. The same year, Pierre Krebs, the chief author and spokesman of the New Right in Germany, became a target of violent protests and attacks while delivering a speech at the University of Vienna. As the subsequent German edition of the New Right quarterly *Elemente* reported, the outbursts of Leftist extremism seemed, ironically, to have enhanced the prestige and importance of the New Right:

> It is now an obvious fact. Our ideas have caught on. Our ideas disturb the profiteers of egalitarianism, be they of the Leftist or Rightist brand. Our ideas increasingly disturb the course of events, because they require an alertness and a force of argument from our adversaries that they do not have.
>
> In short, instead of doing battle on the cultural and intellectual field, instead of showing intelligence, they are showing, their capacity for thought exhausted, their miserable side by openly resorting to violence. Moreover, these entirely Bolshevik and plutocratic crooks use violence with impunity because they can carry out their deeds under the cover of night and fog (*Nacht und Nebel*)...[26]

Meanwhile, the New Right's attempt to increase its following among traditional conservatives in Europe did not have much success. Their incessant criticism of NATO, American influence in Europe and the Judaeo-Christian heritage appeared to many conservative thinkers who were initially sympathetic as an outrageous submission to the Soviet threat. Even more shocking appeared the much-publicised statement

---

(Since 1990, Alain de Benoist's *On Being a Pagan* and *The Problem of Democracy*, as well as Guillaume Faye's *Archeofuturism*, have appeared in English.-Ed.)

26 'Gewalt statt Argumente gegen das Thule-Seminar', *Elemente*, January-March 1987, p. 45.

by de Benoist, in which he contends that Communist totalitarianism poses a lesser threat to Europe than liberal totalitarianism:

> It is true that there are two forms of totalitarianism; different in causes and consequences, but both being dangerous. Totalitarianism in the East imprisons, persecutes and kills the body, but it leaves hope. Totalitarianism in the West creates happy robots. Such totalitarianism 'air-conditions hell' and kills the soul.[27]

In the United States, on the whole, the New Right has been almost entirely ignored, although it did cause some concern among Jewish intellectuals and publishers. Thus, I. R. Barnes, an expert on neo-fascism who teaches in England, wrote in *Mainstream*, a monthly Jewish review published in New York, that the 'sophisticated lions of the New Right have introduced a new tactic of infiltration and the acquisition of cultural power.'[28] And with considerable worry, Barnes assailed the European New Right as an anti-Semitic and pro-Nazi organisation: the New Right culturally transmits fascist and neo-fascist ideas, thereby normalising fascism within an intellectual elite.[29]

In 1987, after a silence of several years, a new controversy about the European New Right flared up in the American conservative press, this time in the monthly magazine *The World and I*, published by the Washington Times Corporation, a publishing company financed by the Korean tycoon Sun Myung Moon. In his review of de Benoist's newest book, *Europe, Tiers Monde, même combat*, the Hoover Institute scholar David Gress deplores the fact that while the French Left has found its way into the respectability of parliamentary democracy, 'Alain de Benoist — once proud to call himself on the Right — adopted the discarded ideas of the Left'.[30] These words were a clear reference to de Benoist's frequent praise of Régis Debray, Antonio Gramsci, and other socialist 'meta-politicians'. Gress writes that 'a man such as de

---

27 This is a famous phrase by Alain de Benoist, the philosophical leader of the European New Right, quoted by *Le Monde*, 28 May 1981, and later repeatedly used by Alain de Benoist, for example in *Europe, Tiers monde, même combat* (Paris: Robert Laffont, 1986), p. 219.

28 I. R. Barnes, "Creeping Racism and Anti-Semitism," in *Midstream*, February 1984, p. 14.

29 *Ibid.*, p. 13.

30 David Gress, 'From the Right to the Left', in *The World and I*, May 1987, p. 437.

Benoist, who was once wrong but interesting, has lent support to these vicious and false ideologies, and in doing so has become dangerous and foolish as well'.[31] In the same issue of *The World and I*, Thomas Molnar, a Hungarian-born American Catholic philosopher and a friend of de Benoist, while commenting on the same book, takes up the defence of the European New Right, and argues in favour of the national independence of the peoples of Europe and the peoples of the Third World:

> Despite the simplification of this thesis, it is unfortunate that de Benoist's critique does not receive a serious hearing in this country. We remain satisfied with our good conscience and regard those who challenge it as either primitive or envious people. We refuse to consider the proposition that American materialism may do damage to others.[32]

The New Right's uncompromising attack on American multinationals and the American diplomatic and military presence in the Third World have prompted Roger Kaplan, the associate editor of *Reader's Digest*, to accuse de Benoist of anti-Americanism. Kaplan writes that de Benoist 'dislikes capitalism, so he easily accepts the completely unverified notion that it requires colonies: that, in short, capitalism begets imperialism'.[33] And with obvious disdain for the New Right's call for a unified and imperial Europe, Kaplan responds: ' "Europe," what is that? The dream of Charlemagne or [that of] Hitler? Europeans have given the world a two thousand year spectacle of murder and mayhem and they expect us to believe that from now on it is going to be all love and cooperation...'[34]

A favourable comment about the New Right, and particularly de Benoist's erudition, came from Paul Gottfried, a senior former editor of *The World and I*. Commenting on the jointly authored book by Molnar and de Benoist, *L'éclipse du sacré*, in which the two authors defend monotheistic and polytheistic worldviews respectively, Gottfried writes

---

31 *Ibid.*, p. 439.

32 Thomas Molnar, 'American Culture: A Possible Threat', in *The World and I*, May 1987, p. 442.

33 Roger Kaplan, 'The Imaginary Third World and the Real United States', in *The World and I*, May 1987, p. 446.

34 *Loc. cit.*

that 'in battling with each other, they marshal staggering amounts of erudition drawn from entire lifetimes of reading. Unlike most American intellectuals, they believe that matters of the soul count for more than public policy issues. I tip my hat to both debaters and commend them for discussing the truly permanent things.'[35]

Some European journals and publications were friendlier to the cultural endeavours of the New Right, in particular the weekly supplement *Le Figaro Magazine*. The publication of *Le Figaro Magazine*, which started in 1978, could boast an audience of over half a million readers by the end of 1979 — something unprecedented in French journalism. Under the leadership of the author Louis Pauwels, a conservative intellectual on good terms with the New Right, *Le Figaro Magazine* opened its columns to its young authors, thus making their ideas more accessible to the wider French public. Had it not been for Pauwels and *Le Figaro Magazine*, these authors would very likely have encountered more difficulty in reaching the higher echelons of French cultural life.[36] Another journal that also showed interest in the ideas of the New Right was the monthly *Contrepoint*, edited by the well-known French intellectual Yvan Blot. *Contrepoint* was a prestigious forum for the distinguished conservative intellectuals of the equally prestigious Club de l'Horloge, a conservative artistic and cultural think-tank known for its connections to French conservative politicians. In recent years, however, the interest of conservative intellectuals from the 'Club d'Horloge' for the ideas espoused by the New Right has been somewhat dampened — presumably on the grounds of the New Right's anti-Americanism and advocacy of religious polytheism.

Another favourable remark about the New Right came from Armin Mohler, a well-known German scholar of contemporary European history. In his essay, 'Wir feinen Konservativen', Mohler contends that

---

35 Paul Gottfried's review of *L'éclipse du sacré*, in *The World and I*, December 1986, pp. 450-453.

36 Louis Pauwels, the former editor of *Le Figaro Magazine*, has significantly distanced himself from the New Right although he continues to acknowledge its great cultural importance: 'I do not regret having contributed, in the 1970s, to the growth of the New Right's audience. Its recent evolution and my own journey have brought a distance between us. But all honest historians will have to remember that the school of thought animated by Alain de Benoist played a decisive role in the disintegration of the Leftist body of doctrine, and the return of cultural power to the Right.' Quoted in *Éléments*, Winter 1985, p. 38.

the defamation staged by the French media against the New Right resembles the witch-hunt that took place earlier in West Germany when the weekly *Der Spiegel* started a campaign against the conservative historian Helmut Diwald. Mohler observes that the liberal media today has a hard time putting the New Right in the 'brown penitentiary corner' because the age of the New Right authors precludes any suspicions of fascism.[37] Mohler notes that the most vehement critics of the New Right are none other than repentant former fascists such as Georg Wolf, from *Der Spiegel,* and the 'political scientist, Maurice Duverger, who began his political career in the footsteps of the fascist leader Jacques Doriot'.[38] At the same time Mohler applauds the cultural and intellectual uniqueness of the New Right, and adds that 'the young French of the New Right can freely expand their range of ideas because their national identity is self-evident to them. The [German] conservatives, after the war, considered it smart to yield their own national question to others...'[39]

Today, the New Right is active in all parts of Europe, although for the reasons enumerated above, its influence has been greatest in France. The authors of the New Right hold regular conferences in Paris and elsewhere in Europe that usually embrace diverse topics ranging from sociobiology to metaphysics, and from medicine to anthropology. It is important to note that other than its 'hard-core' members, whose number remains rather limited, the New Right draws considerable intellectual support from prominent scholars in academia and from world-renowned scientists — although, for a variety of reasons, this support often remains tacit. Academics such as the aforementioned scholar Armin Mohler, the psychologist Hans Jürgen Eysenck, the political philosopher Julien Freund, and many other less-known figures regularly attend the seminars and conferences sponsored by the New Right, during which they critically examine the roots of the contemporary crisis.

The New Right, or the GRECE, which started virtually from nothing, and which was constantly subjected to intellectual ostracism and frequent criticism, has managed to generate considerable intellectual

---

37 Armin Mohler, *Vergangenheitsbewältigung, oder wie man den Krieg nochmals verliert* (Krefeld: Sinus Verlag, 1980), p. 92.

38 *Loc. cit.*

39 *Ibid.,* p. 97.

support, particularly among the *haute intelligence* in Europe. One must, however, specify that its sympathisers, supporters, and members cannot be viewed as a monolithic group with a common political platform. The chief ambition of the New Right has so far consisted of gathering, inspiring, and rehabilitating scientists, writers, novelists, and thinkers critical of egalitarianism and all aspects of social uniformity.

It may be concluded from the above that the New Right has acquired considerable cultural influence in Europe, particularly in the great French scholarly institutions. One of the seductive characteristics of the New Right is its visible openness to all ideological challenges, Left or Right, Fascist and Communist. Such 'organicism' often encompasses ideas of virtually all political currents and crosses the entire social spectrum. In addition, New Right thinkers are often in agreement with some Leftist intellectuals and they also frequently extol the moral and intellectual integrity of some socialist intellectuals, such as Régis Debray. Above all, the New Right always claims to be ready to initiate a dialogue with its intellectual and political foes. Its willingness to debate also provides it with an aura of cultural tolerance, the political consequences of which remain to be seen.

II

THE 'GRAMSCIANISM'
OF THE RIGHT

According to the New Right, the world is a battlefield of ideas, and therefore, the political process in any country is primarily a war of ideas. Culture is the most effective carrier of political ideas because culture mobilises the popular consciousness not only by virtue of ephemeral slogans, but also by a genuine appeal to the historical memory of the people. Reversing the Marxist theorem, the New Right argues that ideas, and not economic infrastructure, constitute the foundation of every polity. The reason that the dominant socialist and liberal ideologies have been politically successful is primarily due to the fact that socialist and liberal theorists have more adroitly instilled cultural consensus in the masses. As a result, modern egalitarian societies are in a position today to assert their historical validity and their allegedly scientific character, since, at any rate, their intellectual leaders had already laid a firm grip on the realm of culture. By using the Gramscian strategy of political conquest, the New Right concedes that the source of political power must be preceded by socio-cultural action. Cultural power is a prerequisite of political power; henceforth, those who are able to leave their imprint on culture will inevitably score gains in the political arena. Culture is not just an ornament or a 'superstructure' to be delivered piecemeal to the people; it is a vital and indispensable part of human development capable of inducing social consensus and providing a ruling elite with lasting political legitimacy.

The New Right conceives of modern liberal and socialist systems as being two worn-out myths that sway the masses not because of their scientific character, but rather thanks to their monopolisation of culture.

The real force that sustains liberalism and socialism is the cultural consensus that reigns more or less undisturbed in the higher echelons of the educational and legal systems. Once these cultural centres of power are removed, the system must change its infrastructure—and not, as Marx claimed, the other way around. The main reason that conservative movements and regimes have been unable to gain lasting political legitimacy lies in their inability to successfully infiltrate the cultural level of society in order to introduce another 'counter-ideology' to the masses. Should conservative movements genuinely desire to become politically consolidated, they must first and foremost elaborate their own cultural strategy, which will ultimately help them to dislodge socialist and liberal leverage in the political arena. One must first conquer the brains before conquering the state, argues the New Right, or to paraphrase Georges Sorel, each political 'aspirant' must first create his powerful secular or spiritual myth in order to win over the masses.[1] Left-wing movements have traditionally been better at understanding the political role of culture than conservative movements. In contrast, modern conservatives naïvely cling to the belief that, in the long run, only economics can dissolve all radical ideologies, including that of their Marxist foes. For the New Right, all political movements are doomed to failure unless they fully grasp the meaning of culture, popular myths, and popular modern sensibilities. Worse, they will forever be prevented from acquiring the political respectability that only culture imparts.

In an effort to decrease the political influence of socialism and liberalism, the New Right proposes a scheme for doing cultural battle by adapting the message that Antonio Gramsci originally intended for Communist intellectuals, consisting in 'being actively involved in practical life, as a builder, an organiser, "permanently persuasive" because he [the intellectual] is not purely an orator...'[2]

Gramsci rejects the role of the intellectual as an 'expert', or what Werner Sombart calls a *Fachmann,* and replaces this role with that of an organic intellectual who is both a popular leader and a 'specialist'.[3] According to Gramsci, 'intellectuals are the "officers" of the ruling class

---

1 Cf. Georges Sorel, *Reflections on Violence* (Cambridge: Cambridge University Press, 2002).

2 Antonio Gramsci, *The Modern Prince and Other Writings* (New York: International Publishers, 1959), p. 122.

3 *Loc. cit.*

for the exercise of the subordinate functions of social hegemony and political government, i.e., of the "spontaneous" consent given by the great masses of the population to the direction imprinted on social life by the fundamental ruling class — a consent which comes into existence "historically" and from [its] prestige..."[4]

In discussing the role of culture as a tool of political conquest, the New Right confers upon it a greater importance that aims at embracing all aspects of social life: the realms of lower education, the media, and even modern popular myths. And in this effort, the New Right follows closely the rule laid down by Gramsci. In contrast to Lenin, who believed that problems could be resolved through the application of absolute state power, Gramsci notes that within each society the state cannot maintain its authority if it fails to acknowledge the importance of popular culture and popular demands. In other words, Marxism, fascism, or liberalism can only attain full legitimacy by relying upon, and if necessary, by following the civil society, whereby they can themselves eventually transform into a civil power. Such power is often invisible, and barely operates in political or legal institutions. Rather, it is an implicit power; *de jure* subservient to the state, but *de facto* being the vehicle of the state. This genuine political power is enhanced when the interaction between the implicit power and the explicit power (the state) is brought to its maximum effect. Should the division between the state and society prevail, and should the 'intellectual minority' which supports it remain permanently hostile to its institutions, it is almost certain that, sooner or later, the regime and its ruling elite will be ousted. The true crisis of legitimacy starts only when the intelligentsia begins to desert the power that lies within the state. The state, consequently, becomes weakened, and the size of its repressive apparatus notwithstanding, it will henceforth continue to exist without the support of its primary social pillar.

Using the Gramscian model of cultural conquest, the authors of the New Right observe that if their ideas are ever to exert political influence, then they must also promote a 'counter-culture' within the existing liberal institutional framework. All past social upheavals, including the French Revolution and even the Industrial Revolution, would not have matured had it not been for a sizeable number of influential thinkers who either wilfully or inadvertently introduced new ideas and new

---

4   *Ibid.*, p. 124.

schools of thought into their societies. According to the New Right, the liberal Right today is committing a cardinal mistake by emphasising the importance of economic efficiency while forgetting that durable political success can only be achieved when coupled with intellectual and cultural gains. This paradox appears even more glaring if one considers that socialist and Communist intellectuals view economics as the basis of history and all aspects of culture as part of the ideological superstructure. In the real political battle, however, the socialists seem to have better understood the role of the cultural superstructure than their conservative colleagues; hence the Leftists' constant and relentless advocacy of 'another education', 'another sensibility', 'another sociology of sex', and so on.[5]

For the New Right, the ongoing 'deideologisation' of European politics has resulted in a gaping cultural vacuum. Marxist ideas having lost cultural supremacy, and liberalism being too incompetent to create a new myth capable of swaying the masses, the time is ripe for the New Right to step in and begin a new cultural war. The New Right argues that as much as Western European societies have tried to remain institutionally conservative, they have been unable to resist various egalitarian and socialistic trends. In the following chapters, we will examine the New Right's view that equality cannot be achieved using the various classical liberal constructs, such as 'equality of opportunity' or the 'right to economic differentiation'. The New Right contends that, in the long run, the liberal proclamation of legal equality must invariably spill over into other spheres, including economics. Consequently, neo-conservative and liberal theorists will not be able to resist socialistic and egalitarian trends in their societies unless they first redefine the concept of *legal* equality. According to the New Right, to do so would first mean to construct a comprehensible conservative ideology. Even the recent realignment of former socialist intellectuals around the liberal and neo-conservative agenda cannot have lasting success because liberal thinkers focus their attention only on the deplorable consequences of Marxism ('The Gulag'), while failing to analyse the egalitarian causes that led to its birth.

---

5   Judging by the number of books published during the 1970s with the title 'towards another sociology of...' the intellectual jargon appears to have its own 'hit parade' of mimicry. For example: Marcel Cohen, *Matériaux pour une sociologie du langage* (Paris: Maspero, 1971); Lucien Goldman, *Pour une sociologie du roman* (Paris: Gallimard, 1964); Michael Lowy, *Pour une sociologie des intellectuels révolutionnaires: l'évolution politique de Lukacs 1909-1929* (Paris: PUF, 1976), etc.

The Treason of the Clerks

By deriding the unfaithful character of former socialist intellectuals, who 'slid from the pinnacle of Mao to a Rotary club',[6] de Benoist draws attention to the eternal fickleness of the European intelligentsia, which seldom shows remorse when changing its old political persuasion. To exemplify this, de Benoist refers to the case of the intellectuals in Vichy France, who were quick to embrace the ideas of fascism, when fascist ideas were in 'cultural' vogue, and who were even quicker to denounce them when socialism came into cultural demand:

> Between 1940 and 1944, no social class rallied to the cause of the occupier more massively than did the intelligentsia. And in this sense, nothing has changed. Intellectuals have again been seduced by the dominant ideology. Poirot Delpech is right in observing that we live in the age of 'collaborationists', who make use of the 'ideological scoop' — i.e., the infallible 'repainted *déjà vu*' that consists of resorting to jargon to impress the fools... For the intellectual Left, this consummate art of self-critical mimesis consists of constantly mounting the pulpit to announce that it is no longer wrong, while simultaneously explaining that it is wrong. And, to top it all off, there are the disillusioned professionals who are launching themselves (good consciousness obliges them!) into the monotheism of an (ideological) whorehouse or the 'gulag-circus', e.g., in the defence of human rights — which never requires any commitment.[7]

These lines may probably add weight to the New Right's contention that the intelligentsia is intrinsically the raw product of the *Zeitgeist*, always eager to replace its slogans once its cherished pundits fall in disgrace. The current intellectual abandonment of Marxism, so prevalent in the modern marketplace of ideas, confirms the fact that Marxism has ceased to exert intellectual magnetism on contemporary intellectuals. The intellectual landscape of today is barren, complains de Benoist:

---

6   This is the title of Guy Hocquenghem's book, *Lettre ouverte à ceux qui sont passés du col Mao au Rotary* (*Open Letter to Those Who Came from the Mao Pass to Rotary*) (Paris: Albin Michel, 1986), reviewed by Guillaume Faye in *Éléments*, under the title 'Hocquenghem vend la mêche', Autumn 1986, pp. 54-56.

7   Alain de Benoist, 'Intelligentsia: les jeux du cirque', *Le Figaro Magazine*, 5 May 1979, p. 82.

[t]here are no more debates in France. No in-depth analyses. By the way, it is always easy to avoid the debate. It suffices to disqualify the adversary. This saves time in having to refute him. One judges the chess-box (the place from which someone talks) rather than the pawn (the discourse itself). One attacks the persons rather than what they write.[8]

The process of intellectual prostitution and the betrayal of former idols that verges on outright political treason has acquired pathological proportions, according to the New Right. And inasmuch as the New Right criticises the former Maoists and Leninists who converted to respectable neo-conservatism, no less strong is its praise for those Leftist intellectuals who have not succumbed to the siren song of neo-conservatism. Among those Leftists is the socialist Régis Debray, who in a vein similar to de Benoist observes:

> When there were three to five million *zeks* in Soviet camps, the entire art world of Paris was hustling into the lobbies of the Soviet embassy. When (now) the least biased experts estimate the number of prisoners of conscience in the Soviet Union at being between one thousand and five thousand, the same people yell in disgust before the fence of the Soviet embassy. This is proof that hatred is not proportional to the 'hateful' — but only to a particular moment and to the forms of our representation.[9]

Thus, for the New Right, the role of the intelligentsia in the Twentieth century has been negative, on the whole. It has consisted of subverting the popular consciousness and creating incompetent political leadership — leadership, in short, which has relied on the corrupted intelligentsia in order to perpetuate its own rule.

The New Right was probably the first cultural movement to introduce the term 'intellectual terrorism', using it to describe its socialist and liberal detractors. To remove those intellectual barriers of 'spiritual terrorism', and to revive its own intellectual heritage, today remains its most important task. It is primarily the cultural heritage of the early European revolutionary conservatives that the New Right is attempting to rekindle, and to this we now turn.

---

8   *Loc. cit.*

9   Régis Debray, *Les Empires contre l'Europe* (Paris: Gallimard), pp. 173, 16-17, quoted in Alain de Benoist, *Europe, Tiers monde, même combat* (Paris: Robert Laffont, 1986), p. 236.

III

THE CONSERVATIVE LEFT OR THE REVOLUTIONARY RIGHT?

The following chapters examine the intellectual heritage of the New Right. Once we have outlined the ideas of some earlier European anti-liberal and anti-socialist authors, it will also be much easier to comprehend the overall cultural and political strategy of the New Right.

It would be erroneous to search for the intellectual antecedents of the European New Right among two or three anti-liberal and anti-Communist thinkers and philosophers of the early Twentieth century. We must again emphasise that hasty analyses of the New Right may end up in academic reductionism that usually defines social phenomena according to some preconceived categories and common denominators. While many predecessors of the New Right, such as Nietzsche, Spengler, or Schmitt, indeed have a reputation for advocating anti-democratic and anti-egalitarian ideas, it must not be forgotten that the New Right often admits its intellectual indebtedness to a number of prominent socialist and even Marxist authors. Nevertheless, despite its efforts to remain unaffected by ideological controversy, the main task the New Right has assigned itself is to restore and even 'rehabilitate' precisely those authors who, due to unfavourable historical circumstances, fell into oblivion or whose works have not received an adequate appraisal on the grounds of their allegedly fascist character. For the purpose of clarity, this book, however, will focus only on those authors who are most relevant in analysing the importance of the New Right and who, later on in our discussion, will be crucial in discussing the crisis of modern politics. I do not, however, mean to do injustice

to authors such as Herder, Fichte, Hölderlin, and some other thinkers, poets, and novelists who do not enter into our immediate discussion, yet who remain instrumental if one wishes to fully understand
the intellectual roots of the New Right.

Undoubtedly, many of the inspirers of the New Right were and still
are the authors who lived during a troubled epoch in Europe; notably, when fascist ideas were still part and parcel of political romanticism for many, before they became part of a dominant system for
a few. Ideas, just like people, are seldom innocent. Having professed
scepticism about democracy, liberalism, and parliamentary democracy during the interwar period of peace is not the same as attacking democracy, liberalism, and parliamentary democracy when the
destiny of millions is at stake. Indeed, many conservative authors for
whom the New Right shows great admiration today were attracted to
fascist ideas, and many more openly collaborated with European fascist regimes. Equally large, however, was the number of those conservative intellectuals who felt betrayed by fascism and yet continued
to believe in their self-styled fascist or proto-fascist ideas. If the logic
is correct that all European radical conservatives share the responsibility for the rise of fascism, then one must also assume that Marx,
Lenin, and Trotsky, not to mention the entire Leftist and liberal post-
war intelligentsia, are also partly responsible for the birth of Stalinism and repression in Marxist countries worldwide.[1] It is true that
Fichte, Wagner, and many other European 'Romantics', as some modern authors argue, may have developed 'proto-fascist' ideas, but the
same criticism could be then levelled against Descartes, Jefferson, and
some Nineteenth century Rationalists who allegedly masterminded
the foundations of modern egalitarian mass society and who even in
part contributed to 'gulag' Communism in the Soviet Union and Eastern Europe. As the old, worn-out saying goes, 'the road to Hell is paved
with good intentions', and one can plausibly speculate that, had it not
been for an array of past and present ideologies, the world today would
be a better place to live.

The debate over the moral responsibility of intellectuals is seemingly endless, and if one genuinely wishes to adhere to the principles of

---

1   The list of European and American Leftist intellectuals who were reluctant to
    criticise Communism 'out of fear of playing into the hands of capitalism and the
    United States' is exhaustive. As we proceed, we shall be referring to their names
    more frequently.

causality, future generations may be justified in discarding intellectuals as an obsolete and harmful social category. Analogously, if one concludes, *a priori*, that the New Right is harbouring fascist ideas simply because it differently evaluates the legacy of some earlier pro-fascist and fascist authors, then the entire present discussion runs the risk of turning into a theory of morals, which is certainly not the purpose of this book. It is undeniable that National Socialism and Fascism made considerable use of the ideas elaborated earlier by some radical conservative and revolutionary conservative thinkers in the first decades of this century. Also, as Armin Mohler observes, the Conservative Revolution was to a great extent a 'treasure trove from which National Socialism [drew] its ideological weapons'.[2] The fact, however, that revolutionary conservative ideas were never implemented in practice may explain why National Socialism has been viewed as a direct outcome of these ideas.

The difficulty in understanding the role of the early revolutionary conservative intelligentsia is also due to the fact that among the revolutionary conservatives there existed immense ideological and personal differences. In describing the odyssey of revolutionary conservative intellectuals, Mohler observes that a small number, especially from predominantly social revolutionary groups, went into exile (such as Otto Strasser, Karl Paetel, and Hans Ebeling). But some traditional conservatives, such as Hermann Rauschning and Gottfried Treviranus, also left the country, although the majority of them decided to stay in Germany.[3] Those who decided to remain in Germany did so less because of admiration for National Socialism, but rather, as Mohler asserts, because they 'hoped to permeate National Socialism from within, or transform themselves into a second revolution'.[4] However, it is hard to deny that, in a manner similar to the many Leftist intellectuals who paid lip service to Stalinism,[5] many conservative intellectuals

---

2   Armin Mohler, *Die konservative Revolution in Deutschland 1918-1932* (Darmstadt: Wissenschaftliche Buchgesellschaft, 1972), p. xxviii.

3   *Ibid.*, p. 6.

4   *Loc. cit.*

5   This was notably the case with some prominent intellectuals who were fervent Stalinists, such as Henri Barbusse, Louis Aragon, and George Lukács. It is also worth noting that many of the so-called anti-Communist dissidents from Communist countries, who seem to have had a great emotional impact on the Western media, were active as commissars, members, or affiliates of their local Communist parties

in the early 1930s also knew their zero hour. Many, indeed, became active spokesmen of National Socialism and lent full support to the fascist police apparatus. Ernst Jünger, once a leading figure in the revolutionary conservative movement in Germany and today one of the direct inspirations of the European New Right, depicted the intellectual 'prostitution' of his former conservative comrades, who went on the payroll of the Third Reich:

> Such people belong to the kind of truffle pigs (*Trüffelschweine*) whom one can find in every revolution. Because the rough, like-minded comrades are unable to locate their cherished opponents, they must resort to the corrupted intelligentsia of higher capacity in order to sniff out, make visible, and then, if possible, attack their opponents with a police crackdown...[6]

One must emphasise that although the Conservative Revolution had the largest intellectual resonance in Germany, it would be erroneous to consider it a purely German phenomenon. It is noteworthy that similar conservative intellectual upheavals took place in virtually all European countries, albeit to a lesser degree. The subsequent rise and demise of National Socialism, while certainly corrupting the ideas of European revolutionary conservative thinkers, also greatly contributed to their inevitable disqualification after the war. Having this in mind, one must wonder whether it is wise to accuse all pre-war revolutionary conservatives of being fellow travellers of fascism, or rather to investigate

---

several decades ago. One of them is the Yugoslav dissident Milovan Djilas (author of a well-known 1957 exposé of the Communist establishment, *The New Class*). Until his ideological conversion, Djilas was a prominent Stalinist spokesman and also the mastermind of the post-war terror in Yugoslavia. Contemporary East European dissidents such as the writer Milan Kundera of Czechoslovakia, the philosopher Leszek Kołakowski, and activist Adam Michnik, both of Poland, were affiliated with the Communist regime in their respective countries during the 1960s. Anatoly Scharansky and Yelena Bonner, two prominent Jewish dissidents in the Soviet Union, were members of the Soviet Communist Party.

6   Quoted in Mohler, *Die konservative Revolution*, pp. 7-8. Jünger wrote these lines in his diary, *Strahlungen* (Tübingen: Heliopolis Verlag, 1955), p. 144, in Paris, 7 October 1942, while he was on active duty as the officer of the Wehrmacht. He fell into disgrace twice; first with the Nazis due to his growing dissatisfaction with their regime, and then, following the war, when he was practically forgotten by a wider public due to his association with them. The New Right has contributed greatly to his recent popularity in France.

individual responsibility, just like among many socialist intellectuals. 'It appears', continues Mohler, 'that the question of individual responsibility is easier to answer because it can be narrowed down to adherence to specific organisations and participation in specific activities.'[7]

Some contemporary conservative critics still continue to debate among themselves about the alleged 'Nazi' character of the pre-war conservative intellectuals. For example, as Peter Viereck asserts, the quoted passage from Mohler's book only 'does a disservice to genuine Burkean and Rankean conservatism by using that term as a part of a nationwide campaign to rehabilitate morally the immoral Rightist fellow-travellers of Hitler.'[8] Viereck sees, in fact, a greater threat in these conservative 'fellow travellers' than in their political masters. While repudiating metapolitics as a socially dangerous phenomenon, Viereck contends that 'without a century of romanticist ideas, seeping downward to all levels and then outward from books into bullets, the well-educated and decent German nation would never have become so uniquely susceptible (gullible) toward a meta-thug. Because unintended political consequences were unforeseen, does not mean that they were unforeseeable...'[9]

The Revolt Against Modernity

It would be naïve to assume that the New Right authors are unaware of the continuing intellectual unpopularity and ostracism that surrounds their conservative predecessors. Yet, four decades after the war, they can easily deny any responsibility for the deeds of their intellectual forefathers by claiming to adhere to the legacy of those conservative authors who never fully got entangled in fascist regimes.

But how did the Conservative Revolution emerge, and what were the political motives of those pre-war conservatives who had chosen a certain *Weltanschauung* that many people after the Second World War found utterly appalling, and which many others, like the New Right, find immensely appealing?

---

7   *Ibid.*, p. 9.

8   Peter Viereck, *Metapolitics: The Roots of the Nazi Mind* (New York: Capricorn Books, 1961), p. ix.

9   *Ibid.*, pp. xxvi, xxvii.

The generation of conservative authors prior to the Second World War protested violently against the rationalist individualism of the liberal social order and against the dissolution of social ties that had burst open with the Industrial Revolution and had swept masses of newly uprooted individuals into new forms of social existence. This was the generation of thinkers that greatly feared the rise of Bolshevism and the ensuing violence that had ominously spread across Europe in the first years following the First World War. According to Zeev Sternhell, an expert on the intellectual origins of fascism, the beginning of the Twentieth century brought in:

> [t]he new sciences of man, the new social sciences, the Darwinian biology, the Bergsonian philosophy, the interpretation of history by Treitschke and Jahn, the social philosophy of Le Bon. The entire Italian political sociology stood up against the postulates on which liberalism and democracy rested. An intellectual climate was thus created which undermined considerably the first foundations of democracy, facilitating enormously the rise of Fascism.[10]

The social order of the morally and financially bankrupt European democracies ultimately drove a sizeable number of sensitive intellectuals into the arms of both socialism and fascism. As Sternhell remarks, for the first time, the majority of European intellectuals began to seriously question the principles of human betterment as well as the belief in indefinite social progress.[11] This 'revolt against modernity', as Julius Evola called it, and which, according to the New Right, represents the cornerstone of the modern crisis, became quasi-universal; it permeated all cultured elites, artists, filmmakers, musicians, painters, and philosophers, only to take its final shape in the realm of politics. During that period, even the line of ideological demarcation between the Right and the Left frequently overlapped. Sternhell writes that in France, for instance, one could observe a massive intellectual defection from the Left to the Right, 'because fascism sometimes drew from the Left and from the Right, and sometimes in some countries more

---

10 Zeev Sternhell, *La Droite révolutionnaire 1885-1914* (Paris: Seuil, 1978), p. 17. (Sternhell later authored another book on the same theme, *The Birth of Fascist Ideology* [Princeton: Princeton University Press, 1994].-Ed.)

11 *Ibid.*, pp. 22-32.

from the Left than from the Right'.[12] In the 1920s and 1930s, all European fascist thinkers, beyond what might separate them on other issues, were in agreement that democratic parliamentary systems were detrimental to national revival and the spirit of historical community. From Giovanni Gentile, the Italian philosopher who, following Aristotle, conceived of man as a 'political animal', through the Belgian Rexist José Streel, who affirmed that the 'individual does not exist in a pure condition', to José Antonio Primo de Rivera, who declared war on Rousseau, all of these conservative intellectuals attacked the foundations of the liberal, 'mechanistic' concept of society that conceives of the people as a simple aggregate of individuals.[13]

The conservative intellectual revolution, also known as the 'organic revolution', engulfed not only Germany but swept over all European countries, stretching its influence even to remote parts of the world. As Mohler notes, the Conservative Revolutionaries comprised 'Dostoyevsky or both Aksakovs for Russia, Sorel and Barrès for France, Unamuno for Spain, Pareto and Evola for Italy, both Lawrence or Chesterton for England, Jabotinsky for Jewry'.[14] One could also include the names of Lothrop Stoddard, Madison Grant, Jack London, Francis Parker Yockey, Ezra Pound, and James Burnham, the theorist of *The Managerial Revolution,* to indicate that even the United States took part in those intellectual upheavals.[15] And all these young intellectuals shared the same idea of the 'earth and the dead',[16] the principles of the absolute subordination of individuals to the collective, and the negation of individual autonomy — the idea that represented the quintessence of organic society.

---

12 *Ibid.*, p. 405.

13 *Ibid.*, p. 409.

14 Mohler, *Die konservative Revolution*, p. 13.

15 See Francis Parker Yockey, *Imperium* (New York: The Truth Seeker, 1962); Ezra Pound, *Impact: Essays on Ignorance and the Decline of American Civilization* (Chicago: Henry Regnery, 1960); Madison Grant, *The Passing of the Great Race* (New York: Scribner, 1916); Lothrop Stoddard, *Lonely America* (New York: Doubleday, 1932), etc.

16 'Earth and the dead' refers to the ideology of the French nationalist Maurice Barrès (1862-1923), who was highly influential on the Conservative Revolution. Barrès believed that the life of a nation must always incorporate these elements if it is to remain rooted. –Ed.

It would be impossible to enumerate the names and examine the ideas of all the authors and intellectual figures who directly or indirectly contributed to the Conservative Revolution in Europe, and who are today exerting an enormous intellectual influence on the New Right. We shall limit ourselves to those authors whose influence was fundamental in shaping its intellectual framework, and who can be justifiably called the precursors of the modern European New Right. The thinkers whom we shall now examine are the German political scientist and jurist Carl Schmitt, the sociologist and economist Vilfredo Pareto, and the historian Oswald Spengler. Naturally, as we proceed, we shall notice that the New Right often refers to its other 'forefathers', such as Friedrich Nietzsche, Martin Heidegger, Georges Dumézil, and many other thinkers and philosophers, who to a great extent can be associated with the New Right's intellectual and cultural heritage. However, given the fact that this book deals with the *political* and *sociological* aspects of the contemporary crisis, and only to some extent with its philosophical and ethical aspects, I decided that Spengler, Pareto, and Schmitt would be the best examples for our present discussion and for our better understanding of the European New Right.

IV

CARL SCHMITT
AND POLITICS AS DESTINY

Like many contemporary German jurists, Carl Schmitt (1888-1982) is an important representative of a school of thought in German and European public law that turned away from the German tradition of legal positivism[1] and tried to broaden the study of law by introducing political and sociological considerations. Schmitt's earlier participation in anti-liberal movements such as the Conservative Revolution, as well as his later involvement with Nazism, is still a subject of controversy, and as the appearance of the New Right shows, this controversy is not likely to end soon.

According to Schmitt, modern society is undergoing a rapid process of 'depoliticisation' and 'neutralisation'. Traditional 'high' politics is nowadays being replaced with 'low' politics and the belief that the role of state authority is increasingly becoming obsolete in modern global society. For Schmitt, depoliticisation is not just a chance result of the modern era or the inevitable consequence of contemporary international economic linkages; it is an original and well-programmed goal of both liberal and socialist societies. But can mankind really escape the grip of politics, asks Schmitt? Politics is a basic characteristic of human life, and despite all attempts to depoliticise the world, politics will continue to be, albeit in a different form, the destiny of all future generations. The inescapable nature of politics is clearly exemplified by the contradiction from which man cannot extricate himself even

---

1 Legal positivism maintains that there is no inherent contradiction between law and morality, and that law is a man-made construction rather than something given by God.-Ed.

when he makes an attempt to do so. All aspects of human life, in all epochs, and despite all efforts, have been the subject of politics. In the Sixteenth century, the political manifested itself in theology, in the Seventeenth century in metaphysics, in the Eighteenth century in ethics, in the Nineteenth century in economics, and in the Twentieth century in technology. Notwithstanding all efforts to displace or subsume the political under either theology or, later, technology, it invariably occurred that each field in its turn became the subject of the political. Although conceived as neutral fields, neither economics nor the modern 'neutral state' (*stato neutrale*) succeeded in fully displacing the political from society; in each instance, each field and every aspect of life was again politicised:

> But in the dialectic of such a development one creates a new domain of struggle precisely through the shifting of the central domain. In the new domain, at first considered neutral, the antitheses of men and interests unfold with a new intensity and become increasingly sharper. Europeans always have wandered from a conflictual to a neutral domain, and always the newly won neutral domain has become immediately another arena of struggle, once again necessitating the search for a new neutral domain. Scientific thinking was also unable to achieve peace. The religious wars evolved into the still cultural yet already economically determined national wars of the Nineteenth century and, finally, into economic wars. [2]

The condition of the political process in modern parliamentary democracies is so pitiful because their internal development has reduced all political discourse to shallow formality. Different opinions are no longer debated; instead, social, financial, and economic pressure groups calculate their interests, and on the basis of these interests they make compromises and coalitions. A modern liberal politician resembles, according to Schmitt, a 'manager' or an 'entertainer' whose goal is not to persuade his opponent about the validity of his political program, but primarily to obtain a political majority. Democracy, liberalism, freedom, and equality are a smokescreen, no more than clichés designed to mask and perpetuate the moral and political bankruptcy of parliamentary systems. For Schmitt, liberal democracies are adept in deforming

2   Carl Schmitt, *The Concept of the Political* (Chicago: The University of Chicago Press, 2007), p. 90.

political semantics by simply renaming their imperial ambitions and territorial acquisitions with anodyne terms such as 'contracts', 'colonies', 'protectorates', and 'mandates'. Different forms of political dependency are thus coming into being in which modern democratic systems rule a heterogeneous populace without, however, making them citizens of the world. For Schmitt this is a salient paradox of modern democracy, all the more so as modern democracy persistently boasts of its 'universal' and 'egalitarian' character. Schmitt writes:

> Even a democratic state, let us say the United States of America, is far from letting foreigners participate in its power structure or its wealth. Until now there has never been a democracy that did not recognise the concept 'foreign' and that could have realised the equality of all men.[3]

And therefore, argues Schmitt, states can never be on equal footing as long as they make distinctions between their own citizens and the citizens of other states and as long as a political actor distinguishes between friend and foe.[4] The demise of radical ideologies, notably Fascism and Bolshevism, followed by the process of the 'deideologisation' of modern society, cannot forestall the crisis of parliamentary democracies because this crisis existed before Fascism and Bolshevism came into being and will likely continue after they are gone. For Schmitt, this crisis is due to the 'consequences of modern mass democracy and in the final analysis from the contradiction of a liberal individualism burdened by moral pathos and a democratic sentiment governed essentially by political ideals'.[5]

Against the modern liberal and Marxist negation of the political, Schmitt opposes the affirmation of the political, and the recognition of the perennial character of political struggle. Referring to Hobbes, Schmitt argues that the notion of the political consists in distinguishing between friend and foe (*amicus* vs. *hostis*). But whereas Hobbes transposes the state of nature to the realm of individuals and states, Schmitt expands upon the same concept by adding global significance to it. In Schmitt's state of nature, the subjects are individuals, countries, empires, nations, classes, and races. The process of depoliticisation,

---

3   Carl Schmitt, *The Crisis of Parliamentary Democracy* (Cambridge: MIT Press, 1986), p. 11.

4   *Ibid.*, p. 12.

5   *Ibid.*, p. 17.

undertaken by both Marxists and liberals in an effort to create a world in which war is impossible, is a dangerous illusion that runs counter to human historical development. Human history in its entirety is primarily a history of perpetual struggle between friends and foes — an ocean of wars with only occasional islands of peace:

> Every religious, moral, economic, ethical, or other antithesis transforms into a political one if it is sufficiently strong to group human beings effectively according to friend and enemy. The political does not reside in the battle itself, which possesses its own technical, psychological, and military laws, but in the mode of behavior which is determined by this possibility, by clearly evaluating the concrete situation and thereby being able to distinguish correctly the real friend and the real enemy.[6]

Having this in mind, how then can perpetual peace be attained, asks Schmitt, and if it can, is such a peaceful and apolitical society really conducive to human betterment?

To this question Schmitt gives the following answer: the will toward political differentiation is the basic characteristic of every human being. Should the unanimous decision be reached someday to merge friends and foes into a common apolitical entity, and provided that differences between friends and foes are forever obliterated, what would happen to those who refuse to join such a depoliticised polity? Would they be allowed to exist, to disagree, or to denounce such a global polity? No, answers Schmitt; the decision would be reached to proclaim total war against those recalcitrant individuals or 'warmongers' who refused to join this depoliticised community. But this time, however, the war would be total and of titanic dimensions, waged, naturally, in the name of eternal principles of justice and peace. The war against war will thus be conducted as the absolute, final war of humanity. Such a 'necessary' war would be particularly intense and inhuman because the enemy is no longer perceived as a person with a sense of justice, but rather as an 'inhuman monster' who needs not only to be repelled, but totally annihilated. 'The adversary', writes Schmitt, 'is thus no longer called an enemy but a disturber of the peace and is thereby designated to be an outlaw of humanity... For the application of such means, a new and essentially pacifist vocabulary has been created. War is condemned but

---

6   *The Concept of the Political*, p. 37.

executions, sanctions, punitive expeditions, pacifications, protection of treaties, international police, and measures to assure peace remain'.[7]

With the preceding statement Schmitt alludes to both liberal and Marxist theorists, to those 'crusaders for peace' who wage their 'last' wars either in the name of manifest destiny or Marx's *Communist Manifesto*. Still, the effort to erase the political by virtue of these final wars cannot be successful since the end result is always the exacerbation of conflict, resulting in increased bestiality and universal violence.

Schmitt, therefore, accepts politics as destiny, because the concept of the political can best provide a decision-maker with a margin for manoeuvring and help him steer away from total wars. The political, for Schmitt, is a necessity that allows the possibility of contained violence that stands in contrast to depoliticised, universal violence. Should man — who is by definition a political being — refuse the political, he then also renounces his own humanity. And to those who use war in order to stop wars, Schmitt responds, 'It is a manifest fraud that to condemn war as homicide and then demand of men that they wage war, kill and be killed, so that there will never again be war.'[8]

Even if all men, hypothetically speaking, were to resolve their differences and decide to live in a perfectly depoliticised society, for what would they be free? Such a society would soon degenerate into a world devoid of life, immersed in economics, morality, and entertainment. Man's life would be reduced to a purely biological existence, devoid of seriousness — and when the seriousness of life is threatened, then the political, along with human existence itself, is also threatened.

Today, continues Schmitt, the much-vaunted neutrality of economics, trade, or technology is deceiving and harmful. Economics, trade, or technology are always instruments and weapons of politics despite efforts in liberal states to counter politics through these seemingly apolitical means. Schmitt accuses liberal society of being intrinsically inhuman and of failing to grasp the meaning of history, and with it, the purpose of man's life. A gullible nation, wishing to be lulled into the politics of peace and to shut itself off from history, is on the verge of committing political suicide. Soon thereafter, another, more politicised nation, like a rapacious predator, will not hesitate to devour it. Or as Schmitt puts it, 'If a people no longer possesses the energy or

---

7   *Ibid.*, p. 79.

8   *Ibid.*, p. 48.

the will to maintain itself in the sphere of politics, the latter will not thereby vanish from the world. Only a weak people will disappear'.[9]

The assumption that post-industrial society, with its developed 'high-tech' network, is more likely to guarantee peace is equally misleading, and to this Schmitt responds that 'today technical inventions are the means of the domination of the masses on a large scale. Radio belongs to a broadcasting monopoly; film, to the censor. The decision concerning freedom and slavery lies not in technology as such, which can be revolutionary or reactionary, can serve freedom or oppression, centralisation or decentralisation'.[10]

Schmitt was among the first to analyse the concept of metapolitics, which he elegantly and with some derision terms 'political romanticism'. To him, no matter whether one cherishes or deplores it, political romanticism is an indispensable motor for creating the legal framework of each society. Likewise, a king can become a deified romantic figure, just as an anarchist conspirator, or the Caliph of Baghdad, can turn into objects of mass veneration. Through political romanticism, ideas and virtues, which may subsequently be denounced as vices and crimes, acquire necessary legitimacy and political credibility. In each epoch, however, political romanticism manifests itself differently. Today one talks about Leftist sensibility, egalitarian brotherhood, and peace on earth; one introduces Leftist and liberal iconography and symbolism, glorifying and deifying the virtues of the prevalent *Zeitgeist*. Here is how Schmitt sees political romanticists:

> Instead of concepts and philosophical systems, their subjectivism leads them to a kind of lyrical rewriting of experiences, which can be combined with a certain organic passivity or, where the artistic gift is absent, to the [above-mentioned] half-lyrical, half-intellectual following of strange activities which accompany political events with glossy characteristics, sloganeering and opinions, emphases and counter-arguments, innuendoes and synthetic comparisons; frequently excited and tumultuous, but always without its own decision, own responsibility, and own danger.[11]

---

9   *Ibid.*, p. 53.

10 *Ibid.*, p. 92.

11 Carl Schmitt, *Die politische Romantik* (Munich and Leipzig: Duncker und Humblot Verlag, 1925), p. 224. (Also available as *Political Romanticism* [Cambridge: MIT Press, 1986]-Ed.)

Political romanticism, continues Schmitt, bears resemblance to 'the lyrical grumbles and trembling of thoughts stemming from somebody else's decisions and responsibilities...' Yet, when push comes to shove, and where real political authority begins, 'political romanticism comes to a stop'.[12]

Schmitt further observes that every political romanticist often demonstrates traits of anarchistic individualism and 'self-awareness' (*Selbstgefühl*) that is usually accompanied by excessive cravings for social messianism and fake philanthropy. Schmitt writes that a political romanticist 'is easily seized by altruistic passions, compassion and sympathy, as well as by snobbish presumptions'.[13] Yet, in real political life, he is unable to think beyond his own emotional subjectivity — which he alters, once another form of political romanticism comes into vogue.

By adapting Schmitt's ideas, the New Right contends that the new romanticists of today, i.e., liberals, socialists, and other political groups 'came' to socialism, liberalism, or egalitarianism more by virtue of sentiment than by cognition, and more by outward symbolism than by inward experience. Yet, despite their innocuous political character, which manifests itself in overt political inactivity, political romanticists are an indispensable social category of every polity and every ideology, because they are the best and most fervent articulators of a political mythology and a political iconography. And as Schmitt observes, where real politics begins, it is a politician who makes decisions — whereby 'political romanticism itself is utilised as a means to unromantic activities'.[14]

On many occasions Schmitt stated that the history of the Twentieth century is being written by the victors and not by the victims. After the war, due to his short affiliation with Nazism, he was stripped of his academic tenure, his books were banned, and he was briefly put in prison. Subsequently, although many German jurists after the war continued to make use of his legal writings, his pre-war popularity was never again restored. Even scholars like Hans Morgenthau, Raymond Aron, and other thinkers of the 'Realist school', whose works strongly bear the marks of Schmitt, seldom ventured to make any reference

---

12 *Loc. cit.*

13 *Ibid.,* p. 226.

14 *Ibid.,* p. 227.

to his writings. Later on in his life, from his self-imposed seclusion in Plettenburg, Schmitt observed with anguish the liberal and Communist efforts to convert politics into morality. The Nuremberg Trials seemed only to have confirmed his apprehensions that, henceforth, 'high politics' would be conducted under the sign of morality, and that in times of large-scale wars, the victim's history, customs and language would inevitably become a subject of political criminalisation:

> Hostility becomes so absolute that even the most ancient sacred differentiation between the enemy and the criminal disappears in the paroxysm of self-righteousness. To doubt the validity of one's own sense of justice appears as treason; to show interest in the opponent's arguments is viewed as treachery; and the attempt to start a discussion is considered the same as agreement with the enemy.[15]

Schmitt found an ardent supporter and a good friend in Julien Freund, a French scholar, today a leading figure of the New Right's 'old guard', and widely acclaimed as Schmitt's successor. Significantly, although Freund fought with the French Resistance during the war, he has been warning that politics must be decriminalised if mankind is to avoid total destruction. In one of his articles on Schmitt, Freund states that the 'behaviour of Carl Schmitt appears to me more honourable than the behaviour of other intellectuals (for example Sartre or Merleau-Ponty) who, when the danger was over, gave us a moralistic lecture on behalf of the liberation movement... My abhorrence for the groundless and no-risk moralising of intellectuals goes back to those days.'[16]

Before the war, Schmitt was one of the most respected and widely read political scientists and jurists in Europe. Then, for a period of time, he fell into semi-disgrace. Judging, however, by the efforts of the New Right, and particularly Julien Freund, the interest in Schmitt may again be experiencing a revival. The fact that some of his books were recently translated into English may signal a new shift in political romanticism.[17]

---

15 See in its entirety Carl Schmitt, *Ex Captivitate Salus, Erfahrungen der Zeit 1945/47* (Cologne: Greven Verlag, 1950), and especially p. 58.

16 Julien Freund, 'Die Lehre von Carl Schmitt und die Folgen', *Elemente* 1, 1986, pp. 21-23.

17 Since the time that this was written, several books about Schmitt have been published in English, and most of his works are now available in English translation.–Ed.

V

OSWALD SPENGLER AND
HISTORY AS DESTINY

In analysing the intellectual forefathers of the European New Right, one often encounters the name of Oswald Spengler (1880-1936), the famous German thinker who exerted a considerable cultural influence on European conservative intellectuals before the Second World War. Although his popularity waned somewhat after the war, Spengler still continues to be a respectable subject of scholarly analysis. His cultural pessimism, which appears sometimes a bit exaggerated, has put his name on the lips of thousands of intellectuals around the world, and one may argue that the appearance of the New Right only attests to a renewed interest in his gloomy prophecies. The terror of modern technology, the rise of totalitarianism in the Soviet Union and Nazism in Germany, and the increasing devaluation of human life may lend some credence to Spengler's premonitory visions about the imminent collapse of Europe — a vision that he outlined in his magnum opus, *The Decline of the West.*

Spengler wrote *The Decline of the West* against the background of the anticipated German victory in the First World War. However, when the war ended disastrously for Germany, his book only corroborated his overwhelming belief that Europe was headed for immediate decline. During Spengler's lifetime the belief in linear human progress and faith in man's innate perfectibility were both still subjects invested with religious fervour, although the aftermath of the war had brought in a sudden wave of scepticism. The mesmerising effects of new technology soon came to be understood not only as a sign of prosperity, but also as an ideal tool for man's annihilation. Inadvertently, and without even knowing it, by attempting to interpret the entire history of Europe, Spengler best succeeded in depicting the history of his own era and his own troubled generation. He was among the first authors who tried to establish a pattern of cultural growth and cultural decay, and in doing so, he conceived of giving to his analysis a deterministic and a certain scientific value. As a result of his endeavours, he wrote 'the morphology of history' — as his work is often termed — although, probably, his work deserves to be renamed a 'biology' of history. The term 'biology' indeed seems more appropriate considering Spengler's inclination to view cultures as living and organic entities afflicted with diseases, plagues, or showing signs of health.

Firstly, Spengler rejects the abstract concept of 'mankind' or 'humanity'. His entire vision of the human species is one of different and opposing peoples, each experiencing its own growth and death. The concept of mankind, writes Spengler, is either a 'zoological expression, or an empty word. But conjure away the phantom, break the magic circle, and at once there emerges an astonishing wealth of actual forms — the Living with all its immense fullness, depth and movement — hitherto veiled by a catchword, a dry-as-dust scheme and a set of personal "ideals".[1]

Spengler was not unaware that the concept of 'world history' encompasses an impressive array of diverse and mighty cultures, each with its own form, own passion, and its own life and death. Thus he writes that 'Cultures, peoples, languages, truths, gods, landscapes bloom and age as the oaks and the stone-pines, the blossoms, twigs and leaves — but there is no aging "Mankind".'[2] All cultures grow in their own 'sublime futility' (*erhabene Zwecklosigkeit*), and human will can never reverse this process.

For Spengler, each culture passes through various cycles or different historical 'seasons'. First there is the period of early cultural blossoming, or the springtime of culture. Then comes the period of maturation, which Spengler alternately calls summer or autumn, and finally comes the period frozen in self-destructiveness, or the end of culture, which Spengler calls civilisation. This cyclical flow of history is an inevitable predicament of all cultures, although historical

---

1   Oswald Spengler, *The Decline of the West*, vol. 1 (New York: Alfred A. Knopf, 1962), p. 17.

2   *Ibid.*, vol. 1, p. 21.

timing may vary according to a different nation, geographical area, or epoch. In the field of politics and statecraft, the established historical cycle is exactly the same, whereby the political process undergoes a period starting with the early phase of maturation, and ultimately ending in decay. Accordingly, the closing years of the First World War, when Spengler was completing his work, had witnessed the passing of the feudal rule of landed aristocracy in Germany and its merging into budding forms of parliamentary plutocracy — soon to be followed by the rise of 'mobocracy' and then Caesarism.

Spengler was convinced that the future of each civilisation could be fairly well predicted, provided that exact historical data is available. Just as the biology of human beings has a well-defined life span, resulting ultimately in biological death, in a similar way each culture possesses its own ever-aging 'data' that usually lasts no longer than a thousand years — namely, the period that separates the springtime of a culture from its eventual historical antithesis: the 'winter', or civilisation. The choice of a thousand years period before the decline of culture begins corresponds to Spengler's certitude that after that period, every society has to face its imminent self-destruction. Likewise, after the fall of Rome, the rebirth of European culture started in the Ninth century with the Carolingian dynasty. After the painful process of growth, self-assertiveness and maturation, a thousand years later, in the Twentieth century, the life of Europe is coming to its definite historical close. Spengler, however, does not explain how culture is born, and what sustains its life. To him this remains a mystery, inaccessible to human cognition.

As Spengler and his contemporary successors among the New Right see it, European culture has nowadays transformed itself into a civilisation that is currently being threatened by an advanced form of social, moral, and political decay. After the Industrial Revolution, Europe had passed the stage of culture, and is experiencing today, and in the most acute form, the winter of its life. New forms of political life have emerged in Europe, marked by the ideology of economism and the rule of plutocracy. All sectors of social life are being reduced to an immense economic transaction. And since nobody can ever be fully satisfied, and everybody yearns for more, it is understandable that masses of people will seek a change in their existing communities. This craving for 'change' will be translated into the incessant decline of the sense of public responsibility, followed by uprootedness and social anomie, which will inevitably and ultimately lead to Caesarism, or totalitarianism. Finally, before the 'muscled regimes' can come into full effect, democracies will be marred by moral and social convulsions, political scandals, and horrendous corruption on all levels of society. 'Through money', writes Spengler, 'democracy becomes its own destroyer, after money has destroyed intellect.'[3] Furthermore, as Spengler observes, the transition from democracy into mobocracy will be facilitated when the tyranny of the few is replaced by the tyranny of the many:

> But the same things recur, and as a *necessary* result of the European-American liberalism — 'the despotism of freedom against tyranny', as Robespierre put it. In lieu of stake and faggots there is the great silence. The dictature of party leaders supports itself upon that of the Press. The competitors strive by means of money to detach readers — nay, peoples — *en masse* from the hostile allegiance and to bring them under their own mind-training. And all that they learn in this mind-training, is what it is considered that they should know — a higher will puts together the picture of their world for them. There is no need now, as there was for Baroque princes, to impose military-service liability on the subject — one whips their souls with articles, telegrams, and pictures (Northcliffe!) until they *clamour* for weapons and force their leaders into a conflict to which they *willed* to be forced.[4]

Hardly any palliative can be found against this predetermined process of social decay. Europe has grown old, unwilling to fight, and its political and cultural inventory has been depleted. Consequently it is obliged to cede its cultural supremacy to more primitive and barbaric nations and races that are less susceptible to pacifism and masochistic guilt. The end of Europe thus being sealed, a new culture, a new nation, and a new cycle of history begins. European man has lost his sense of historical relativism, yet he naïvely thinks that his 'irrefutable truths' and 'eternal verities' will forever remain valid and eternal for all people in the world. If a modern European desires to recognise the temporary nature of his historical position, continues Spengler, he must finally start thinking beyond his narrow 'frog perspective' (*Froschperspektive*), and develop different attitudes towards different

---

3   *Ibid.*, vol. 2, p. 464.

4   *Ibid.*, vol. 2, p. 463.

political convictions and principles. What do Parsifal or Prometheus have to do with an average Japanese citizen, asks Spengler? What is the importance of Sophocles for an Indian, 'and for the modern Chinese or Arab, with their utterly different intellectual constitutions, "philosophy from Bacon to Kant" has only a curiosity-value'.[5]

Spengler was the first to note the plurality of histories and their unequal distribution in time and space. His contemporary, Heinrich Scholz, a 'Spenglerian' himself, in commenting on Spengler's work observed that when history is not seen as a unified phenomenon, but instead manifests in polycentric occurrences, then it also cannot be considered a continuum; rather it must disintegrate into autonomous and clearly separated cyclical occurrences, the number of which is determined by the centres in which life is concentrated in creative archetypes.[6] Drawing on Spengler's remarks, the New Right also contends that it is now Europe's turn to live in the fulcrum of moral, social, and political decay. Henceforth, it would be erroneous to envision, as many liberal and socialist authors do, that the 'West' or Europe will continue to be used as a frame of reference for non-European nations:

> History is not an uninterrupted, and in its final result, unpredictable development of European man; instead it is a *curriculum vitae* of many cultures having nothing in common except the name — because each of them has its own destiny, its own life and its own death.[7]

But how can one distinguish between culture and its antithesis, that is to say, civilisation, asks Spengler? To this he answers that civilisation is the entropy of culture; it is the course of life in which all productive energy becomes exhausted; it is culture that lives on its own past. One can describe civilisation as a legitimate and sterile daughter of culture. Civilisation is the product of intellect, of completely rationalised (*durch-rationalisierter*) intellect. Civilisation means uprootedness, and this uprootedness develops its ultimate form in the modern megalopolis. The force of the people against massification, creativity

---

5   *Ibid.*, vol. 1, p. 23.

6   For the entire discussion see the review of Spengler's book by Heinrich Scholz, *Zum 'Untergang des Abendlandes'* (Berlin: Verlag von Reuther und Reichard, 1920), p. 10.

7   *Ibid.*, p. 11.

vs. decadence, ingeniousness vs. rationality — these are some of the most visible signs that distinguish culture from civilisation:

> Culture and Civilisation — the living body of a soul and the mummy of it. For Western existence the distinction lies at about the year 1800 — on the one side of that frontier life in fullness and sureness of itself, formed by growth from within, in one great uninterrupted evolution from Gothic childhood to Goethe and Napoleon, and on the other the autumnal, artificial, rootless life of our great cities, under forms fashioned by the intellect. Culture and Civilisation — the organism born of Mother Earth, and the mechanism proceeding from hardened fabric.[8]

But Spengler's construction of history also shows some contradictions. In spite of his assertions that the Nineteenth century was the period of advanced social decay, in all spheres of life magnificent works were created that even Spengler would have characterised as reminiscent of Classical achievements. For Scholz, Spengler's assertions concerning the irreversible loss of ancient Greek culture do not appear persuasive in view of the continuing interest in the Graeco-Roman spirit, and notwithstanding the fact that the Hellenic *polis* is a thing of the past. Scholz argues that despite the historical gap, thinkers such as Socrates and Plato are part of the modern cultural heritage, just as they were in the summertime of European culture, notably in the Seventeenth century.

Probably the biggest ambiguity that surrounds Spengler's interpretation of history lies in his inveterate pessimism, particularly when he argues about the irreversible decline of European culture. In his well-known essay, 'Pessimism?', written as a rebuttal to his critics, Spengler contends that man must reconcile himself to his historical destiny. He adds that, 'The first thing that confronts man in the form of Destiny is the time and place of his birth. This is an inescapable fact; no amount of thought can comprehend its origin, and no will can avert it. Moreover, it is the most decisive fact of all. Everyone is born into a people, a religion, a class, an age, a culture.'[9]

---

8   *The Decline of the West*, vol. 1, p. 353.

9   Oswald Spengler, 'Pessimism?', in *Selected Essays* (Chicago: Henry Regnery, 1967), p. 143.

Man is so much constrained by his historical environment, writes Spengler, that all his attempts to change his destiny are hopeless. And against all these flowery theories, all liberal and socialist philosophising about the 'glorious future', about the duties of humanity and the essence of ethics—speculating about the future is pure nonsense. Spengler sees no other avenue of redemption except by declaring himself a fundamental and resolute pessimist in regard to the 'goals of humanity':

> As I see it, humanity is a zoological entity. I see no progress, no goal or path for mankind, except perhaps in the minds of Western progress-mongers. In this mere mass of population I can distinguish no such thing as a 'spirit', not to speak of a unity of effort, feeling, or understanding.[10]

Yet, following his espousal of historical indeterminacy, Spengler confuses his reader with a purely Faustian exclamation: 'No, I am not a pessimist. Pessimism means not to see any more tasks. I see so many unsolved tasks that I fear we shall have neither time nor men enough to go at them.'[11] These words do not seem to fit into the patterns of historical pessimism that he earlier elaborated so passionately, all the more so as in his later works he advocates force and the warrior's toughness in order to stave off Europe's collapse. Thus, one may easily conclude that Spengler elegantly extols historical pessimism, or 'purposeful pessimism' (Zweckpessimismus), as long as it fits into the scheme of the irreversible decay of European society; however, once he perceives that cultural and political loopholes are available for the moral and social regeneration of Europe, he quickly reverts to the eulogy of power politics.[12] Similar characteristics are often found among many German romanticists and social thinkers, notably Nietzsche, Treitschke, and to a great extent among the New Right authors themselves. One may wonder, after all, why should somebody worry about

---

10 *Ibid.*, p. 147.

11 *Ibid.*, p. 148.

12 Notably in 'Is World Peace Possible?', *Selected Essays*, p. 205: 'Peace is a desire, war is a fact; and history has never paid heed to human desires and ideals. Life is a struggle involving plants, animals, and humans. It is a struggle between individuals, social classes, peoples, and nations, and it can take the form of economic, social, political, and military competition.'

the destiny of Europe, if this destiny had already been predetermined, if the cosmic dice have already been cast and all political and cultural efforts appear hopeless? Moreover, in an effort to mend the unmendable, by advocating the Faustian mentality and will to power, Spengler seems to be emulating the optimism of the socialists, rather than the ideas of those reconciled to impending social catastrophe. This ambiguity often dominates the works of the authors of the New Right who, while subscribing to a cyclical concept of history, deplore, along with Spengler, that every historical cycle has to run its course and eventually yield its force to another cycle. In short, on one hand one can observe the deep *Kulturpessimismus* and resignation to the unavoidable decline of Europe, while on the other, we are witnessing the glorification of a Faustian will to power.

These ideas constitute the fundamental part of the New Right's concept of history. Yet, no matter how dismal and decadent modern society appears to be, no matter what the outcome of the struggle is, or how threatened Europe appears, the New Right insists that it is still worth *dying for Europe as an honourable warrior*. By quoting Alexander Zinoviev in the Preface to one of his books (the 'historical optimist counts on nothing and on nobody'), de Benoist basically suggests that one must lay down one's life for Europe as a fighter, although the battle already appears lost.

VI

VILFREDO PARETO AND POLITICAL PATHOLOGY

Few thinkers have left such a pervasive influence on the European New Right as the Franco-Italian-Swiss political sociologist and economist Vilfredo Pareto (1848-1923). At the beginning of the Twentieth century, Pareto was an influential and respected political thinker, although after the Second World War his popularity rapidly declined. The fascist experience in Europe, which used and abused Pareto's intellectual legacy, undoubtedly contributed to his subsequent fall into intellectual disgrace.

Pareto's political sociology is hardly compatible with the modern liberal or socialist outlook on the world, an outlook of which Pareto was one of the most ardent critics. Throughout his work, Pareto meticulously scrutinised the energy and the driving force that lies behind political ideas and beliefs. Consequently, he came to the conclusion that ideas and beliefs often dissimulate pathological characteristics irrespective of their apparent utility and validity. Some modern students of Pareto, such as Guillaume Faye, went so far as to draw a close parallel between Pareto and Freud, observing that while Freud attempted to uncover pathological behaviour among seemingly normal individuals, Pareto tried to unmask social and political aberrations that lie camouflaged in the most respectable ideologies and political beliefs.[1]

In general, argues Pareto, each government tries to preserve its political institutions and internal harmony by *a posteriori* justification of its political behaviour; a behaviour that stands in sharp contrast to

---

1   Guillaume Faye, 'Pareto "doxanalyste",' *Nouvelle École*, no. 36, Summer 1981, pp. 73-80.

its *a priori* political objectives. In practice, this means that governments have a tendency to 'sanitise' their improper and often criminal
behaviour by simply appropriating self-serving labels such as 'democracy', 'democratic necessity', and 'struggle for peace'. It would be wrong,
however, to assume that such improper behaviour is exclusively the
result of a governmental conspiracy of some corrupt politicians bent
on fooling the masses. The great majority of politicians, and also ordinary people, are inclined to view a social phenomenon as if this phenomenon was reflected in a convex mirror. As a result, they assess the
value or the objectivity of this phenomenon only after they have first
deformed its objective reality. Thus, a particular social phenomenon,
such as a riot, a coup, or a terrorist act, is often perceived through the
prism of an individual's convictions, which usually leads to opinions
based on the relative strength or weakness of these convictions. It is
a very serious error, argues Pareto, to assume that a leader of some
oppressive regime is always a liar or a crook just because his subjects
(or constituents) feel cheated or oppressed. Rather, it is more likely
that such a leader is a victim of self-delusions, which in all honesty
he considers 'scientific' and truthful, and which he wishes to benevo-
lently share with his subjects (or constituents). To illustrate the power
of self-delusion, Pareto points to the example of socialist intellectuals
and observes that 'many people are not socialists because they have
been persuaded by reasoning. Quite the contrary; these people acqui-
esce to such reasoning because they are [already] socialists'.[2]

In his essay on Pareto's *doxanalysis*,[3] Guillaume Faye notes that
the subject of scandal for liberals and socialists is Pareto's tendency to
compare modern ideologies to neuroses, to latent manifestations of
simulacra and unreal affects — especially when these ideologies (e.g.,
socialism, liberalism, Christianity) present rational and 'scientific'
aspects. In Freud's theory, the complexes manifest themselves in obses-
sive ideas, neuroses, and paranoia. In Pareto's theory, the 'ideological complexes' manifest themselves in obscure ideological *derivatives*
which evoke 'historical necessity', 'self-evident' truths, or economic
and historical determinism.[4]

---

2   Vilfredo Pareto, *Les systèmes socialistes* (Paris: Marcel Giard, 1926), vol. 1, p. 12.

3   *Doxanalysis*, which is derived from the Greek *doxa* (opinion), is the technique of
    separating the emotional components from the rational parts in a belief system.

4   Guillaume Faye, *ibid.*

For Pareto, no belief system or ideology is fully immune from pathological influence, although in due course of time each belief system or ideology must undergo the process of demythologisation. The ultimate result will be the decline of a belief or an ideology as well as the decline of the elite that has put these beliefs and ideologies into practice.

Like many European conservatives before the war, Pareto was scornful of the modern liberal and socialist myth which holds that constant economic growth creates social peace and prosperity. For him, as well as for Oswald Spengler and Carl Schmitt, no matter how sophisticated some belief or ideology may appear, it is certain that in the long run it will ultimately decay. Not surprisingly, Pareto's attempts to denounce the illusion of human progress, as well as to 'uncover' the nature of socialism and liberalism, prompted many contemporary theorists to distance themselves from his thought.

Pareto argues that political theories seldom become attractive on the grounds of their presumably empirical or scientific character — although, of course, they all claim to be scientific and empirical — but primarily because they can exert an enormous sentimental force upon the masses. For example, in the latter days of the Roman Empire, it was an obscure religion from Galilee that, in a short time, mobilised masses of gullible people, willing to die, willing to be tortured, and willing to torture others once their religion seized the reins of power. In the Age of Reason, the prevailing 'religion' among the educated people was rationalism and the belief in boundless human improvement. After that came the 'self-evident' ideology of liberalism and 'scientific' Marxism and the belief in human equality. According to Pareto, depending on each historical epoch, pathological complexes are likely to give birth to different ideological derivatives — although their irrational essence will always remain the same. Since people need to transcend reality and make frequent excursions into fantasy and the imaginary, it is natural that they resort to religious and ideological symbols, however aberrant these symbols may subsequently appear to them. In analysing this phenomenon, Pareto takes the example of Marxist 'true believers', and notes that '[t]his is the current mental framework of some educated and intelligent Marxists in regard to the theory of *value*. From the logical point of view they are wrong; from the practical point of view and that of utility for their cause, they are probably right.'[5] Unfortunately, continues Pareto,

---

5   Vilfredo Pareto, *op. cit.*, vol. 1, p. 310.

these true believers who clamour for change know only what to destroy and how to destroy it, but are full of illusions as to what they have to replace it with, '[a]nd if they could imagine it, a large number among them would be struck with horror and amazement'.[6]

The pathological components of ideology are so powerful that they can completely obscure reason and the sense of reality, and in addition, they are not likely to disappear even when they take on a different 'cover' in a seemingly more respectable myth or 'self-evident' ideology. For Pareto, this is a disturbing historical process of which there is no end in sight:

> Essentially, social physiology and social pathology are still in their infancy. If we wish to compare them to the physiology and pathology of man, it is not to Hippocrates that we have to go, but far beyond him. Governments behave like an ignorant physician, randomly picking drugs in a pharmacy and administering them to a patient.[7]

So what remains of the much-vaunted liberal and socialist progress, asks Pareto? Almost nothing, given that history continues to be a perpetual and cosmic eternal return, with victims and victors, heroes and henchmen alternating in their roles, bewailing and bemoaning their fate when they are in a position of weakness, and abusing the weaker when they are in a position of strength. For Pareto, the only language people understand is that of force. And with his usual cynicism he adds, '[t]here are some people who imagine that they can disarm the enemy by complacent flattery. They are wrong. The world has always belonged to the stronger, and will belong to them for many years to come. Men only respect those who make themselves respected. Whoever becomes a lamb will find a wolf to eat him'.[8]

For Pareto, nations, empires, and states never die from foreign conquest but exclusively from suicide. When a nation, a class, a party, or a race becomes too degenerate or corrupted — which seems to be the predicament of every group — then another, more powerful party, class, nation, or race will surface and win over the masses, irrespective of the utility or validity of the new political theology or ideology:

---

6   *Ibid.*, vol. 1, p. 317.

7   *Ibid.*, vol. 1, p. 320.

8   Vilfredo Pareto, 'Danger of Socialism', in Placido Bucolo (ed.), *The Other Pareto* (New York: St. Martin's Press, 1980), p. 125.

A sign which almost always accompanies the decadence of an aristocracy is the invasion of humanitarian sentiments and delicate 'sob-stories' that render it incapable of defending its position. We must not confuse violence and force. Violence usually accompanies weakness. We can observe individuals and classes, who, having lost the force to maintain themselves in power, become more and more odious by resorting to indiscriminate violence. A strong man strikes only when it is absolutely necessary — and then nothing stops him. Trajan was strong but not violent; Caligula was violent but not strong.[9]

The downtrodden and the weak will always appeal to the sense of justice of those who rule, but the moment they grab the reins of power they will become as oppressive as their former rulers. Moreover, if by chance some nation happens to display signs of excessive humanity, philanthropy, or equality, it is a certain symptom of its terminal illness. Soon another political actor will appear with enough virility and force to convince the masses that life is equally possible under a different brand of 'justice':

> I realise that someone could answer to me that the Christians, too, called for freedom when they were oppressed, but that as soon as they came to power, they in their turn oppressed the pagans. Today, the orthodox socialists, oppressed, call for freedom but, tomorrow, if they are in power, will they give it to us...? Hope alone remains in Pandora's box. We can only console ourselves with hypotheses since reality is so grim.[10]

Deluded by dreams of justice, equality, and freedom, what weapons do liberal democracies have today at their disposal against the 'downtrodden' masses worldwide? The New Right observes that the sense of guilt among Europeans in regard to Africans, Asians, and other downtrodden populations has paralysed European decision-makers, leaving them and Europe defenceless against tomorrow's conquerors. For, had Africans or Asians been at the same technological level as Europeans, what kind of a destiny would they have reserved for Europeans? This is something indeed that Pareto likes to speculate about:

9   Vilfredo Pareto, *Les systèmes,* vol. 1, pp. 37-38.
10 Vilfredo Pareto, 'Danger of Socialism', p. 127.

All peoples that are horrified by blood to the point of not knowing how to defend itself sooner or later will become the prey for some bellicose people. There is probably not a single foot of land on earth that has not been conquered by the sword, or where people occupying this land have not maintained themselves by force. If Negroes were stronger than Europeans, it would be Negroes dividing Europe and not Europeans dividing Africa. The alleged 'right' which the peoples have arrogated to themselves with the title 'civilised' to conquer other peoples whom they got accustomed to calling 'uncivilised' is absolutely ridiculous. Rather, this right is nothing but force. As long as Europeans remain stronger than Chinese, they will impose their will upon them, but if the Chinese become stronger than Europeans, these roles will be reversed...[11]

Might always comes first, and those who assume that their passionate pleas for justice and brotherhood will be heeded by those who were previously enslaved are gravely mistaken. New victors, in general, always teach their former rulers that signs of weakness result in proportionally increased punishment. To lack resolve in the hour of decision, to willingly surrender oneself to the anticipated generosity of new rulers, is a characteristic of degenerate individuals, and as Pareto writes, it is desirable for society that such individuals disappear as soon as possible.[12] Should, however, the old elite be ousted and a new 'humanitarian' elite comes to power, the cherished ideas of justice and equality will again appear as distant and unattainable as ever. Possibly, argues Pareto, a new elite will be even worse and more oppressive than the former one, all the more as the new 'world improvers' (*Weltverbesserer*) — as Spengler calls them — will not hesitate to make use of the most obscene verbal acrobatics to justify their oppression.

The New Right observes that despite his shortcomings, imperfections, and silence on the issue of value systems, Pareto strongly challenges the postulates of egalitarian humanism and faith in democracy, in which he sees not only utopias but also errors and lies endorsed by vested interests. Although Pareto dissects a certain pathological character in every ideology, he nonetheless acknowledges that ideas and beliefs are indispensable as a unifying and mobilising factor for every society. When he, for example, affirms the absurdity of some doctrine,

---

11 Vilfredo Pareto, *Les systèmes*, pp. 38-39.

12 *Ibid.*, especially on p. 67.

he does not at all suggest that a doctrine or an ideology must be harmful to society. In fact, this same ideology may be very beneficial to society. In contrast, when he affirms the utility of some doctrine, he does not imply that it must be experimentally truthful. On the matters of value, however, Pareto remains silent. For him, the dichotomy 'good vs. bad' is ridiculous and inappropriate in studying social phenomena.

The New Right portrays Pareto's methodology as belonging to the tradition of *intellectual polytheism*. With Hobbes, Machiavelli, Max Weber, and Carl Schmitt, Pareto rejects the widespread modern belief in economic progress and human advancement. Pareto also opposes every form of reductionism in studying social phenomena and argues that the world contains many truths and a plurality of values, with each being 'truthful' within the confines of a given historical epoch and a specific people. The New Right notes that 'in this sense, the sociology of Pareto, just as the anthropology of Gehlen, the political science of Carl Schmitt, or the psychology of Jung, provides us not with the *theses,* but with the *method* and *concepts* conducive to establishing a global conception of the human phenomenon'.[13] Furthermore, Pareto's relativism concerning the meaning of political 'truths' invariably leads him to the demystification of those doctrines and ideologies that view themselves as 'objective'. As Faye writes, Pareto denies that there is any form of objectivity in the modern dominant ideologies (socialism and liberalism), and instead, he views both of them as a 'cover' for specific ruling elites. Faye adds that 'Pareto's *doxanalysis* has committed a sin in *unmasking* modern political ideologies, and especially those, such as Marxism, which portrayed themselves as objective and demystifying'.[14]

Pareto's theory of illogical actions and sentimental influence irks many modern theorists worldwide, often to the point that trying to edit and publish his books becomes difficult. In the recently published edition of Pareto's essays, Ronald Fletcher writes in the Preface that he was told by the 'market researchers of British publishers that Pareto is "not on the reading list" and is "not taught" in current courses on sociological theory in the universities'![15] Such a response from publishers

---

13 *Nouvelle École,* no. 36, Summer 1981, editorial, p. 12.

14 Guillaume Faye, *ibid.* pp. 73-80.

15 Preface by Ronald Fletcher in *The Other Pareto* (New York: St. Martin's Press, 1980), p. x.

is quite predictable given Pareto's cynicism toward democracy, which often bears the marks of political nihilism.

Nonetheless, almost a century after his death, Pareto's books command respect among even those critics and scholars who are the least inclined to accept his political ideas. Also, one of these days, the influence Pareto exerted on his contemporary as well as future disciples must be examined. Of course, the names of Gustave Le Bon, Gaetano Mosca, Robert Michels, and later Joseph Schumpeter and Raymond Aron quickly come to mind.[16]

Fletcher writes that while dealing with the post-war schools of thought, such as 'systems analysis', 'behaviourism', 'reformulations', and 'new paradigms', important works are often ignored or simply rejected on the grounds of their presumably 'undemocratic' influence. In the process, the great erudition of Pareto, ranging from linguistics to economics, from knowledge of Hellenic literature to modern sexology, has often been overlooked and neglected. Nevertheless, regardless of whether one agrees or disagrees with Pareto, it is worth noting that his analyses can still be useful in studying the pathology of all ideologies, including those of Leftist and liberal intellectuals. As we observe today the relentless conversion of former Marxists in the East and the West to the respectable ideology of liberalism, it may be wise to take another look at Pareto.

---

16 Pareto's writings influenced an entire generation of thinkers and politicians, who in a similar vein attempted to demonstrate that so-called democratic states carry the germs of their own destruction. This includes Gaetano Mosca, *The Ruling Class* (New York: McGraw-Hill, 1939); Robert Michels, *Political Parties* (New York: Dover Publications, 1959); and especially Gustave Le Bon, *Psychologie politique* (Paris: Les Amis de Gustave Le Bon, 1984) and *The Crowd* (New York: Viking Press, 1960). On p. 314 of *Psychologie politique*, Le Bon writes, 'Clergy, socialists, anarchists, etc., are close varieties of the same psychological specimen. Their soul is bent under the weight of similar illusions. They have an identical mentality, cherish the same things, and respond to the same needs with hardly different means'.

VII

THE PAGAN RIGHT

U p to this point, one may contend that the New Right is not so new in view of the fact that the authors whom the New Right claims as its spiritual forefathers are already known to a wider public of both Leftist and conservative intellectuals. But the New Right is 'new' insofar as it attempts to apply the ideas of the previously discussed authors differently to the contemporary and ever-changing European political environment. Furthermore, a salient element that the New Right has introduced into its criticism of modern politics, and that probably underscores its entire political, ethical, and philosophical importance, is its emphasis on the value of ancient European paganism and polytheism.

This chapter examines the New Right's criticism of Biblical monotheism and contrasts it with the description of religious polytheism such as it manifested itself in pre-Christian European paganism. It limits itself to the cursory description of polytheism and paganism originating on the European continent. The Indian pantheon of gods and deities, as well as the manifestation of paganism in other non-European cultures, will not be examined. It must be emphasised that the New Right's criticism of monotheism is basically aimed at the Judaeo-Christian legacy in Europe and not against other monotheistic religions elsewhere in the world. The central figure in our discussion is again the leader of the New Right, the philosopher Alain de Benoist. As will be noted, de Benoist's arguments are strongly influenced by Friedrich Nietzsche, Martin Heidegger, and Louis Rougier; in short, the conservative authors and philosophers who have played a decisive role in the philosophical formation of the New Right.

We have already seen that, for its advocacy of ancient European paganism and polytheism on the one hand and its criticism of Biblical monotheism on the other, the New Right quickly came to be stigmatised by many contemporary conservative critics. Therefore, it should not come as a surprise that even initially sympathetic supporters of the New Right gradually became somewhat resentful of its constant glorification of polytheism and its hostility towards the Judaeo-Christian heritage. This resentment grew further as fears emerged that the New Right was trying to revive old European pagan worship and cults, which for many justifiably bore a resemblance to earlier National Socialist attempts to 'dechristianise' and 'repaganise' Germany.[1] To make things worse, the New Right's attacks against Christian dogma antagonised those intellectuals who had initially shown considerable sympathy for its anti-Communist and anti-liberal ideas. Soon, the debate about European paganism vs. Judaeo-Christianity came to be known in Parisian conservative circles as a game of 'monopoly' — an obvious reference to the ongoing clash between adherents of a monotheistic and a polytheistic concept of the world, respectively. As long as the New Right limited itself to criticising liberalism, Communism, and modern mass society, it could count on definite conservative support. Once it began to target the political legacy of Judaism, Christianity and the existence of a single omnipotent god, however, even the most sympathetic followers found ample reasons for scepticism and fear. The parallel between the New Right and the earlier Nazi efforts to remove the Judaeo-Christian heritage from Germany turned out to be so conspicuous that it could not be easily hidden.

---

1   See notably Alfred Rosenberg, *The Myth of the Twentieth Century* (Sussex: Historical Review Press, 2004), and works by the prominent German scholar Hans F. K. Günther, a sympathiser with National Socialism, who in the 1920s and 1930s wrote a great number of books and articles on racial topics, such as *The Racial Elements of European History* (Sussex: Historical Review Press, 2007). After the war, however, due to a different ideological atmosphere, Günther's subject matter became less inflammatory, such as *Religious Attitudes of the Indo-Europeans* (Sussex: Historical Review Press, 2001), in which he espouses the virtues of the Indo-European pagan cosmology. Also worth noting is the name of Wilhelm Hauer, *Deutscher Gottschau* (Stuttgart: Karl Gutbrod, 1934), who significantly popularised Indo-European mythology among National Socialists. See pp. 240-254 of the same book, where Hauer discusses the difference between Judeo-Christian Semitic beliefs and European paganism. Some of Hauer's writing was translated in *Germany's New Religion* (London: George Allen and Unwin, 1937).

Whatever one may think about the seemingly obsolete or even derogatory connotation of the phrase 'European paganism', it is certain that this often derogatory label is largely a result of the historical and political influence of Christianity. Jean Markale writes that, etymologically, paganism is related to the beliefs and rituals that were observed in European villages and the countryside. But paganism, in its modern version, can also mean a certain sensibility and a way of life — a phenomenon that stands in contrast to the Judaeo-Christian heritage in Europe. To some extent European peoples continue to be 'pagans' because their national memory often contains allusions to ancient myths, fairy tales, and folklore that bear the peculiar marks of pre-Christian themes. Markale observes that 'the dictatorship of Christian ideology has not silenced those ancient customs; it has only condemned them to the shadow of the unconscious.'[2]

In European culture, polytheistic beliefs began to dwindle with the rise of Christianity. In the centuries to come, it was to be expected that the European thought, whether in theology or, later on, in sociology, politics, history, or psychology — in short, their entire perception of the world — would gradually come under the influence of Judaeo-Christian monotheistic beliefs. David Miller, in his book *The New Polytheism*, observes that the centuries-long impact of Judaeo-Christian monotheism has considerably altered the European approach to all social sciences as well as its overall perception of the world. Following the consolidation of the Judaeo-Christian belief in Europe, the world came to be understood according to fixed concepts and categories governed by the logic of 'either-or', 'true or false', 'good or evil' — with seldom any shading between the two. Miller, nevertheless, doubts that Judaeo-Christian monotheism can continue to be a valid approach in understanding the complex social reality of the contemporary world, a world that is replete with choices and intricate social differences that stubbornly refuse all simplistic categorisation.[3]

In the European popular consciousness, the centuries-long and pervasive influence of Christianity has significantly contributed to

---

2 Jean Markale, 'Aujourd'hui l'esprit païen?' in *L'Europe païenne* (Paris: Seghers, 1980), p. 16. The book contains pieces on Slavic, Celtic, Latin, and Graeco-Roman paganism. Alain de Benoist was also a contributor to the book, 'Le domaine grec et romain', pp. 251-363.

3 For a comprehensive discussion see the valuable book by David Miller, *The New Polytheism* (New York: Harper and Row, 1974), p. 7, and *passim*.

the modern view that holds any celebration of paganism, or for that matter any nostalgia for Graeco-Roman polytheism, as irreconcilable with contemporary society. Thomas Molnar, a Catholic philosopher who is sympathetic to the New Right, notes that modern adherents of neo-paganism, including the authors of the New Right, are certainly more ambitious than their predecessors Nietzsche, Heidegger, Evola, and Spengler. Thus, Molnar writes, the aim of the New Right is not so much to return to the worship of the ancient European deities as it is to forge another civilisation, or rather, a modernised version of 'scientific and cultural Hellenism', considered a common receptacle of traditional wisdom for all European peoples. With clear sympathy for the 'polytheistic' endeavours of the European New Right, Molnar adds:

> There is no question of conquering the planet but rather to promote an *oikumena*[4] of the peoples and civilisations that have rediscovered their origins. Thus, the assumption goes that the domination of stateless ideologies, notably the ideology of American liberalism and Soviet socialism, would come to an end. One believes in rehabilitated paganism in order to restore to the peoples their genuine identity that existed before monotheist corruption.[5]

Anxious to dispel the myth of pagan 'backwardness', and in an effort to redefine European paganism in the spirit of modern times, the New Right has gone to great lengths to present its meaning in a more attractive and scholarly fashion. De Benoist summarises the New Right's position regarding the idea of a pagan revival in Europe in the following words:

> Neo-paganism, if in fact there is such a thing, is not a cult phenomenon — as imagine not only its adversaries, but also sometimes well-intentioned groups and covens who can be described as often clumsy, sometimes unintentionally comical, and perfectly marginal... There is something else that seems especially important to watch out for today, at least according to the idea we have of it. It is less the disappearance of paganism than its re-emergence under primitive or puerile forms, kin to that 'second religiosity' that Spengler rightly described as one of the characteristic traits of cultures in decline. This is also what Julius Evola wrote about as 'generally corresponding to a phenomenon of escape,

---

4   Greek: 'the inhabited world'.-Ed.

5   Thomas Molnar, 'La tentation païenne', *Contrepoint*, 15 June 1981, p. 53.

alienation, and confused compensation, which is of no serious consequence on reality...something hybrid, decrepit, and sub-intellectual.[6]

As much as paganism exerted some influence on the Romantic poets
and philosophers of the early Nineteenth century, particularly in Germany and England, it must be noted that it never turned into a subject
of passionate elucidation and scholarly debates, as the authors of the
New Right have recently conferred upon it. One may contend that Pareto, Spengler, Sorel, and other anti-Christian thinkers, although imbued with 'polytheistic' beliefs and resentment of Christian dogma,
never went so far as to conceive of Christianity as the sole factor of
European political and cultural decay. One had to wait for Nietzsche
to begin accusing Christianity of being the main cause of the modern
crisis. Therefore, it must not come as a surprise that the New Right,
and particularly de Benoist's criticism of Judaeo-Christianity, bears a
striking similarity to Nietzsche's earlier observations.

Like Nietzsche, de Benoist argues that Christianity has introduced
an alien 'anthropology' into Europe that is today directly responsible for the spread of egalitarian mass society and the rise of totalitarianism.[7] In his dialogue with Molnar (*L'éclipse du sacré*), de Benoist
defines totalitarianism as a system which claims to possess a unique
truth; a system that upholds the idea of an absolute good vs. an absolute evil; and a system where the idea of the enemy is identified with its
concept of evil — and who is therefore to be physically exterminated
(cf. *Deuteronomy* 13). In short, observes de Benoist, Judaeo-Christian
universalism set the stage for the rise of modern egalitarian aberrations, particularly in Communist systems:

> That there are totalitarian regimes 'without God' is quite obvious — the
> Soviet Union, for example. These regimes, nonetheless, are the 'inheri-
> tors' of Christian thought in the sense in which Carl Schmitt demon-
> strated that the majority of modern political principles are secularised
> theological principles. They bring down to earth a *structure of exclusion;*

---

6   Alain de Benoist, *On Being a Pagan* (Atlanta: Ultra, 2004), p. 10. The quote by
    Evola is from *Ride the Tiger*.

7   Alain de Benoist, *L'éclipse du sacré* (Paris: La Table ronde, 1986), especially the
    chapter 'De la sécularisation', pp. 198-207.

the police of the soul yield their place to the police of the state; the ideological wars follow upon the religious wars.[8]

Similar conclusions are shared by the philosopher Louis Rougier, who
represents the 'old guard' of the New Right, and whose philosophical research was also directed toward the rehabilitation of European
pagan thinkers. In his book, *Celse contre les chrétiens* (*Celsus Against
the Christians*), Rougier writes that Christianity very early came under
the influence of both Iranian Zoroastrian dualism and the eschato-
logical visions of Jewish apocalyptic beliefs. Accordingly, the Jews, and
later on the Christians, adopted the belief that the good, who presently
suffer, will be rewarded in the future. 'There are two empires juxta-
posed in space', writes Rougier, 'one governed by God and his angels,
the other by Satan and Belial.'[9] The consequences of this largely dualistic vision of the world, argues Rougier, resulted, over a period of time,
in the Christian portrayal of their political enemies as always wrong, as
opposed to the Christian's own position, invariably right. For Rougier, Graeco-Roman intolerance never assumed such total and absolute
proportions of religious exclusion; the intolerance towards Christians,
Jews, and other sects was sporadic and was usually aimed at certain
religious customs deemed contrary to Roman common law (such as
circumcision, human sacrifices, and sexual or religious orgies).[10]

By cutting themselves off from Europe's polytheistic roots and by
accepting Christianity, Europeans gradually began to adhere to a vision
of the world that emphasised the equality of souls and the importance
of spreading God's gospel to *all* peoples, regardless of creed, race or
language (*Paul; Galatians* 3:28). For his part, de Benoist sees in Christian universalism a form of 'Bolshevism of Antiquity', and notes that
in order to fully grasp the meaning of modern egalitarian doctrines,
particularly Marxism, one must first trace their origins in Christianity:

> According to the classical doctrine of the development and degrada-
> tion of cycles, the egalitarian theme has entered our culture from the
> stage of *myth* (equality before God), and proceeded to the stage *of
> ideology* (equality before people); after that, it has passed to the stage
> of '*scientific pretension*' (affirmation of the egalitarian *fact*). In short,

---

8   *Ibid.*, p. 233.

9   Louis Rougier, *Celse contre les chrétiens* (Paris: Copernic, 1977), p. 67.

10   *Ibid.*, p. 89.

we have proceeded from Christianity to democracy, and after that to socialism and Marxism. The most serious reproach that one can level against Christianity is that it has inaugurated this egalitarian cycle by introducing into European thought a *revolutionary anthropology*, with a *universalist and totalitarian* character.[11]

Authors such as Ludwig Feuerbach and Bertrand Russell, whose intellectual legacy is being significantly revived by the New Right, also argue that Judaeo-Christian monotheism and religious exclusiveness presupposes an underlying idea of universalism, as well as the establishment of a single, undisputed truth.[12] The consequence of Christian belief in ontological oneness, i.e., that there is only one God and therefore only one truth, results in an effort to obliterate or ignore all other possible 'truths' and values. For de Benoist, the belief in equality before one god paves the way for a one-dimensional world, with a one-dimensional history and a one-dimensional logic. Accordingly, each occurrence of Christian intolerance could be interpreted as a violent response against those who have departed from the belief in Christ. Hence we have this concept of Christian 'false humility' that Rougier mentions in his discussion about the Christian attitude towards Jews. Although almost identical in their worship of one god, the clash between Christians and Jews was bound to occur, because Christians could never quite reconcile themselves to the fact that they also worship the deity of those whom they abhor as a people who killed this same deity. Moreover, whereas Christianity is meant to be a universalist religion, proselytising in all corners of the world, Judaism is a strictly an ethnic religion of the Jewish people.[13] For de Benoist, Judaism sanctions its own nationalism, in contrast to Christian nationalism, which is constantly belied by its own universalist logic. 'Christian anti-Semitism', suggests de Benoist, 'can therefore correctly described as a neurosis.'[14]

---

11 Alain de Benoist, 'L'Eglise, L'Europe et le Sacré', in *Pour une renaissance culturelle* (Paris: Copernic, 1979), p. 202.

12 Ludwig Feuerbach, *The Essence of Christianity* (New York: Harper, 1957). Also Bertrand Russell, *Why I am Not a Christian* (New York: Simon and Schuster, 1963).

13 Rougier, *Celse contre les chrétiens*, p. 88.

14 Alain de Benoist, *On Being a Pagan*, p. 119.

To the critics who argue that polytheism is a thing of the prehistoric and primitive mind, incompatible with modern societies, de Benoist responds that paganism, as he sees it, is not a return to 'paradise lost' or a nostalgia for the Graeco-Roman order. To pledge allegiance to 'paganism' means primarily an attempt to return to the roots of Europe's historical origins, as well as to revive some sacred aspects of life that existed in Europe prior to the rise of Christianity. As to the alleged 'supremacy' or 'modernity' of Judeo-Christianity over the 'backwardness of Indo-European polytheism', de Benoist responds that in terms of modernity, Christian religions may be considered no less ridiculous and obsolete than the religions of pagan Europeans:

> Just as yesterday we had the grotesque spectacle of Christian missionaries worshipping their own *gris gris* [fetish] while denouncing 'pagan idols', it is somewhat comical today to witness the denunciation of the (European) 'past' by those who ceaselessly boast of the Judaeo-Christian continuity and are always presenting for our edification the 'ever relevant' examples of Abraham, Jacob, Isaac, and other proto-historical Bedouins.[15]

For the New Right, Judaeo-Christian monotheism has substantially altered the modern approach toward understanding history and politics. Judaeo-Christianity has assigned a specific goal to history, the end result of which is a gradual, but definite devaluation of all past events which *did not* display the sign of God's theophany. According to the authors of the New Right, the Judaeo-Christian rationalisation of the historical process precludes the reassessment of one's own national past, and in addition, it significantly contributes to the 'desertification' of the entire world. Ernest Renan, a predecessor of the New Right,

---

15 *Ibid.*, p. 11. Alain de Benoist has been at odds with the so-called conservative *nouveaux philosophes*, who attacked his 'paganism' as a tool of intellectual anti-Semitism, racism, and totalitarianism. In response, de Benoist levels the same criticism against the *nouveaux philosophes*. See his article, 'Monothéisme-polythéisme: Le grand débat', *Le Figaro Magazine*, 28 April 1979, p. 83. He writes, 'Like Horkheimer, like Ernst Bloch, like Lévinas, like René Girard, what B.-H. Lévy desires is less of 'audacity', less of ideal, less of politics, less of power, less of the State. Less *of history*. What he expects is the *accomplishment* of history, the end of all adversity (the adversity which corresponds to the Hegelian *Gegenständlichkeit*), discarnate justice, universal peace, the disappearance of frontiers. The birth of a *homogeneous* society, where the "wolf will lie with the lamb and the panther sleeps with the goat" (*Isaiah* 11:6)'.

observed earlier that Judaism is oblivious to the notion of the sacred, because the 'desert itself is monotheistic'.[16] Quoting Harvey Cox's *The Secular City*, de Benoist writes that the loss of the sacred — which is today resulting in the *Entzauberung* of the modern polity — is the 'legitimate consequence of the impact of Biblical faith on history... The disenchantment of nature begins with the creation, the desacralisation of politics with the exodus and the deconsecration of values with the Sinai covenant, especially with its prohibition of idols'.[17] Continuing with a similar analysis, Mircea Eliade, a long-time sympathiser of the New Right, adds that Judaic resentment of pagan idolatry stems from the rationalistic character of Mosaic law. More than in any other monotheistic religion, writes Eliade, Judaism has rationalised all aspects of man's life through a myriad of prescriptions, laws, and interdictions:

> Desacralisation of Nature, devaluation of cultural activity, in short, the violent and total rejection of cosmic religion, and above all the decisive importance conferred upon spiritual regeneration by the certain return of Yahweh was the prophets' response to the historical crises menacing the two Jewish kingdoms.[18]

The New Right rejects the idea of some of its critics that Christian religions, notably Catholicism, are also able to preserve the sacred. De Benoist writes that Catholicism owes its manifestation of the sacred (holy sites, pilgrimages, Christmas and Easter festivities, and its pantheon of saints) to the indomitable undercurrent of pagan and polytheistic sensibility that has kept resurfacing in Catholic beliefs.

Paganism, as he sees it, is less a religion in the Christian sense of the word, but rather a certain type of 'spiritual equipment' that stands in sharp contrast to the religion of Jews and Christians. Therefore, if Europe is to stave off spiritual chaos, it needs to replace a monotheistic vision of the world with a polytheistic vision of the world — which alone can guarantee the 'return of the gods' and the plurality of *all* values. In other words, the return to paganism can significantly help

---

16 Ernest Renan, *Histoire générale des langues sémitiques* (Paris: Imprimerie Impériale, 1853), p. 6.

17 Alain de Benoist, *L'éclipse*, p. 129, quoting Harvey Cox, *The Secular City* (New York: Macmillan, 1965), p. 15.

18 Mircea Eliade, *Histoire des croyances et des idées religieuses* (Paris: Payot, 1976), p. 369 and *passim*.

to re-evaluate history and to restore those values which have been obliterated by Judaeo-Christianity. In contrast with Christian humility and fear of God, paganism stresses courage, personal honour, and spiritual and physical self-overcoming. In his book *The Religious Attitudes of the Indo-Europeans,* Hans F. K. Günther, a conservative German anthropologist, remarks that:

> ...Indo-European religiosity is not rooted in any kind of fear, neither in fear of deity nor in fear of death. The words of the latter-day Roman poet, that fear first created the Gods (Statius, *Thebais,* III, 661: *primus in orbe fecit deos timor*), cannot be applied to the true forms of Indo-European religiosity, for wherever it has unfolded freely, the 'fear of the Lord' (*Solomon, Proverbs* 9:10; *Psalms* 111:30) has proved neither the beginning of belief nor of wisdom.[19]

Unlike a Christian, a pagan is encouraged to assume complete responsibility before history because he is the only one who can give history a meaning. In his comments on Nietzsche's attitude towards history, Giorgio Locchi of the New Right writes that in pagan cosmogony, man alone is considered a forger of his own destiny (*faber suae fortunae*), exempt from Biblical or historical determinism, 'divine grace', or economic and material constraints.[20] In the same vein, some other authors of the New Right emphasise the difference between the pagan tragic and heroic attitude towards life as opposed to the Christian sense of *guilt* and fear of God. For the New Right author Sigrid Hunke, the pagan mentality consists of:

> [e]ssentialisation of life, since both life and death have the same essence and are always contained in both. Life, which can be confronted with death at any moment, renders the future permanent in each instant, and life becomes eternal by acquiring an inscrutable profundity, and by assuming the value of eternity.[21]

---

19 Hans F. K. Günther, *The Religious Attitudes of the Indo-Europeans,* translated by Vivian Bird and Roger Pearson (Sussex: Historical Review Press, 2001), p. 19.

20 See Giorgio Locchi, 'L'Histoire', *Nouvelle École,* nos. 27-28, Autumn-Winter 1975, pp. 183-190.

21 Sigrid Hunke, *La vraie religion de l'Europe,* translated by Claudine Glot and Jean-Louis Pesteil (Paris: Le Labyrinthe, 1985), p. 253. The book was first published under the title *Europas eigene Religion: Der Glaube der Ketzer* (Bergisch Gladbach: Gustav Lubbe, 1980).

For Hunke, along with other authors of the New Right, in order to remedy the crisis of modern society one must first abandon the dualistic logic of religious and social exclusion, 'a logic of exclusion which has been responsible for extremism not only among individuals, but also among parties and peoples, and which, starting from Europe, has disseminated into the world this dualistic split which has acquired planetary proportions'.[22] To achieve this ambitious goal, the New Right suggests that Europeans first give a different meaning to history.

The Terror of History

Contrary to the Judaeo-Christian dogma which asserts that historical time starts from one unique father, in European paganism there are no traces of the beginning of time; instead, historical time is a perpetual recommencement, the 'eternal return', emanating from multiple and different fathers. In pagan cosmogony, writes de Benoist, time is the reflection of a non-linear conception of history — a conception in which the past, the present, and the future are not perceived as moments irrevocably cut off from each other, or following each other along a single line. Instead, remarks de Benoist, the past, the present, and the future are perceived as dimensions of each actuality.[23] In contrast, Judaeo-Christian monotheism excludes the possibility of historical return or 'recommencement'; history has to unfold in a predetermined way by making its way towards a final goal.

Undoubtedly, Judaeo-Christian dogma does admit that man may have a history but only insofar as history is bestowed with an assigned goal, a *certain* goal, and a *specific* goal. Should a man, however, continue to cling to his ancient concept of history that evokes the *collective memory* of either his tribe or people, he runs the risk of provoking Yahweh's anger. De Benoist notes that in the place of pagan organic solidarity or communal ties, the monotheism of the Bible attempts to create divisions. Yahweh forbids 'mixtures' between the present and the past, between people and the divine, between Israel and the *goyim*.[24]

---

22 *Ibid.*, p. 274.
23 Alain de Benoist, *L'éclipse*, p. 113.
24 *Ibid.*, p. 132.

According to de Benoist, one can encounter two concepts of history among pagans. The first concept presents the classical image of the historical becoming that operates in cycles. The other concept presupposes the image of history having a beginning only incidentally — but ignoring the predictable and determined finality. In Indo-European pagan cosmogony it is incumbent upon each people to assign a role to its own history, which means that there cannot exist 'self-appointed' peoples occupying the central place in history. By the same token, just as it is erroneous to speak about one truth or one single god, it is equally wrong to maintain that all of humanity must pursue the same and unique historical direction as proposed by Judaeo-Christianity.

The Judaeo-Christian concept of history suggests that the flow of historical time is mono-linear and, therefore, limited by its significance and meaning. Henceforth, for Jews and Christians, history can only be apprehended as a totality governed by a sense of an ultimate end and historical fulfilment. History for both Jews and Christians appears at best *parenthetical*, at worst, an ugly episode or a 'valley of tears' which must one day be erased from the Earth and transcended in Paradise. In the modern secular city, the idea of paradise can either be transformed into a notion of 'classless' society, or the apolitical and ahistorical consumer society. Here is how de Benoist sees it:

> Legitimisation by the future that replaces legitimisation of the eternal authorises all uprootedness, all 'emancipations' from identity in its original form. This *utopian* future that replaces a *mythic* past is, incidentally, always the generator of deceptions, because the paradise that it announces must constantly be put off to a later date. Temporality is no longer a crucial element in the development of an individual who tries to grasp the game of the world — temporality is pursued via one goal, reached from one end; it is an *expectation* and no longer *communion*.
>
> To submit the unfolding of world history to an obligatory outcome means, in fact, to trap history within the reign of objectivity, which reduces the possibilities for choices, orientations and projects.[25]

Consequently, the Judaeo-Christian belief will place all hopes in the future, since the future is thought to be able to 'rectify' the past and thereby assume the value of redemption. Time for Jews and Christians

---

25 *Ibid.*, pp. 155-156.

is no longer reversible, and therefore, each historical occurrence acquires the meaning of divine providence, of God's finger, or theophany. Moses received the Law at a *certain* place and during a *certain* time, and Jesus later preached, performed miracles, and was crucified at a *specifically* recorded time and place. These divine interventions in human history would never happen again. Eliade summarises this in the following words:

> Under the 'pressure of history' and supported by the prophetic and Messianic experience, a new interpretation of historical events dawns among the children of Israel. Without finally renouncing the traditional concept of archetypes and repetitions, Israel attempts to 'save' historical events by regarding them as the active presence of Yahweh.
>
> Messianism gives them a new value, especially by abolishing [historical events'] possibility of repetition *ad infinitum*. When the Messiah comes, the world will be saved once and for all and history will cease to exist.[26]

Now, directly commanded by the will of Yahweh, history functions as a series of theophanies or *events,* with each event becoming irrevocable and irreversible. As Pierre Chaunu, a well-known contemporary French historian, observes, the rejection of history is a temptation of those civilisations which emerged out of Judaeo-Christianity.[27]

These observations necessitate some comments. If one accepts the idea of the end of history, as both Christians and Marxists maintain, to what extent can the entire suffering throughout history be explained? How is it possible, from liberal and Marxist points of view, to 'redeem' past oppressions, collective sufferings, deportations, and humiliations that have filled the pages of history? This is a fundamental problem which shall be discussed in more detail in the second part of this book. Suffice to say that this enigma only underscores the difficulty regarding the concept of unresolved justice in egalitarian (both liberal and Marxist) society. If a truly egalitarian society ever becomes a reality, it will inevitably be a society of the 'elect' — of those who, as Eliade notes, managed to escape the 'pressure of history' by simply being born at the

---

26 Mircea Eliade, *The Myth of the Eternal Return: Cosmos and History,* translated from French by Willard R. Trask (Princeton: Princeton University Press, 1965), pp. 106-107.

27 Pierre Chaunu, *Histoire et foi* (Paris: Edition France-Empire, 1980).

right place at the right time. Similar views are held by the conservative theologian Paul Tillich, who writes that such 'equality' would result in immense historical inequality, since it would do injustice to those, who, in Arthur Koestler's words, perished with a 'shrug of eternity'.[28] Eliade illustrates the futility of modern ideologies of 'social improvement', for instance, when he mentions how south-eastern Europe had to suffer for centuries simply because it happened to be in the path of Asiatic invaders and Ottoman conquerors. Eliade notes that due to the fortunes of geography and history, Eastern Europeans have never been charmed by modern historicism, and instead, in times of great political and social catastrophes, they subconsciously sought solace in the traditional 'pagan' justification of cyclical history.

The New Right concludes that for a Christian it is Christianity that defines the value of a human being, for a Jew it is Judaism that gauges someone's 'chosenness', and for a Marxist it is not the quality of a man that defines his class, but rather the quality of the class that defines the man. One thus becomes 'elected' by virtue of his affiliation to his religious belief or his class. Yahweh, similar to his future secular successors, is a jealous god, and in this capacity he is opposed to the presence of other gods and values. He is a 'reductionist', and whatever exists beyond his fold must be either punished or destroyed. Not surprisingly, throughout history, the monotheistic 'true believers' have been encouraged, in the name of 'higher' goals, to punish those who had strayed away from Yahweh's assigned path.

In contrast, writes de Benoist, '[a] system that accepts a limitless number of gods not only accepts the plurality of the forms of worship that address them, but also, and especially, the plurality of mores, social and political systems, conceptions of the world for which these gods are so many sublimated expressions'.[29] It follows from this that pagans, or believers in polytheism, are considerably less inclined to intolerance. Their relative tolerance is primarily attributable to the acceptance of the notion of the 'excluded third party' (*der ausgeschlossene Dritte*), as well as the rejection of Judaeo-Christian dualism. In

---

28 See Paul Tillich, *The Eternal Now* (New York: Charles Scribner's Sons, 1963), p. 41 and *passim*. 'Shrug of eternity' are the last words Koestler uses in his novel *Darkness at Noon* (New York: The Modern Library, 1941), p. 267. Koestler was sympathetic to the European New Right, and in fact advocated similar ideas. See Alain de Benoist, 'Un homme supérieur', *Éléments*, no. 45, Spring 1983, pp. 5-12.

29 Alain de Benoist, *On Being a Pagan*, p. 110.

Judaeo-Christian belief, relative, different or contradictory truths cannot exist, since Judaeo-Christianity excludes everything that is not compatible with the division between the concept of good and evil. Eliade writes that the 'intolerance and fanaticism characteristic of the prophets and missionaries of the three monotheistic religions have their model and justification in the example of Yahweh'.[30] In contemporary secular systems, this means that the opposite, the undecided, those who have not taken sides, and those who refuse modern political eschatologies become the target of ostracism or persecution.

Thus, for the New Right, the chaos of modern society has primarily been caused by Biblical monotheism. In the very beginning of its development in Europe, Judaeo-Christian monotheism set out to demystify and desacralise the pagan world by slowly supplanting ancient pagan beliefs with the reign of the law. During this centuries-long process, Christianity has gradually removed all pagan vestiges that coexisted with it. For the authors of the New Right, the desacralisation and the *Entzauberung* of life and politics has not resulted from Europeans' chance departure from Christianity, but rather from the gradual disappearance of the pagan notion of the sacred. Never has Europe been so saturated with the Judaeo-Christian mentality than at the moment when churches and synagogues are virtually empty.

In the following pages we shall see how the New Right deals with what Louis Dumont calls the 'genesis and triumph of modern egalitarian and economic ideologies'. We shall also examine why according to the New Right, economism and egalitarianism constitute the main vectors of totalitarianism. Needless to say, for the New Right, all modern belief systems, including liberalism and Communism, represent secular progenies of Judaeo-Christianity.

---

30 Mircea Eliade, *Histoire des croyances et des idées religieuses* (Paris: Payot, 1976), vol. 1, p. 194.

PART TWO

THE EGALITARIAN MYSTIQUE: THE ROOTS OF THE MODERN CRISIS

'No matter how our future may look, either as an Arcadian dream of impeccable parliamentary democracy, or as a nightmare of totalitarian darkness — the future belongs to the police state.'

—Friedrich Sieburg, *Die Lust am Untergang*

'It suffices to amputate a people from its history and memory in order to open up the avenue of egalitarianism.'

—Jean Cau, *Discours de la décadence*

INTRODUCTION

In the preceding chapters we have seen that the authors of the New Right, as well as some of its predecessors, consider Christianity, liberalism, and Marxism to be the main instigators of the modern crisis. Many of these authors, whose arguments were summarised by Alain de Benoist, maintain that modern liberalism and Marxism, embodied today by America and the Soviet Union respectively, advocate the same values — i.e., egalitarianism, globalism, and economism. Although the implementation of these values differs significantly in America and the Soviet Union, they are nonetheless the main source of legitimacy for both systems.

The purpose of the second part of this book is to examine the New Right's criticism of modern liberalism and Communism, and the underlying belief of these two ideologies in the dogma of equality. In the following chapters extensive reference will be made to some conservative authors who, although sharing the same or similar ideas with the New Right, are independent of the New Right.

The New Right argues that, with minor exceptions, both modern liberalism and Marxism wish to impose on all nations the ideals of equality, human rights, democracy, and economic progress. To counter this globalist and universalist trend, spearheaded by America and the Soviet Union, the New Right urges all nations, and particularly European nations, to disengage themselves, culturally and politically, from both superpowers, and from both liberalism and Marxism, and join in the common fight for the 'cause of the peoples'. In other words, instead of a vague belief in universal human rights, the New Right stresses the primacy of national rights; instead of abstract and elusive dreams of egalitarian democracy, and the myth of eternal economic progress, the New Right espouses a return to the 'roots' and the foundation of organic societies.

The following pages will examine why the New Right, and some other conservative authors, see in liberalism and Marxism two major causes of the modern crisis. The New Right persistently emphasises the fact that that the vague concepts of equality, democracy, and economic progress very often lend themselves to serious political manipulations that in turn always create new political disappointments. The New Right's main thesis is that when equality is left unchecked, society is doomed to sway into 'democratic totalitarianism'. Conversely, when equality is limited to the constitutional and legal sphere, serious economic inequalities and permanent pockets of poverty are bound to persist. In short, according to the New Right, the inherent economic contradictions of liberalism *inevitably* set the stage in which Communism becomes a desirable system that ultimately leads to totalitarian democracy. Here is how de Benoist summarises this point:

> Liberalism reveals its 'schizophrenic' character and constitutional impotence in view of the fact that it is a regime which *simultaneously* generates inequality and, by abhorring inequality, creates the theoretical foundations of its own legitimacy. This is the reason why liberal politicians never have *anything* with which to oppose their socialist critics except better *efficiency* — in short, the guarantee of better success in attaining the same objectives.[1]

This part of the book will proceed in the following manner: in the chapter 'The Metaphysics of Equality', we shall briefly outline the origins of egalitarian ideas and their impact on the future development of liberal and socialist thought. This chapter will show that the Judaeo-Christian heritage made a significant contribution to the rise of egalitarian ideas in modern societies, and that despite the alleged separation of the Church from political power in Western societies, political discourse in liberal democracies continues to borrow heavily from the Judaeo-Christian legacy. We shall also try to pinpoint the main difference between liberal and socialist perceptions of equality and their permanent dispute over the concept of economic equality.

The chapter 'The New Right and the Elusive Equality' critically examines the liberal concept of legal equality, human rights, and the

---

1   Alain de Benoist, 'L'ennemi principal', in *Éléments*, no. 41.

equality of economic opportunity from the perspective of conservative thinkers. This chapter is largely devoted to the authors of the New Right and some conservative authors whose views often parallel those of the New Right. It is very important to specify that none of the authors mentioned in this chapter publicly espouses legal *inequality* or, for that matter, challenges *all* political practices in liberal societies. Their endeavour basically consists of exposing flaws in the liberal theory of human rights and equal economic opportunity. Furthermore, it will be seen that the authors under investigation share a deep-rooted fear that these flaws may ultimately eclipse the elementary notion of human liberty. Some of the authors, who will be singled out in our discussion, are the New Right theorists Louis Rougier, de Benoist, Pierre Krebs, and other conservatives, such as Max Scheler, Antony Flew, and many others. We shall also briefly explore how these authors come to terms with the much-vaunted liberal concept of legal equality and economic 'equal opportunity' and why they maintain that some liberal theoretical premises are untenable in practice.

For the New Right, the fundamental problem with liberalism is its self-contradictory attitude towards equality. The New Right emphasises time and again that equality cannot be controlled; once it is proclaimed in the legal and political fields, equality must run its full course in all other fields, including the field of economics. Accordingly, equal legal rights make no sense, unless they are backed up by equal *economic* rights, i.e., rights to equal shares of affluence. For the New Right, Marxist theorists are much more consistent in formulating their doctrine of natural rights, insofar as Marxists claim that economic equality is a fundamental part of natural rights. In other words, for the New Right, liberals have done a meagre job of promoting economic equality, and as a consequence, they have made themselves permanent targets of socialist, and especially Marxist, opponents. Here is how de Benoist sees it:

> Far from becoming immunised against Communism, liberalism finally *makes* Communism acceptable — and acceptable in a triple form. It makes it acceptable by disseminating the egalitarian ideal, which, at the same time, it is itself incapable of achieving. Thus, [liberalism] introduces in a mild form the aspiration that is the basis of Communism itself.

Finally, it makes Communism acceptable, by distilling an ideology of technomorphic conditioning that makes people oblivious to real liberty, and above all, that makes them ready to accept socialism on the grounds of the irrepressible taste for equality and security.[2]

The chapter '*Homo Economicus*' analyses the nature of modern liberal societies. Similar to the New Left, the New Right labels liberal systems 'soft' totalitarianisms: on the one hand liberalism alleges that its main concern is liberty, yet on the other hand, its internal dynamics constantly demonstrate that its real concern is economics, consumerism, and the cult of money. For the New Right, liberalism is basically the ideology of economics and ethics, of money and morals, since practically all social and human phenomena are reduced to the realm of economic transactions. The economic reductionism in liberal countries gradually leads to social alienation, the obsession with privacy and individualism, and most important, to ethnic and national uprootedness or *Entwurzelung*. Consequently, when the breakdown of ethnic ties occurs, liberal societies are left with social atomisation, followed by what Othmar Spann calls 'the battle of all against all' (*bellum omnium contra omnes*), which leads directly to Communist totalitarianism.

As the reader will note, this part is more descriptive, and it basically portrays some of the social consequences of what de Benoist terms the 'schizophrenia of liberalism'. For the New Right, the next logical step in egalitarian dynamics is the transition from liberalism to Marxist socialism or 'democratic totalitarianism'. The chapters 'Totalitarianism and Egalitarianism' and '*Homo Sovieticus*' will attempt to lay out the New Right's own theory of totalitarianism. In addition, it will also focus on some totalitarian practices in former Communist systems.

It must be emphasised that the New Right, and some contemporary conservative authors in Europe, significantly revise the earlier theories of totalitarianism. In fact, all of our authors agree that unbridled egalitarianism, coupled with the myth of economic progress, provides the framework for 'totalitarian democracy', which in their view is also the most extreme form of totalitarianism. Some of the authors who shall be reviewed are Michel Maffesoli, Claude Polin, and de Benoist.

It is important to note that the authors in question frequently refer to socialist countries in Eastern Europe and the Soviet Union as

---

2   *Loc. cit.*, April- May 1982, p. 45.

'Communist', and therefore in these two chapters we shall also adopt this label without necessarily giving it a derogatory connotation, as is often the case among some conservatives. Needless to say, there are important differences between socialist Sweden and the socialist Soviet Union and, consequently, in order to stress these differences, I deemed it more appropriate to use the denomination 'Communist' as a description of social reality in the Soviet Union. In the light of *glasnost* and *perestroika,* many liberal theorists would no longer consider the Soviet Union to be a 'totalitarian' country, and would instead probably prefer to label it as 'authoritarian'. As already indicated at the beginning of this book, there is unfortunately no uniform political vocabulary on which social scientists could agree in designating social phenomena. To be sure, many contemporary authors today would reject the very idea of a totalitarian Soviet Union.

The political discourse which the authors of the New Right use concerning the concept of totalitarianism could indeed lead to some misunderstandings. For example, it is no secret that the New Right refers to modern liberal societies as 'soft totalitarianisms'; a label that would probably strike many liberals as unjust and unfounded. In contrast, many socialist countries often depicted liberal countries as 'totalitarian' without, however, admitting their own totalitarian natures. Undoubtedly, even Stalin conceived of his society as the greatest democratic achievement.

For the New Right, liberal societies, by becoming socially transparent, and by reducing freedom to economic 'freedom', deliberately renounce higher spiritual values, and thus they invariably reveal their proto-totalitarian character, despite the seeming social and political pluralism that they so fervently espouse. For Claude Polin, a renowned French conservative scholar, individualism, economism, and egalitarianism are the main ingredients of the totalitarianism that lies dormant in long-standing liberal societies. On the other hand, for Alexander Zinoviev, a Russian dissident and a highly regarded expert on logic who has also had a crucial impact on the New Right and the European conservative scene, the Soviet Union is a perfect Communist society, highly democratic, and above all, a society which successfully created a new specimen, *Homo sovieticus.* Zinoviev, who shares astounding similarities in terms of his epistemology and social analyses with Pareto, Polin, and de Benoist, is convinced that Soviet Communism has truly achieved equality on *all* levels of society, regardless of the unpalatable consequences that the Soviet people have had to endure in achieving this equality. As we shall see in our concluding chapter, Zinoviev maintains that the Gulag was not at all a chance result of history, or a totalitarian departure from democratic principles; instead it was the ultimate form of democratic and egalitarian aspirations that would have been implemented with or without Marx and his scientific socialism.

Naturally, amidst such a variety of different terms and different conceptualisations by different conservative authors, it is often hard to agree on the most suitable terminology. Therefore, it is imperative that this book convey a message that would be acceptable to the authors mentioned above, irrespective of the different wordings that they assign to their concepts. For Maffesoli, Zinoviev, Polin, de Benoist, Dumont, and probably some other authors, true totalitarianism is not national, but international. True totalitarianism is not the oppression of the few over the many; it is the oppression of the many over the few. As Polin summarises, 'Totalitarianism is the total terror of all against all at all moments' (*terreur totale de tous sur tous à tous les instants*). Modern liberal and socialist countries have been able to realise this peculiar brand of terror.

For the New Right, humanity is headed towards totalitarian chaos whose main cause is the incipient Judaeo-Christian belief in egalitarianism. This is finally the fundamental teaching of the European New Right regarding the genesis and the outcome of the egalitarian and democratic ideal.

I

THE METAPHYSICS OF EQUALITY

The idea of equality is probably as old as mankind itself. Although egalitarian experiments were known to have taken place very early in history and about which there is scant information, it was with Judaism and, later on, Christianity, that we can trace with greater certainty the genesis and the gradual consolidation of the modern belief system of egalitarianism. This chapter will limit itself to the cursory examination of the rise and the consolidation of the egalitarian ideal in Western thought.

A number of authors of liberal, socialist, and conservative persuasion maintain that the modern ideal of equality owes a significant debt to the early Jewish prophets. Thus the French author Gérard Walter, in his book *Les origines du communisme,* maintains that the roots of the modern egalitarian ideal and the belief in brotherhood and democracy can best be traced to Judaea and early Jewish scriptures.[1] In a similar vein, the American scholar Emanuel Rackman, in his piece 'Judaism and Equality', writes that Judaism derives the idea of equality from the fact that God created only *one* man from whom all humanity is descended. He notes:

> That all men have only one progenitor was held to mean that all human beings are born equal. They enjoy this equality by virtue of the very fact that they were born, even if they never attain to the faculty of reason.[2]

1 Gérard Walter, *Les origines du communisme* (Paris: Payot, 1931), 'Les sources judaïques de la doctrine communiste chrétienne', pp. 13-65. Compare with Vilfredo Pareto, *Les systèmes socialistes* (Paris: Marcel Girard, 1926), vol. 2, 'Les systèmes métaphysiques-communistes', pp. 2-45.

2 Emanuel Rackman, 'Judaism and Equality', in *Equality,* edited by J. Roland Pennock and John W. Chapman (New York: Atherton Press, 1967), p. 155.

Rackman, in fact, sees the decisive importance of Judaism for the development of natural rights, and later human rights, which subsequently became the cornerstone of the American doctrine of natural rights. He adds:

> This was the only source on which Thomas Paine could rely in his *Rights of Man* to support the dogma of the American *Declaration of Independence* that all men are created equal. And this dogma was basic in Judaism.[3]

Similar views are held by the American scholar Milton Konvitz, who maintains in his book *Judaism and the American Idea* that within the framework of the religious system, it was impossible for the liberal 'Founding Fathers' to arrive at the philosophy of equality in the absence of a belief in ethical monotheism, i.e., the belief in one God. Konvitz writes:

> At bottom the democratic faith is a moral affirmation: men are not to be used merely as means to an end, as tools; each is an end in himself; his soul is from the source of all life... no matter how lowly his origin, a man is here only by the grace of God — he owes his life to no one but God. He has an equal right to pursue happiness; life, liberty and the pursuit of happiness are his simply by virtue of the fact that he is a live human being.[4]

The Judaic ideal is the kingdom of heaven, equality, and peace, and it can be said that these principles also played a considerable role in modern liberal and socialist thought. Along with the idea of fraternity and liberty, equality is today held as an operative idea behind democratic thought. Furthermore, it is worth noting that the idea of equality first emerged as the absolute equality of souls before God and, until at least the late Seventeenth and Eighteenth centuries, did not necessarily imply that all people must have equal legal and political rights. One may argue that the effort of some Rationalist thinkers, including even Locke, Mill, and Rousseau, primarily consisted of transforming the Christian egalitarian ideal into a form that was suitable for a secular

---

3   *Loc. cit.*

4   Milton Konvitz, *Judaism and the American Idea* (Ithaca and London: Cornell University Press, 1978), p. 71.

world that was slowly but surely witnessing the erosion of Church authority. Charles Rihs, in his well-documented book *Les philosophes
utopistes*, sees in Mably, Condorcet, and later Rousseau, millenarian
secular prophets whose ideas about a just society were in many aspects
similar to early Judaic prophecies.[5]

In the Eighteenth century, another secular impetus to egalitarian
ideas sprang up from Protestant scholars, the admirers of *jus naturale*
(natural law), Grotius, Pufendorf and Vattel, who hoped that with the
Reformation the gates of equality for the budding bourgeoisie were at
last thrust open. Subsequently, with the gradual secularisation of life
and the rise of the bourgeois class, the dogma of *jus naturalis* began to
emerge in early liberal societies, and eventually came to be known as
'human rights' and equal rights before the law. Carl J. Friedrich summarises this point in the following words:

> Legal equality before the law is in a sense the secular version of equal-
> ity before God; both God and the Law transcend the individual and his
> needs. Yet they suggest that in very essential respects, human beings
> are entitled to be treated as if they were equal.[6]

When one looks in retrospect at the political gains of egalitarian dogma,
one can clearly see its permanent progress through history. Even the
Catholic Church, which in the Nineteenth century denounced human
rights, democracy, and liberalism as 'un-Christian inventions' in its
encyclicals, such as *Quanta Cura* and *Syllabus Errorum*, has often portrayed itself as a champion of these same values since the Second World
War, particularly since the Second Vatican Council.[7] Ernst Troeltsch,
Louis Rougier, and Werner Sombart, who may also be associated with
the legacy of 'revolutionary conservatism', noted quite some time ago

---

5   Charles Rihs, *Les philosophes utopistes* (Paris: Marcel Rivière, 1970). Compare
    with the interesting essay by Norman Cohn, 'Medieval Millenarism', in *Millennial
    Dreams in Action* (New York: Schocken, 1970). On p. 33, Cohn says that 'more
    than in any other religion, Jewish religion centres on the expectation of a future
    Golden Age; Christianity inherited that expectation'.

6   Carl J. Friedrich, 'A Brief Discourse on the Origin of Political Equality', in *Equality*,
    p. 227.

7   In the 1864 encyclicals *Quanta Cura* and *Syllabus Errorum*, the Vatican strongly
    condemned democracy and liberalism. After the Second World War, and espe-
    cially after 1966, the position of the Vatican toward democracy and liberalism has
    obviously changed.

that it is no accident that liberalism has grown solid roots precisely in those countries that showed a strong attachment to *the Bible* and especially to the *Old Testament*.[8] Troeltsch writes that the Calvinist version of Christianity, as it developed in the United States, became a receptacle for the development and consolidation of the egalitarian ideal, from which later sprang the pacifist, internationalist cast of mind, and the belief in universal human rights.[9] More recently, Jerol S. Auerbach, in his piece 'Liberalism and the Hebrew Prophets', asserted that liberals in America, Jews and Christians alike, have traditionally resorted to quoting Hebrew prophets in order to frame the indictment of social ills. He writes:

> Liberalism is still good for the Jews, according to the conventional wisdom, because liberal values express fidelity to prophetic ideals. [And] commitment to the rule of law (the legacy of *Torah*) reinforced by a passion for social justice defines the Biblical heritage of American democracy.[10]

---

8   Ernst Troeltsch, *The Social Teaching of the Christian Churches* (New York: Harper, 1960), p. 64 in the German edition; Werner Sombart, *The Jews and Modern Capitalism* (Glencoe, Illinois: Free Press, 1951). On p. 44, Sombart writes that 'what we call Americanism is nothing else, if we may say so, than the Jewish spirit' (*geronnenes Judentum*). Also Louis Rougier, *La Mystique démocratique: ses origines, ses illusions,* prefaced by Alain de Benoist (Paris: Éditions Albatros, 1983), especially Chapter V, 'Le protestantisme et le capitalisme', pp. 187-221. The book was first published in 1929, and had a considerable influence on conservative audiences in Europe. Also by the same author, *Du paradis à l'utopie* (Paris: Copernic, 1977), pp. 133-201.

9   Troeltsch, *op. cit.*, p. 310 (p. 768 in the German edition). And the passage on 'Naturrechtlicher und liberaler Character des freikirchlichen Neucalvinismus', pp. 762-772. Compare with Georg Jellinek, *The Declaration of the Rights of Man and of Citizens* (Westport: Hyperion Press, 1979). On p. 77, Jellinek writes that '[t]he idea of legally establishing inalienable, inherent and sacred rights of the individual is not of political but religious origin.'

10 Jerol S. Auerbach, 'Liberalism and the Hebrew Prophets', in *Commentary*, vol. 84, no. 2, August 1987, p. 58. Compare with Ben Zion Bokser in 'Democratic Aspirations in Talmudic Judaism', in *Judaism and Human Rights*, edited by Milton Konvitz (New York: W. W. Norton, 1972). On p. 146, Bokser writes that 'The Talmud ordained with great emphasis that every person charged with the violation of some law be given a fair trial and before the law all were to be scrupulously equal, whether a king or a pauper.'

For Carl Schmitt, who has already been discussed in previous chapters, the 'political theology' of liberalism and socialism continues to borrow from Jewish and Christian eschatology, albeit by bestowing its discourse with a more secular flavour.[11] This view is shared by the New Right which also concurs that the ideal of equality, human rights, constitutionalism, and universalism represent the secular transposition of non-European, Oriental, and Judaeo-Christian eschatology.

Liberal or Socialist Equality?

When liberal authors maintain that all men are equal, it is not to say that men must be identical. It is important to note that for liberal thinkers, equality has never meant identity, and liberalism has nothing to do with uniformity. To assert that all men are equal, in liberal theory, means that all men should be first and foremost treated fairly and their differences acknowledged. It was the intimate feeling among liberal theorists that the idea of equality and the idea of liberty are interrelated. Both ideas sprang up from the same faith in the common humanity of man and respect for each individual. John Locke, a thinker who played a decisive role in the development of liberal thought, wrote:

> [We] must consider a state also of equality, wherein all the power and jurisdiction is reciprocal, no one having more than another; there being nothing more evident than that creatures of the same species and rank, promiscuously born to all the same advantages of nature, and the use of the same faculties, should also be equal one amongst another without subordination or subjection, unless the Lord and Master of them all should by any manifest declaration of his will set one above another.[12]

Some liberals, such as Richard H. Tawney, although acknowledging the innate differences among people, as they manifest themselves in differing human capacities and intelligence, maintain that liberalism

---

11 Cf. Carl Schmitt, *Political Theology* (Cambridge: MIT Press, 1985), pp. 35-46. Schmitt writes on p. 36, that '[a]ll significant concepts of the modern theory of the state are secularised theological concepts...'

12 John Locke, *On Civil Government* (London: J.M. Dent and Sons, 1924), p. 118, in chapter 'Of the State of Nature', § 4.

must strive to make equality of opportunity accessible to everybody, because only in that way will the differences between the privileged and the unprivileged in society gradually become less glaring. In a significant passage from *Equality*, Tawney writes:

> The important thing, however, is that it [equality] should not be completely attained, but that it should be sincerely sought. What matters to the health of society is the objective towards which its face is set, and to suggest that it is immaterial in which direction it moves, because whatever the direction, the goal must always elude it, is not scientific but irrational.[13]

The problem, of course, arises when the idea of equality becomes associated with the demand for economic equality, which in turn may bring about theories that depart significantly from the liberal legacy. From Babeuf to Marx, many socialist theorists have repudiated the often huge economic discrepancies in liberal society—a society that often prides itself on legal equality and the respect for human rights. The avowed goal of socialists, and particularly Marxist theorists, was the removal of those economic barriers and the creation of a society in which equal economic opportunity would also be translated into equal economic outcomes. In the famous passage from *The Critique of the Gotha Program*, Marx clearly outlined his criticism of liberal equality in these words:

> Hence *equal rights* here [in liberalism], means in principle *bourgeois rights*. This *equal* right is an unequal right for unequal labour. It recognises no class differences, because everyone is only a worker like everyone else; but it tacitly recognises unequal individual endowment and thus productive capacity as natural privileges.

Therefore Marx proposes his vision of a society that would bring about true equality:

> In a higher phase of Communist society, after the tyrannical subordination of individuals according to the distribution of labour, and thereby also the distinction between manual and intellectual work, have disappeared, after labour has become not merely a means to live,

---

13 Richard H. Tawney, excerpt from *Equality*, in *The Idea of Equality*, edited by George L. Abernethy (Richmond: John Knox Press, 1959), p. 238.

but is in itself the first necessity of living... then and only then can the narrow rights of bourgeois rights be left far behind, and society inscribe on its banner: 'From each according to his capacity, to each according to his need.'[14]

For Marxists, economic wealth is commonly singled out as the most important form of inequality. Logically, if the ownership of the means of production is no longer held in the hands of the few, then the 'legal' superstructure will also change its nature, and along with it, the bourgeois definition of human rights will need to be amended. This is a rather important point, which shall be discussed later, particularly when we start examining the causes of the frequent failure of the liberal crusade for human rights in the former Communist countries of Eastern Europe and the former Soviet Union. John Rees makes the following point in his book *Equality:*

> [The] Marxist is sufficiently committed to stressing the importance of ownership in the productive instruments to regard this fact as a prime and decisive factor in generating social inequalities; hence his conviction that social ownership and control of these instruments is necessary and sufficient for achieving a classless society.[15]

The transfer of property from the bourgeoisie to the workers would probably spell the doom of capitalism, although if one follows the logic of equality, it does make some sense to envision a society in which the idea of equality would also incorporate equality of economic conditions.

For David Thomson, socialist equality is neither feasible nor desirable, since this would spell the doom not only of capitalism, but also bring about the end of culture and civilisation.[16] Nonetheless, Thomson realises that in contemporary liberal societies the craving for equality can become so pervasive that it can totally obscure the love of liberty. This is an important element of our discussion to which we shall be referring more often as we proceed. Many authors, across the entire ideological spectrum, seem to be in agreement that, despite

14 Karl Marx, *Critique of the Gotha Programme* (New York: International Publishers, 1938), pp. 9-10.

15 John Rees, *Equality* (New York: Praeger Publishers, 1971), p. 35.

16 David Thomson, *Equality* (Cambridge: Cambridge University Press, 1949), p. 9.

its significant achievements in political and legal rights, liberalism has not been very successful in implementing economic rights for all people. Thomson remarks, not without irony:

> Many who would stoutly defend with their dying breath the rights of liberty and equality...(as would many English and American liberals) shrink back with horror from the notion of economic egalitarianism.[17]

It comes as a surprise, especially to the New Right, that the idea of equality, which is widely accepted in liberal societies in the form of guaranteed legal, religious, and political rights, is commonly skirted in the economic arena. One may accept the hypothesis that if all social and political inequalities are man-made, the unresolved economic inequality in liberal countries is the product of real people, too. It is worth recalling that as soon as the prospect of legal equality appeared as a viable reality in Seventeenth century political thinking, it automatically came under fire from those who thought of it as insufficient and selective in implementation. For example, Sanford Lakoff notes that the egalitarian idea provided not only the budding bourgeoisie of the Seventeenth century with ammunition, but also radicals such as Thomas Müntzer, Gerard Winstanley, and countless other figures, who were not satisfied with an emasculated (legal) equality; the equality which probably accommodated the needs of the bourgeoisie but failed to announce that peasants and workers should also enjoy the same political rights and, above all, share an equal part of the wealth. As Lakoff notes, what Müntzer or Winstanley wanted was economic equality for the masses.[18] Thus, instead of bringing people together, the liberal definition of equality, from its very incipience, managed to create a serious social rift and in addition, set the stage for often violent attacks by socialistic and Communistic opponents. Louis Rougier traces the contradiction between legal and economic equality in the egalitarian ideal to Judaism and its successor, Christianity. In his book *La mystique démocratique*, Rougier writes that Judaism and Christianity, by regarding justice as the equal distribution of riches, turned a

---

17 *Ibid.*, p. 79.

18 Sanford Lakoff, 'Christianity and Equality', in *Equality,* edited by J. Roland Pennock and John W. Chapman (New York Atherton Press, 1967), pp. 128-130.

moral problem into an economic problem, and consequently deliberately pushed all social discourse into the *economic* forefront. He notes:

> By proclaiming that wealth is a divine benediction, Judaism, with its
> modern substitute Puritanism, has been the generator of modern cap-
> italism. Yet, by proclaiming that wealth is very often unequally distrib-
> uted, and that it does not always go to the just who suffer the odious
> inequity of being poor—Judaism has been a prime purveyor of the
> democratic mystique, and its logical conclusion: socialism.[19]

The great concern for the New Right, and some other conservative
authors, is its deep-seated doubt in the liberal capacity to stave off the
irreversible demand for *more* equality. Given the contemporary dynamics of egalitarian discourse, it is likely that if economic opportunities or resources suddenly become scarce, total economic equality,
and with it the rise of totalitarian democracy, may become the only viable alternative. It is worth noting that even the French Revolution was
not a complete and successful revolution for many who had originally
welcomed it as an advent of a new and just epoch. Thus, Babeuf maintained that equality cannot just stop at the threshold of mere legal-
ism; it must continue its course to absolute equality which would entail
economic equality. This is how he put it in his *Manifesto of the Equals*:

> The French Revolution is only the forerunner of a much greater, much
> more solemn, revolution which will be the last... Begone, hideous dis-
> tinction of rich and poor, of masters and servants, of governing and
> governed... In the cry of equality, let the forces of justice and happiness
> organise themselves.[20]

It is needless to argue how much Babeuf's proclamation influenced
Marx and future Marxist leaders, but it is also interesting to note a
strange millenarian resonance that echoes in Mably, Condorcet, Rousseau, Babeuf, and later on, in Marx — a resonance that carries the same
millenarian emotional appeal that Paul once addressed to the Galatians: 'There is neither Jew nor Greek, there is neither bond nor free,

---

19 Louis Rougier, *La mystique démocratique*, p. 184. See the passage in its entirety, 'Le
    Judaïsme et la Révolution sociale', pp. 184-185.

20 Quoted in David Thomson, *Equality*, pp. 85-86.

there is neither male nor female; for ye are all one in Christ Jesus.' (*Galatians* 3:28)

One may agree with Thomson that the appetite for equality grows with the taste of it — and this is precisely where the New Right and some other conservative theorists see the greatest threat to liberty.

II

THE NEW RIGHT AND THE ELUSIVE EQUALITY

The following chapter provides an extensive critique of various egalitarian manifestations in modern societies. The New Right and several other American and European conservatives examined in this chapter have some serious misgivings about the concepts that 'all men are born equal', of human rights, and the equality of (economic) opportunity — in short, all those concepts that are today widely held as fundamental elements in modern liberal societies. One of the tasks of these authors is to point to the flaws in egalitarian beliefs and contrast them with the importance of the particular national and historical identities of different peoples with diverse cultures.

The New Right contends that, due to the legacy of fascism, many theories critical of egalitarianism have not received adequate attention on the grounds of their alleged anti-democratic character. As a result, some authors, particularly in the fields of genetics, anthropology, and ethology, whose ideas are critical of some widely accepted assumptions in both liberal and socialist societies, have remained practically unknown to a larger audience. Drawing on the work done by Arthur R. Jensen, Konrad Lorenz, Hans J. Eysenck, and some other scientists, the New Right asserts that various assumptions about the equality of men need to be significantly revised, put into appropriate social context, and additionally, the social sciences should use some data more extensively that have been made available through research in the fields of the natural sciences. Firstly, the New Right posits that men are born with different qualities and that acquired and inborn skills and capacities significantly affect man's future political and social role. Furthermore, argues the New Right, it is necessary to view each human being as a unique creature whose overall behaviour and the subsequent political socialisation depend considerably on hereditary and cultural factors, as well as values and norms absorbed within his tribal, national, racial, and ethnic environment.

One of the reasons that there is still a great deal of confusion surrounding the concept of human equality is probably due to its careless and ambiguous use. Equality of what? For example, the inequality of competence, and the inequality of outcome have been accepted largely as valid principles by the majority of people in liberal democracies, although even these principles appear deficient to the authors of the New Right. How is somebody's competence to be gauged, what is the role of the changing socio-economic structure on the psychology of modern citizens, and how does the role of hereditary factors determine the equality of competence, inquires the New Right? What role is played by the factor of one's historical, national or racial memory, particularly when the scourge of racism threatens society? Why, to put it bluntly, have some nations invented the Gatling gun in order to enslave some other nations — and why not the other way around? For example, the controversial dispute about genetic and racial inequality, which has raged in the United States and Europe for quite some time is seen by the New Right as corroborating its own thesis that to believe or not believe in equality is rather a matter of sentiments that may either be refuted or proven by scientific inquiries.[1] Hans J. Eysenck, the

---

1   The American journal, *American Psychologist,* July 1972, pp. 660-661, critically commented on persistent attacks by the 'environmentalists' against the proponents of hereditary factors, with these words: 'The history of civilisation shows many periods when scientific research or teaching was censured, punished or suppressed for non-scientific reasons, usually for seeming to contradict some religious or political belief... Today, a similar suppression, censure, punishment, and defamation are being applied against scientists who emphasise the role of heredity in human behaviour. Published positions are often misquoted and misrepresented; emotional appeals replace scientific reasoning; arguments are directed against the man rather than against the evidence (e.g., a scientist is called 'fascist', and his arguments are ignored). A large number of attacks come from non-scientists, or even anti-scientists, among the political militants on campus. Other attacks include academics committed to environmentalism in their explanation of almost all human differences. And a large number of scientists, who have studied the evidence and are persuaded of the great role played by heredity in human behaviour, are silent, neither expressing their belief clearly in public, nor rallying strongly to the defence of their more outspoken colleagues.' The petition was signed first by

English psychologist and philosopher, and also an avowed supporter of the New Right, persistently argues in his writings that the general intelligence of people, including special skills, is strongly determined by heredity. To a great extent hereditary factors are decisive for man's future socialisation. Eysenck notes:

> A recognition of this essential human diversity, based as it is on genetic factors at present beyond our control, would save us untold misery, and release our energies from vain struggle to confine other people's behaviour within chains of our own devising. It is very difficult to think of somebody else's views as being just as sane, just as reasonable, just as likely to promote happiness as our own, when his views conflict with ours.[2]

Eysenck insists that modern societies must consider the fact that people are bio-social organisms, and that 'each attempt to neglect biological factors in our behaviour, or to refute them, leads to absurd consequences'.[3] For Eysenck the 'rational man of the Enlightenment — the economic man, cherished by economists — this, and other fallacies have been given to us as desirable patterns of human nature'.[4] In his piece 'Vererbung und Gesellschaftspolitik -die Ungleichheit der Menschen und ihre gesellschaftspolitischen Auswirkungen', Eysenck notes:

> The [second] application of the principle of biological and genetic determination in human behaviour concerns human diversity. As a result of specific gene patterns that stand in diverse relationship with the changing environment, segments of the human species differ in endless forms from each other.[5]

---

fifty scientists from the United Kingdom, who were later joined by scientists from other parts of Europe and America. Among the signatories were Francis Crick, Hans Eysenck, Richard J. Herrnstein, Jacques Monod, Arnold Gehlen, Garrett Hardin, etc.

2 Hans Jürgen Eysenck, *The Inequality of Man* (London: Temple Smith, 1973), p. 33.

3 Hans Jürgen Eysenck, 'Vererbung und Gesellschaftspolitik: die Ungleichheit der Menschen und ihre gesellschaftspolitischen Auswirkungen', in *Die Grundlagen des Spätmarxismus*, with contributions from Horst Nachtigall, Ernst Topitsch and Rudiger Proske (Stuttgart: Verlag Bonn Aktuell, 1977), pp. 10-11.

4 *Ibid.*, p. 10.

5 *Ibid.*, p. 33.

Refuting the socialist and liberal reductionist model of society, Konrad Lorenz, a world-renowned ethologist, a Nobel Prize winner, and a supporter of the New Right, suggests that it is necessary for politicians and political scientists to pay greater attention to the biology of man when examining social and political aberrations in modern societies. In his book, *The Waning of Humaneness*, Lorenz deplores that the modern mystique of equality is often oblivious to the multifarious dimensions of the human personality, and he adds that men are unequal at the moment of their conception. In the chapter 'The Pseudodemocratic Doctrine', Lorenz writes:

> Among the factors stabilising the technocratic system belongs the doctrine of the absolute equality of all humans, in other words, the erroneous belief that the human is born as a *tabula rasa*, a blank tablet, a clean slate, and that his entire personal identity and personality are determined, initially, by the learning process. This doctrine, in which unfortunately many people still believe even today with nothing less than religious fervour, had its origin, as Philip Wylie shows us in his book *The Magic Animal*, in a misrepresentation of a famous phrase found in the American *Declaration of Independence* drafted by Thomas Jefferson. There it states 'that all men are created equal'.[6]

Lorenz's observations are paralleled by Richard J. Herrnstein, a former professor of psychology at Harvard University, and also one of the frequently quoted sources of the New Right. In his controversial article entitled 'I.Q.', first published in *The Atlantic Monthly*, and subsequently reproduced in Eysenck's book, *The Inequality of Man*, Herrnstein strongly condemns the modern myth of equality, and argues that this myth may seriously impair the elementary notion of freedom. Herrnstein writes:

> The spectre of Communism was haunting Europe, said Karl Marx and Friedrich Engels in 1848. They could point to the rise of egalitarianism for proof. From Jefferson's 'self-evident truth' of man's equality, to France's *égalité* and beyond that to the revolutions that swept Europe as Marx and Engels were proclaiming their *Manifesto*, the central political fact of their times, and ours, has been the rejection of aristocracies and privileged classes, of special rights for 'special' people. The vision of a classless society was the keystone of the *Declaration of*

6   Konrad Lorenz, *The Waning of Humaneness* (Boston: Little, Brown, 1987), p. 178.

Independence as well as the *Communist Manifesto*, however different the plan for achieving it.[7]

Lorenz goes one step further and writes that as effective and noble as the *Declaration* appeared in the Eighteenth century, it was almost inevitable that its message would gradually become a subject of quasi-religious veneration and frequent political manipulations. Lorenz actually sees in modern democratic ideologies a carefully planned 'state religion', designed by 'lobbyists of large industry and by the ideology of Communism. [This] pseudo-democratic doctrine continues to exert tremendous influence on public opinion and on psychology'.[8] Referring also to the proclamation of the American *Declaration*, in which he sees the benign form of the future irreversible rise of egalitarianism, Lorenz notes:

> As effective as the *Declaration* was, so was also the subsequent double distortion of the phrase's logic; the first incorrect deduction was that if all humans had ideal conditions for development, they would develop into ideal beings. From this incorrect deduction it was further inferred, in another logical somersault, that all humans at birth are absolutely identical.[9]

Drawing from the above-mentioned authors, the New Right asserts that the belief in equality rests more on the principles of social desirability inherited in secular forms from Judaeo-Christian scholasticism than on the facts established by scientific analysis. According to Pierre Krebs, one of the philosophers of the New Right, the contemporary theories of the egalitarian mythos deliberately associate a pseudo-science (historical materialism) with a messianic catechism (the universalist dogma), which are in turn implemented on each level of society. Accordingly, this myth of egalitarianism must either resort to the explicit 'raw' power, such as in Marxist states, or to the 'soft' economic conditioning that functions as a leading principle behind technocratic liberal countries.[10] The inevitable result is a tendency to regard each

---

7   Richard J. Herrnstein, 'I.Q', quoted in Eysenck, *The Inequality of Man*, p. 214.

8   Lorenz, *The Waning of Humaneness*, p. 180.

9   *Ibid.*, p. 179.

10 Pierre Krebs, 'Gedanken zu einer kulturellen Wiedergeburt', in *Das unvergängliche Erbe: Alternativen zum Princip der Gleichheit*, prefaced by H. J. Eysenck,

human being as a pliable being, and to reduce all human phenomena to a single cause, notably economics. In the process of this 'levelling', argues Krebs, the role of heredity, the role of national consciousness, the importance of popular and ancient mythology and religion is significantly neglected, if not totally obliterated. Citing Alain Peyrefitte, a conservative French politician, Krebs writes that 'the assumption that all people at birth are endowed with the same talents, and that all peoples possess the same energies is the result of spiritual confusion regarding human evolution, which would once have been considered insanity'.[11]

Krebs further writes that contemporary racism and violent nationalism usually occur in multi-cultural and multi-racial societies, notably when a dominant and larger ethnic group feels that an alien minority or smaller ethnic group threatens its national and historical identity. Accordingly, a large nation coexisting with a smaller ethnic group within the same body politic will gradually come to fear that its own historical and national identity will be obliterated by a foreign and alien body unable or unwilling to share the same national, racial, and historical consciousness. When racism or racial exclusion occur, they can basically be traced to the individuals and peoples who feel more and more alienated from their former communal bonds. Krebs implicitly argues that in multi-racial and multi-cultural environments, abstract human rights will make very little sense. Indeed, such an environment may become eventually harmful to all ethnic and racial groups coexisting with each other. He notes:

> Egalitarian structures that lump together essentially different and, indeed, even opposite peoples leads in the first stage to the deficient adaptation of individual ethnic groups (which in turn results in the sense of uprootedness among the larger group). After all contradictions and differences have been levelled out, the second stage sets in with the general and uniform adaptation that manifests itself in a form of massification (*Vermassung*).[12]

---

with contributions by Alain de Benoist, Peter Binding, and Jörg Rieck (Tübingen: Grabert Verlag, 1981), p. 18.

11 Quoted in Krebs, *op. cit.*, p. 20.

12 Krebs, *Ibid.*, p. 24.

Consequently, according to Pierre Krebs and Hans J. Eysenck, the aberrant and inevitable aggressive behaviour that usually accompanies racism is in part the response of a stronger group to the prospects of impending uprootedness. Referring to aggressive behaviour among humans, Eysenck, in his usual pessimistic tone, notes that 'among the majority of people the reptile brain (*das reptile Hirn*), or paleocortex, plays, unfortunately, a predominant role over the sense of reason, and it cannot be influenced by sweet appeals to the senses, or by rational preaching'.[13] For Lorenz, political violence and aggression cannot be resolved by simple legal measures; human aggression lies in man's own phylogenesis that no amount of belief in human perfectibility can solve. In his book, *Civilized Man's Eight Deadly Sins*, in the chapter 'Genetic Decay', Lorenz notes:

> [The] belief, raised to a doctrine, that all men are born equal and that all moral defects of the criminal are attributable to the defects in his environment and education, leads to attrition of the natural sense of justice, particularly in the delinquent himself; filled with self-pity, he regards himself as the victim of society.[14]

For the authors of the New Right, man cannot be regarded as a *tabula rasa* or as an abstract being, but instead, each aspect of his humanness has to be taken into account. As Pierre Krebs remarks, the elements of man are mythological, historical, biological, and psychological. 'Because', adds Krebs, 'we are a people of a specific heritage, of roots, of tradition, and thinking'.[15] The continuing massification and anomie in modern liberal societies are basically a sign of the modern refusal to acknowledge man's innate genetic, historical and national differences as well as his cultural and national particularities — the features that are increasingly being supplanted with a belief that human differences occur only as a result of different cultural environments. Krebs notes:

> The uniformity of the human species has gradually stifled overall motivations that otherwise make the most ideal and most profound reasons to live. The levelling (*Gleichstellung*) of all individuals has gradually destroyed the personality. The process of population

---

13 Eysenck, 'Vererbung und Gesellschaftspolitik', *op. cit.*, p. 29.

14 Konrad Lorenz, *Civilized Man's Eight Deadly Sins* (London: Methuen, 1974), p. 49.

15 Krebs, *op. cit.*, p. 25.

massification has gradually destroyed peoples. The generalisation of *one* 'truth' has influenced the integrity of all other 'truths'.[16]

Often accused of advocating social Darwinism and sociobiology, the New Right persistently denies the charges that its intent is to *reduce* human beings to a single factor of biological determinism. To this and similar accusations, the New Right responds that 'biological reductionism' would significantly invalidate its own pluralistic and 'polytheistic' concept of the world, and contradict its main thesis that rejects *all* forms of determinism: historical, economic, and biological alike. Nonetheless, the New Right does not shy away from acknowledging the importance of some authors such as Georges Vacher de Lapouge and Ludwig Woltmann, and insists that these racialist authors be studied with fewer ideological prejudices.[17] For his part, Konrad Lorenz notes that:

> [O]ur present-day caricature of a liberal democracy has reached the culminating point of an oscillation. At the opposite extreme, reached by the pendulum not long ago, are Eichmann and Auschwitz, 'euthanasia', racial hate, massacre, and lynch law. We must realise that, at both sides of the point the pendulum would indicate if it ever stopped moving, there are *genuine values:* on the 'left' the value of free, individual development; on the 'right' the value of social and cultural soundness. It is the excess *of both* that leads to inhumanity.[18]

In the editorial of the New Right's quarterly, *Nouvelle École*, entitled 'Darwinisme et société', the New Right reiterates that of all animals, man *alone* is not obligated to adhere to his nature as a species. Placed in permanent malleability, he is 'open to the world', that is, he is capable not only of adapting himself to new social structures but also of creating new ones. His biological constitution is not a fatality.[19] As de Benoist reminds us, 'in the capacity of a human being, for man, culture

---

16 Krebs, *op. cit.*, p. 30.

17 Alain de Benoist, 'Ludwig Woltmann et le darwinisme allemand ou le socialisme prolet-aryen', in *Nouvelle École*, Summer 1982, pp. 87-98.

18 Lorenz, *Civilized Man's Eight Deadly Sins*, p. 50.

19 'Darwinisme et société', in *Nouvelle École, op. cit.*, p. 13.

has primacy over nature, and history has primacy over biology. Man *becomes* by creating from what he already is. He is the *creator himself.*[20]

The Rights of the Peoples or Human Rights?

Modern liberal and socialist ideologies, observe the authors of the New Right, demonstrate the same globalist design to erase the plurality of nations and supplant diverse national consciousnesses with the universal belief in 'generic man' and one humanity. For the New Right, the chief axiom of liberalism and socialism is the dogma consisting of human rights and the unity of mankind — a dogma inherited from the Judaeo-Christian eschatology, and subsequently transposed in a secular form into the modern world. Pierre Bérard, a historian affiliated with the New Right, in his piece 'Ces cultures qu'on assassine', writes that *Genesis* postulates that the totality of people are descended from one and the same original couple. 'This archetype of generic and universal man sets forth a paradigm which establishes the unity of species within the framework of the zoological apparatus — which, in the last analysis, boils down to reducing culture to nature.'[21] This archetype of common humanity stands in sharp contrast to pagan thought, which uses each person's historical and geographic environment, that is, 'a place as a centre of crystallisation of cultural identity', as a reference.[22] The implicit message of the *Declaration of Independence* regarding human rights involved the assumption that universal human rights precede narrow communal or national rights, and that the American-adopted legal principles could be valid for all peoples on Earth, regardless of their national origin. Bérard notes that the American and French declarations, by intending to be universal, in fact became the most pernicious expression of Western (Judaeo-Christian!) ethnocentrism. The *Declaration* posits that what is viewed as self-evident by Western peoples, must also be self-evident for non-Western peoples. The end result is the loss of one's cultural and national memory. Bérard writes:

---

20 *Loc. cit.*

21 Pierre Bérard, 'Ces cultures qu'on assassine', in *La cause des peuples* (Paris: Le Labyrinthe, 1982), p. 27.

22 *Ibid.*, p. 26.

Historically, human rights are the ideological expression of Jacobinism. They today become the expression of Western ethnocentrism (*occidentalo-centrisme*) — the underlying discourse of the new international order. And in all cases they could justify genocidal crusades.[23]

Identical views are shared by de Benoist in his piece 'Pour une déclaration du droit des peuples', in which he argues that the proclamation of the same rights for all peoples leads in the long run to the deprivation of its own specificity for all peoples. 'People exist', writes de Benoist, 'but a man by himself, the abstract man, the universal man, that type of man does not exist'.[24] For de Benoist, man acquires his full rights only within his own community and by adhering to his national and cultural memory. He writes:

> The real subject can exist only in the capacity of a subject that has been reconnected (*sujet réel* vs. *sujet relié*) — reconnected to particular heritages, to particular adherences. In other words, there cannot be a subject preceding its associations; no subject can exist to which some characteristics could be attributed outside all associations....
>
> The category of 'people' cannot be confounded with language, race, class, territory, or nation alone. A people is not a transitory sum of individuals. It is not a chance aggregate. It is a reunion of the inheritors of a specific fraction of human history, who, on the basis of their sense of a common identity, develop the will to pursue their own history and give themselves a common destiny.[25]

For the authors of the New Right, culture and history are the 'identity cards' of each people. Once the period of assimilation or integration begins to occur, a people will be threatened by extinction — extinction that, according to de Benoist, does not necessarily have to be carried out by physical force or by absorption into a stronger and larger national unit, but very often, as is the case today, by the voluntary or involuntary adoption of the Western Eurocentric or 'Americano-centric' liberal model. To counter this Westernisation of nations, the New Right and its chief spokesman, de Benoist, oppose all universalisms — 'this universalism which has its origins in the Biblical assertion of common

---

23 *Ibid.*, pp. 32-33.

24 Alain de Benoist, 'Pour une déclaration du droit des peuples', in *La cause des peuples*, p. 55.

25 *Ibid.*, pp. 55-56.

ancestry, and which, since the beginning of the Seventeenth century, has incessantly inspired profane egalitarianism.[26]

To the universalist model of modern egalitarian doctrines, the New Right opposes the *nominalist* concept of the world; a concept that posits that each reasoning proceeds from the particular to the general, and hence that national rights must also precede international human rights. De Benoist claims that the anti-egalitarian view is by definition a nominalist view.[27] Similar views are held by Armin Mohler in his piece 'Nominalistische Wende', in which he argues that in contrast to universalism, nominalism sets out from the assumption of human singularity, relativity, and the cultural diversity of peoples.[28] De Benoist reiterates this point with the following words:

> Diversity is something positive, because all genuine richness rests on it. The diversity of the world lies in the fact that each people and each culture possesses its own norms, whereby each culture sets upon itself its own sufficient structures, i.e., a framework whose internal order cannot be changed at will without changing all the other parts. Here starts also a fundamental criticism of totalitarianism, whose main historical sources we identify in monotheism.[29]

Similar remarks were made earlier by other conservative authors, notably Louis Rougier and Max Scheler, to whom the authors of the New Right often refer in framing their critique of liberalism and socialism. Thus, Scheler once remarked that love for humanity and 'the religion of human rights' are akin to a form of social *ressentiment* that usually emerge when society is in the throes of rapid disintegration, and plagued by hyper-individualism. Scheler wrote that 'the love of humanity emerged primarily as a protest against the *love of fatherland,* and consequently it became a protest against every organised community'.[30]

---

26 *Ibid.,* p. 58.

27 Alain de Benoist, 'Gleichheitslehre, Weltanschauung und Moral', in *Das unvergängliche Erbe,* pp. 77-105.

28 Armin Mohler, 'Die nominalistische Wende: ein Credo', in *Das unvergängliche Erbe,* pp. 55-74.

29 Alain de Benoist, 'Gleichheitslehre', *op. cit.,* p. 87.

30 Max Scheler, *Das Ressentiment im Aufbau der Moralen* (Leipzig: Verlag der weissen Bücher, 1915), p. 187. (Translated into English as *Ressentiment* [New York: Free Press of Glencoe, 1961].-Ed.)

When a people loses its consciousness, argued Scheler, its uprooted members readily resort to ill-defined and utopian ideals that are generally aimed at the moral 'improvement' of the entire world.

Scheler's words are paralleled by Rougier who sees in abstract human rights a denial of one's own roots. Rougier argues that the concept of human rights may often appear devoid of any meaning unless understood within the framework of man's community or nation. In his 'organic' conception of human rights, Rougier writes that each right presupposes three elements: an active subject of the right, an object of this same right, and finally a passive subject, that is, another individual to whom a holder of such rights can refer.[31] According to Rougier, man can fully enjoy his rights, and define his liberty, only when he lives in communion with a people sharing the same destiny and the same culture. Rougier writes:

> An isolated man has no rights. An individual derives his rights when he enters a relationship with other fellow creatures, that is, from the fact that he lives in society. By virtue of his nature, man has therefore no rights anterior to society, nor rights that would be imposed on society. His individual rights can emerge only as a result of a juridical status of the society in which he lives. He has therefore no rights except those which society grants him.[32]

For the New Right and its 'ideologue' Louis Rougier, the organic community is the only valid reference for someone's rights, whereby a person's rights can be enhanced, measured, or curtailed only by the degree of a community's generosity or the lack thereof. To the advocates of universal human rights, the authors of the New Right oppose a view that each person is first defined by his birth, heritage, a country of origin, and the value system inherited from his community. De Benoist wittily remarks, 'I see a horse but I do not see horsehood' (*Ich sehe ein Pferd, aber ich sehe keine Pferdheit*).[33] Similar views were once jokingly expressed by the conservative Joseph de Maistre in his sharp critique of liberal democracy in France. He wrote that during his travels he had seen 'Frenchmen, Italians, Russians, and so on; thanks to

---

31 Louis Rougier, *La Mystique démocratique*, p. 49.

32 *Ibid.*, p. 50.

33 Alain de Benoist, 'Gleichheitslehre', *op. cit.*, p. 78.

Montesquieu, I even know that one can be Persian; but I must say, as for man, I have never come across him anywhere.'[34]

Numerous indeed were the conservative authors who wrote critically about liberal democracy and equality before the Second World War, and on whose heritage the New Right draws significantly. In a manner similar to Carl Schmitt, the German conservative jurist, Fritz Buchholz wrote that every new amendment, bill, or legislation introduced into the legal system of liberal societies significantly invalidates the principle of equal rights, since each legal change further implies differentiation among citizens. Buchholz observed:

> Absolute equal rights are a purely theoretical hypothesis. Such equality could only be implemented in a legal system in which any formation of the constantly diverse and different reality of life no longer occurs; this equality could consist only of a unique legal clause (*Rechtssatz*), i.e., 'All people have same rights'. Each further restrictive clause would imply further differentiation. Such a legal system would be the end of law and community. Absolute equal rights means, therefore, the negation of the legal system itself.[35]

Furthermore, in the course of history, rights are subject to change, and they, as a result, must validate changes in a country's mores, customs, and the prevalent system of beliefs. 'The rights of peoples, in contrast', remarks Buchholz, 'are in their content determined by the natural qualities of a people and can be understood as the innate value system of a community.'[36]

For his part, Louis Rougier sees an additional obstacle in the universal implementation of human rights. He notes that even if supposedly, in the future, the principles of equal human rights were thoroughly and fairly implemented, they would only enhance the inequality towards those who never had a chance to enjoy them in the past, in short, those

---

34 Joseph de Maistre, *Considerations on France* (Cambridge: Cambridge University Press, 2003), p. 53. De Maistre further writes, 'The question is not whether the French people can *be free* with the constitution they have been given, but whether they can be *sovereign*.' *Ibid.*, p. 37.

35 Fritz Buchholz, *Gleichheit und Gleichberechtigung in Staats- und Völkerrecht* (Bleicherode am Harz: Verlag Carl Nieft, 1937), p. 41.

36 *Ibid.*, p. 28.

countless millions of people who had spent their lives in slavery, glaring injustice and inequality. Here is how sees it:

> Maybe the realisation of integral justice at the end of human evolution would be tantamount to the largest inequality, capable of forever disqualifying the cosmos morally. The privileges of the latecomers would cause the aggravation of glaring injustice to be inflicted upon those of their ancestors who were the artisans of their egotistical happiness.[37]

From the observations by Louis Rougier, Carl Schmitt, Fritz Buchholz, and some other conservative authors, the New Right reaches the conclusion that due to their deterministic nature, egalitarian doctrines are bound to always create new disappointments and as a result are compelled to adopt a rather hostile attitude towards history. The liberal and socialist notion of history, according to the New Right, defines history as 'the dark ages' — a notion that is today being supplanted with the secularised formula of 'man being a final and finished creature'.

De Benoist argues that man can only define his liberty and his individual rights as long as he is not divorced from his culture, environment, and temporal heritage. '[Man] does not live on Mars, he does not live on a lone island, or in the kingdom of the blessed, but *here and today,* and in a very specific society.'[38] For his part, Pierre Vial, an editor of the New Right's publications, observes that all egalitarian beliefs are proto-totalitarian, 'since each totalitarian system aims at destroying the identity of peoples, by first attacking as a priority their *culture*'.[39]

Undoubtedly, argues Vial, although both liberal and socialist societies deny any ties to totalitarianism, one way in which they stand in tacit agreement is in their belief that nations and peoples are vestiges of the past, and that they must be replaced with an internationalist and global order. Vial writes:

> Today, more than ever before, it is peoples that in their irreducible specificity constitute a major obstacle to the universalism of 'a system that kills peoples'. This system is founded on the ideology of hedonism and narcissist well-being — the common objective of liberalism

---

37 Louis Rougier, *op. cit.*, p. 111.

38 Alain de Benoist, 'Gleichheitslehre', *op. cit.*, p. 90.

39 Pierre Vial, 'Servir la cause des peuples?', in *La cause des peuples,* p. 69.

and socialism, which secularises the Christian dogma of personal salvation.[40]

Although liberal and socialist forms of totalitarianism may differ, and indeed may find themselves in violent conflict against each other, Vial asserts that they are both destructive to the cultural and historical identity of all peoples on Earth:

> Hard totalitarianism: this is the totalitarianism which the Tibetan people have to endure. Soft totalitarianism: the one that operates by virtue of imposing the Western-American cultural model diffused through the media across the entire world.[41]

Some conservative authors, to whose ideas the New Right often refers, observe that the concept of human rights can very often have very inhumane consequences, and that under a certain set of circumstances, the worst despotism can derive legitimacy from the principles of human rights. This is the thesis that we already encountered in our earlier descriptions of Carl Schmitt and that has recently been addressed again by the conservative scholar Jean-Jacques Wunenburger.

Wunenburger writes that the political rationality concerning the issue of human rights may lead to the subordination of cultural and national diversities to a unique right, i.e., to a triumph of subjective rights and ethnocentrism:

> In other words, the idea of nature functions gradually as a weapon against the organic conception of a social corpus, according to which each man is a member of a differentiated and hierarchical totality. The new political rationalism finds in atomism and mechanism the categories of thought that invalidate the holistic vision of society propitious to Classical and Medieval philosophy. Thus, a society, stripped of its specific nature, becomes an artifact whose function rests solely on the attributes of the individual.[42]

---

40 *Ibid.*, p. 71.

41 *Loc. cit.*

42 Jean-Jacques Wunenburger, 'Les droits de l'homme, du fondement philosophique à l'illusion idéologique', in *Contrepoint*, nos. 50-51 (1985), pp. 102-103.

The possible abuse of the principles of human rights, continues Wunenburger, becomes quite real when the social advancement of the individual in modern society is simultaneously accompanied by the further abstraction of the concept of universal human rights. It may very often happen, argues Wunenburger, that in the name of human rights some undesirable individuals, some categories of people, and sometimes entire nations, particularly in Communist countries, can be flatly described as 'elements hostile to peace'. In the name of universal principles, a certain category of people can thus be easily termed 'monsters' and consequently denied any legal help under the assumption that monsters cannot be humans. Human rights, thus, can become a powerful 'juridical weapon' against all those who may be perceived as unworthy of them. Similarly to Carl Schmitt, Wunenburger observes the danger of abusing the concept of human rights:

> This new and rational form of social exclusion implies the paradoxical idea of an exceptional right (law) for certain crimes separately characterised as 'crimes against humanity'. According to the right applied to the human species, the criminal *de facto* denies the humanity of his victim without, however, depriving himself of enjoying natural rights. [Only] the equal dignity conferred upon all people is removed from him. In contrast, some criminals are absconded from the logic and the justice of human rights, and will be subsequently deferred to an exceptional justice — in view of the fact that their crimes may have been perpetrated not against the humanity inherent in particular victims, but against humanity considered as a whole. Henceforth, the criminal is denied his own quality as a reasonable being; he becomes a pervert, a monster. Therefore, by making possible this particular category 'crimes against humanity', the reason of jurisprudence takes an enormous risk in becoming so insidiously tied together to a judiciary mechanism that is not very reasonable.[43]

Drawing on similar observations, de Benoist notes in his piece on terrorism that the worst enslavement and state terrorism can thus find their legitimacy in the abstract doctrine of human rights. For de Benoist, 'the idea that liberal societies derive their legitimacy from the free exercise of sovereign power automatically eliminates any right to

---

43 *Ibid.*, p. 106.

resistance and insurrection.[44] Although the New Right's theories concerning the concept of human rights appear sometimes contradictory, one must nonetheless agree that the New Right has at least understood to what extent the seemingly noble principle of human rights can be abused.

The most glaring example of such abuse can be observed in those countries in which some individuals are viewed by the prevalent jurisprudence as traitors, monsters, lunatics, and criminals — and are usually subject to exceptionally harsh treatment. Ironically, the same individuals may often be portrayed, under different circumstances and in some other countries, as 'heroes', 'freedom fighters', etc.

For the authors of the New Right, the so-called democratic states in both the East and the West enjoy immense privileges in defining their own version of human rights; they can launch preventive terrorist attacks against individuals and countries that are pronounced to be terrorists *a priori*. As de Benoist writes, 'State terrorism derives its legitimacy from the reasoning of the state, whereas the terrorist derives his legitimacy, in the majority of cases, by refusing to accept the reasoning of the state'.[45] To paraphrase Carl Schmitt from our earlier chapter, if some country derives its legitimacy from the principle of human rights and democracy, any attempt to challenge the country's democracy may be viewed as insanity or as a crime against democracy. The New Right observes that between Ezra Pound, the American poet who was put in a psychiatric asylum after the war by the American authorities, and the Russian dissident, Vladimir Bukowski, a psychiatric victim of the Soviet system, there is no difference. Modern systems can, in this way, justify state terror, deportations, and the imprisonment of dissidents in psychiatric hospitals in the name of higher goals, democracy, and human rights. Some of the practices of such distorted implementations of democracy and human rights will be analysed in greater detail in our last chapter, which deals with Communist totalitarianism.

---

44 Alain de Benoist, 'Terrorisme: le vrai problème', in *Éléments*, Winter 1986, p. 7.
45 *Ibid.*, p. 15.

III

HOMO ECONOMICUS:
THE BATTLE OF ALL AGAINST ALL

The indictments that the New Right levels against liberalism are manifold, yet the main ones are directed against the liberal concept of equality and the liberal attempt to render the entire political arena subservient to the realm of economic activities. The following chapter will therefore examine how the New Right and some other authors, such as Othmar Spann, Carl Schmitt, Louis Dumont, Murray Milner, and Antony Flew come to terms with the liberal belief in economic progress and equal economic opportunity and why, according to the New Right, liberalism is defenceless before Communist totalitarianism. In doing so we shall thus set the stage for our last chapter, which deals with the New Right's description of Communist totalitarianism.

For the authors whose ideas are discussed in this chapter, liberalism and socialism are essentially two different offshoots of the same belief in egalitarianism and economism. For the New Right, given that liberalism is unsuccessful in attaining economic equality, the viable and likely equality becomes 'equality in poverty'. This perfect equality in poverty the French philosopher Claude Polin calls Communism.

The authors of the New Right note that the liberal rejection of historical materialism, as well as the liberal, sentimental espousal of human rights and human dignity, does not quite match the prevalent unequal and egoistic rules characterising the liberal market. Guillaume Faye, a sociologist of the New Right, alleges that the more modern liberal societies subscribe to the idea of universal human rights and dignity, all the more, ironically, do they tend to legitimise their power structure through ruthless economic competition and the monitoring of the fiduciary activities of the entire body politic. 'More than in any other epoch', writes Guillaume Faye, 'money, the instrument of the social and economic relationship, the means of surveillance and rule, has become the ultimate criterion; indeed, *the language* of Western civilisation'.[1]

Louis Dumont, an author to whom the New Right owes a great deal in devising its own criticism of liberalism, sees in economism and egalitarianism a natural outgrowth of secularised Judaeo-Christian dogma, noting that 'just as a religion gave birth to politics, politics in turn will be shown to give birth to economics'.[2] Henceforth, in the liberal doctrine, writes Dumont in his book *From Mandeville to Marx*, man's pursuit of happiness comes to be associated with the pursuit of economic activities. Dumont writes:

> [T]he substitution of man as an individual for man as social being was possible because Christianity warranted the individual as a *moral* being. The transition was thus made possible from a holistic social order to a political system raised by consent as a superstructure on an ontologically given economic basis.[3]

Dumont's observations were anticipated earlier in the Twentieth century by Werner Sombart who, in his book *The Quintessence of Capitalism*, wrote that the two main pillars of liberalism are economics and ethics — because for a liberal politician economics is a perfect expression of morality. For an individual to engage in economic activities, notes Sombart, means also to secure for himself 'secular salvation'.[4] It can be inferred from Sombart's remarks that liberal societies are prone to adopt a rather hostile attitude to traditional forms of politics, and in fact, as Schmitt suggests, the prime objective of liberalism is to eliminate the notion of the political and replace it with the notion of economics. Schmitt writes:

---

1   Guillaume Faye, 'La fin du bas de laine', in *Éléments*, no. 50, Spring 1984, p. 30.

2   Louis Dumont, *From Mandeville to Marx: The Genesis and Triumph of Economic Ideology* (Chicago: The University of Chicago Press, 1977), p. 16.

3   *Ibid.*, p. 59.

4   Werner Sombart, *The Quintessence of Capitalism* (New York: Howard Fertig, 1967), especially 'Holy Economy', pp. 105-120.

Under no circumstances can anyone demand that any member of
an economically determined society, whose order in the economic
domain is based upon rational procedures, sacrifice his life in the
interest of rational operations.[5]

For Guillaume Faye, economic activities in liberalism stand in caus-
al relationship with the belief in legal equality. He writes that 'with
the beginning of the Seventeenth century the egalitarian ideology sets
forth the premises for a political science which no longer conceives of
a people as a specific historical reality.'[6] From now on, continues Faye,
all individuals in liberalism are interchangeable. 'What counts are the
mechanisms (the systems), institutions and laws, aimed at producing
the same effects everywhere.' For political and historical consciousness, liberalism substitutes practical consciousness, whose goal is to
instil in each individual the uniform and rational behaviour that consists of endless and repetitious economic transactions.[7] Ultimately, reminds de Benoist in his book *Die entscheidenden Jahre*, 'the merchant
[liberal] society is condemned to death, because nobody within it is
willing to die for it.'[8]

Many conservative authors, including those of the New Right,
observe that despite apparent ideological differences between Marxist
socialism and classical liberalism, liberalism often provides a similar
'Marxist' deterministic interpretation of history and politics. If there
is one thing in which liberals and Marxists seem to be effectively in
agreement, writes de Benoist, it is their common hostility to power
politics and history. Consequently, both assume that the realm of economics is the best cure for social and political problems. In an editorial
published in *Éléments*, it is observed:

Whatever their economic systems seem to be, socialist and liberal
societies converge on one essential point: they are *economic* systems.
Founded on a conception of the world that is exclusively economic,
these societies propose in the last analysis the same human ideal: the

---

5   Carl Schmitt, *The Concept of the Political,* p. 48.

6   Guillaume Faye, *Le système à tuer les peuples* (Paris: Copernic, 1981), p. 96.

7   *Loc. cit.*

8   Alain de Benoist, *Die entscheidenden Jahre* (Tübingen: Grabert Verlag, 1982), p.
    53, and the entire chapter 'Wider den Individualismus', pp. 51-55.

economics of the market and free exchange for the former; central planning and nationalisation for the latter.[9]

Following in the footsteps of Schmitt, Faye notes that politics in liberal systems is often viewed as an embarrassment, a *pis aller*, a nuisance — something that could create tensions at any time, cause a dangerous social polarisation, and eventually disrupt the peaceful course of liberal democracy. Guillaume Faye asserts that with liberalism in particular, the belief prevails that economic growth alone can solve all social and political contradictions. In his book *Contre l'économisme*, he writes:

> Given that economics has come to be viewed in Marxism and liberalism as the only means of achieving social justice, and understood by them as the equalisation of material conditions, the result has been the emergence of sentiments of injustice much stronger than before. Indeed, economics is by definition a place of domination. Trying to create out of it the means of emancipation is an absurdity that provokes social schizophrenia, already known to us.[10]

If by chance liberal countries happen to encounter some social and political difficulties, those difficulties will be blamed on 'too much' politics and the departure from the sacrosanct economic rules. Accordingly, all traces of politics must be subdued and replaced by apolitical economics. By the same token, the former notion of the state must be reduced to the *Minimalstaat*, or a *stato neutrale*, as Schmitt called it. Drawing on Schmitt's observations, de Benoist writes:

> The market represents a model construction that must demonstrate the least possible power, i.e., the minimum of the political. This is the real precondition of its efficiency. Mistakes or failures of the system are always explained by claiming that there is still too much [political] power.[11]

---

9 'L'économie organique', (unsigned), quoted in *Pour une renaissance culturelle*, edited by Pierre Vial (Paris: Copernic, 1979), pp. 54-55.

10 Guillaume Faye, *Contre l'économisme* (Paris: Le Labyrinthe, 1982), p. 10.

11 Alain de Benoist, *Die entscheidenden Jahre*, p. 34, and the entire chapter 'In der kaufmännisch- merkantilen Gesellschaft geht das Politische ein', pp. 32-38. For a strong criticism of the liberal model of world development, see de Benoist's book which received a favourable critique in France, *Europe, Tiers Monde, même*

In liberalism, continues de Benoist, individuals function solely as isolated economic units whose historical or national attachments are often regarded as mere vestiges of the past. The continuing adherence to historical or national consciousness, the love of one's tribe or clan, may appear suspicious and even harmful in a society in which all strong convictions threaten to render economic transactions precarious.

Some conservative critics of liberalism such as Othmar Spann, to whom the New Right frequently refers, wrote earlier in the Twentieth century that instead of slowing down the rise of socialism, liberalism in fact accelerates its proliferation. Spann critically observed that although the liberal economic game presupposes all people as equal, the unequal outcome of this game indicates that the economic contestants were unequal from the very beginning of the game. Conditions, goods, and commodities differ from one country to another and so do the talents of the people who are involved with the liberal market. Consequently, in the process of liberal economic development, as Spann argued, material inequality will appear to grow and grow as long as liberal economic activity is in the process of expansion. How can liberals still adhere to the concept of natural rights, inquired Spann, when liberal systems accept economic inequality as something given, and indeed as something conducive to economic growth? For the proponents of natural rights, argued Spann, to which liberals seemingly subscribe, under no circumstances can it be admitted that each individual enters the economic competition on a different footing. In fact, according to Spann, natural rights presuppose that *all* people must be equal regardless of what their material circumstances happen to be. Spann notes:

---

combat (Paris: Robert Laffont, 1986), especially the chapter, 'Le "développement" en question', pp. 99-132. De Benoist and other authors of the New Right, contrary to Western neo-conservatives, advocate economic and cultural 'coupling' with African and Middle Eastern countries. See Pierre Brader in *Éléments,* no. 62, Spring 1987, pp. 25-32. About the inadequacy of the liberal model of development for Third World countries, see Pierre Bérard, 'Louis Dumont: anthropologie et modernité', in *Nouvelle École,* no. 39, Autumn 1982, pp. 95-115. Interestingly, the thesis of the New Right on 'pluralistic' economic development is reminiscent of some new theories of development. Cf. Vrajenda Raj Mehta, *Beyond Marxism: Towards an Alternative Perspective* (New Delhi: Manohar Publishers, 1978). Vrajenda holds the view that liberal economic development is often on a collision course with the cultural and political diversity of non-Western countries.

Undoubtedly, the essence of capitalism is individualism, but not the kind of individualism whose origins are natural rights — i.e., the individualism which in fact excludes competition and the war of all against all (*bellum omnium contra omnes*), and which, additionally, in its original contract (*Urvertrag*), abolishes the right of the stronger to victory. The essence of capitalism is Machiavellian individualism that awards the stronger with victory and laurels. [12]

Continuing with Spann's arguments, the New Right remarks that it is understandable why liberalism from its incipience has always been under attack by both conservative and Leftist opponents. For socialists, liberalism has not gone far enough in implementing equality; for conservatives, liberalism has already gone too far in implementing it. Hardly had liberal economic freedom been proclaimed than conspirators of all sorts began to undermine it. For the authors of the New Right, liberalism contradicts itself by proclaiming social and political equality while seriously neglecting economic equality. It sets the stage for something that it now refuses to bring to its logical historical conclusion.

These arguments seem to be paralleled by an observation made by Spann, who wrote that 'the often-heard statement is in this sense correct, that liberalism and socialism are fruits from the same tree.'[13] One could add that socialism has probably had a more implacable logic.

Faced with the immense wealth that surrounds him, a deracinated and atomised individual is henceforth unable to rid himself of the fear of economic insecurity, irrespective of the degree of his guaranteed political and legal equality. Spann remarked that as long as economic activities were subordinated to the realm of politics, an average individual had at least some feeling of security, regardless of how miserable his economic position may have been. Now, in a society that has broken those organic and hierarchical ties and supplanted them with the anonymous market, man belongs nowhere. As Spann noted, 'mankind can reconcile itself to poverty because it will be and remain poor forever. But to the loss of estate (*Stand*), existential insecurity, uprootedness, and nothingness, the masses of affected people can never

---

12 Othmar Spann, *Der wahre Staat* (Leipzig: Verlag von Quelle und Meyer, 1921), p. 120.

13 *Loc. cit.*

reconcile themselves'.[14] The result is social anomie, apathy, and the galloping sense of uncertainty, which in times of great economic stress may give birth to all forms of totalitarian temptations.

The New Right concludes that the economic reductionism of liberalism leads to the exclusion of practically all other spheres of human activities and particularly those which lie in the realm of cultural and spiritual endeavours. 'To judge the value of a system on the basis of the efficiency of its economy', writes de Benoist, 'means in reality to set up economics as a model or a desirable pattern'.[15] Similar views are supported by other conservative authors who, although acknowledging the awesome dynamics of liberal economic growth, do not hesitate to call liberalism, such as Schumpeter does, a system of 'creative destruction'.[16] For Claude Polin, the author who will be discussed in the following chapter, 'the survival of the liberal economic system is solely made possible by a constant effort to run ahead of itself'.[17] These views are also shared by the conservative author Ernst Forsthoff, who wrote that the pattern of liberal development is beset by contradictions, because this pattern constantly creates new needs and new disappointments. Forsthoff remarked:

> Neither the invention of the automobile, nor the plane, nor the radio has satisfied human needs. Instead it has created new ones. Today, half of the labour force in the United States produces goods unknown at the turn of the last century.[18]

The issue that preoccupies the authors of the New Right is the possible extent and limits of liberal economics. What will happen if liberal societies must suddenly face a devastating financial disruption? What will happen if a sudden shrinkage of economic opportunities sets in,

---

14 *Ibid.*, p. 123.

15 Alain de Benoist, *Die entscheidenden Jahre*, p. 72, and the entire chapter, 'Der Ökonomismus führt zum Egalitarismus und Kommunismus', pp. 65-73.

16 Joseph A. Schumpeter, *Capitalism, Socialism and Democracy* (New York: Harper and Row, 1975), p. 165 and *passim* in the chapter 'Decomposition'.

17 Claude Polin, *Libéralisme, espoir ou péril?* (Paris: La Table ronde, 1984), p. 27 and *passim.*

18 Ernst Forsthoff, *Der Staat der Industriegesellschaft* (Munich: Beck Verlag, 1971), p. 35.

followed by the pressing popular demands for more egalitarian distribution of economic wealth?

Equal Economic Opportunity or the Opportunity to Be Unequal?

Many conservative authors have pointed out some serious flaws in the liberal concept of economic opportunity, the concept that posits that all people are equal at the outset of the economic game. We have already seen that, for Spann, economic competition cannot be conducted between two economic contestants in such a way that their stakes would be annulled and losses forgiven after each round of their economic transactions have been completed. The liberal concept of economic opportunity is devoid of meaning unless it specifies the conditions and circumstances in which this opportunity manifests itself. Thus, writes John Schaar in his piece 'Equality of Opportunity and Beyond', equality of opportunity is a rather misleading concept, which, if properly understood, should read: 'Equality of opportunity for all to develop those talents that are highly valued by a given people at a given time'.[19] In other words, if one follows Schaar's logic, should the whims of the market determine that some items, commodities, or human talents are more in demand or more marketable than some other commodities or talents, it will inevitably follow that some people will experience an acute sense of inequality and injustice. Schaar writes:

> This is inherent in any society, and it forms an insurmountable barrier to the full development of the principle of equal opportunity. Every society encourages some talents and contests, and discourages others. Under the equal opportunity doctrine, the only men who can fulfil themselves and develop their abilities to the fullest are those who are able and eager to do what society demands they do.[20]

Consequently, the unpredictable behaviour of the liberal market can significantly advantage some individuals while seriously disadvantaging

19 John H. Schaar, 'Equality of Opportunity and Beyond,' in *Equality*, p. 230. Compare with Robert Nisbet, 'The Pursuit of Equality', *Public Interest*, no. 35, Spring 1974, pp. 103-120. Also 'The Fatal Ambivalence', *Encounter*, December 1976, pp. 10-21.

20 Schaar, *ibid.*, p. 236.

others. Moreover, to make the problem worse, argues Schaar, the apolitical and neutral *Minimalstaat*, originally thought to be the best means to defuse ideological conflict and power politics, could, under specific circumstances, exacerbate the inequities caused by the liberal social contract with consequences that may be devastating for the entire society. Schaar summarises this prospect in the following words:

> The person who enters wholeheartedly into this contest comes to look upon himself as an object or commodity whose value is set, not by his own internal standards of worth but by the valuation others placed on the position he occupies. Thus, when the dogma of equal opportunity is effectively internalised by the individual members of a society, the result is humanly disastrous for the winners as well for the losers. The winners easily come to think of themselves as being superior to common humanity, while the losers are almost forced to think of themselves as something less than human.[21]

For many conservative critics, the endless competition in the liberal market is a frightening prospect for the future of liberalism. The unpredictable nature of economic growth, with its unstable market, may induce the majority of people, as Lorenz earlier indicated, to consider *economic security* and *economic equality* preferable to the notion of liberty and free economic competition. These views are exemplified by Murray Milner in his book *The Illusion of Equality,* with these words:

> Status insecurity is a necessary part of a society which has both significant inequality and equality of opportunity. Such insecurity usually produces anxiety. Hence we see how equality of opportunity produces the combination of anxiety about one's own status but a de-emphasis on the status consciousness towards others. Stressing equality of opportunity necessarily makes the status structure fluid and the position of individual within it ambiguous and insecure.[22]

The race for riches, with its uncertain results, generates undesirable political consequences, especially when equality of opportunity, as Antony Flew suggests, turns into an open competition for scarce resources, and when different people start employing those resources

21 *Ibid.*, p. 235.
22 Murray Milner, *The Illusion of Equality* (Washington and London: Jossey-Bass, 1972), p. 10.

differently. Similar to Milner, in his book *The Politics of Procrustes*, Flew notes:

> Equal chances in this sense not merely are not necessarily, they necessarily cannot be, equiprobabilities of success. A 'competition' in which the success of all contestants is equally probable is a game of chance or a lottery, not a genuine competition.[23]

To which Milner adds:

> Such a race is necessarily tiring. Extended indefinitely, it could lead to exhaustion and collapse.[24]

Jean Baechler comes to identical conclusions in his piece 'De quelques contradictions du libéralisme'. Success, just as failure, observes Baechler, is always cumulative, for the simple reason that a previous success, be it in the form of someone's heritage or a 'marketable talent', presents a considerable asset for his future economic competition. It is a truism, says Baechler, that a person who has started with more money certainly has more chances of succeeding than the one who has no money. He observes:

> The facts speak for themselves in the matters of economics where the march towards monopoly in a given sector is inexorable as long as counter-forces are not active. By the same token, when a diplomatic and strategic space is divided among many sovereign units, the imperial unification in the long run is inevitable. Within the interior of one unit the rich have more chances to become richer than the poor, just as the powerful have to reinforce their power. In the competition for power the rich are advantaged just as the powerful are advantaged in the pursuit of their affluence.[25]

On the basis of the foregoing observations, the New Right tries to resolve the following problems: what are the limits of liberal economic growth, and can liberty be threatened by the rising demand for equality? Can the belief in egalitarianism and economism eventually be

23 Antony Flew, *The Politics of Procrustes* (New York: Prometheus Books, 1981), p. 111.

24 Milner, *op. cit.*, p. 11.

25 Jean Baechler, 'De quelques contradictions du libéralisme', *Contrepoint*, no. 21, May 1976, p. 45.

forestalled in order to prevent the rise of totalitarian democracy? And can a society which is increasingly using economics as a paradigm for human happiness be called a truly pluralistic society?

None of these abovementioned authors share the belief that unbridled egalitarianism and economism can be compatible with liberty. As Baechler says, 'Whoever promises the instauration of liberty *and* equality is a liar, a fool, or an ignorant person.'[26] In fact, all our authors seem to be in agreement that even if liberalism becomes successful in arresting egalitarian dynamics and economic inequality, it will solely return to the same position of *status quo ante bellum* — i.e., the return to the starting point, knowing, however, that sooner or later it will be plagued by the same problems. For Claude Polin the liberal *Minimalstaat*, or as he calls it *l'état providence*, is one stage towards the real 'tyranny, that of all against all, and which has the name of Communism.'[27]

It is to this peculiar 'terror of all against all at all moments' that we now turn in order to understand the New Right's description of totalitarianism.

---

26 *Ibid.*, p. 49.

27 Claude Polin, 'Le libéralisme et l'état providence ou le double dépit amoureux', *Contrepoint*, no. 50-51, 1985, p. 69.

IV

TOTALITARIANISM AND EGALITARIANISM

'The spirit of totalitarianism is the absence of all spirit.'
—Claude Polin, *L'esprit totalitaire*

The notion of totalitarianism is unusually vague. In modern political discourse the word *totalitarianism* is more often used to discredit or insult a political opponent than to actually denote someone's political orientation. Undoubtedly, it is much easier to describe the *effects* of totalitarianism than the *causes* of totalitarianism. The majority of political scientists and sociologists more or less agree that totalitarianism is a serious social pathology, yet few of them are in perfect agreement as to what causes its proliferation. For a variety of reasons it is impossible to arrive at a comprehensible definition of totalitarianism because the countries that demonstrate totalitarian characteristics often boast their love of freedom, or their attachments to democratic principles. Moreover, one may also argue that the definition of totalitarianism significantly hinges on the social scientist himself. It is not difficult to predict that a socialist scholar will assess somewhat differently the notion of totalitarianism than will his conservative or liberal colleague.

Having this in mind, this chapter has a manifold and probably somewhat ambitious purpose. In the first several pages I shall briefly review several theories of totalitarianism that were developed by such renowned scholars as Raymond Aron, Hannah Arendt, and Jacob L. Talmon. After that, I shall proceed with the New Right's own analysis of totalitarianism. In the conclusion of the chapter, I shall describe some practical manifestations of totalitarianism which, according to the social critic Alexander Zinoviev and the authors of the New Right, are best observable in Communist *and* in liberal societies.

Needless to say it would be impossible to review or analyse all the different theories of totalitarianism. Therefore, I shall limit myself to a cursory description of totalitarianism by selecting those authors who, to some extent, may be tied into the overall argument of this book and whose theories have gained considerable credibility in the academic community.

Before we proceed, it is very important to stress that the authors of the New Right, while not entirely rejecting the liberal analyses of totalitarianism, considerably revise them. By drawing on the works of Claude Polin and Alexander Zinoviev, we shall try to observe to what extent the New Right shares some of the former theories regarding totalitarianism, and to what extent it rejects them as outmoded and empirically unverifiable. Furthermore, in order to illustrate the intricacies of the 'totalitarian temptation' we shall occasionally refer to Michel Maffesoli, Alain Besançon, and Louis Dumont, whose observations have also been embodied in the New Right's own theory of this very passionate and disturbing social phenomenon that has yet to be fully understood.

The Problem

Totalitarianism, according to many authors, is not just a simple form of despotism. If it were, then one could argue that the origins of totalitarianism can be traced to medieval societies, or that totalitarianism still thrives in many contemporary authoritarian countries. Some political scientists, like Zbigniew Brzezinski and Carl J. Friedrich, have noted that in seeking to trace the roots of totalitarianism, social scientists have argued almost every possible link. Thus they write in their book, *Totalitarian Dictatorship and Autocracy,* that 'Marx and Hegel, Nietzsche and Hobbes, Kant and Rousseau, Plato and Aristotle, St. Augustine, Luther, and Calvin — all have been charged with having forged the ideas that became weapons in the arsenal of the totalitarians'.[1] In spite of the fact that there are different theories of totalitarianism,

---

1   Carl J. Friedrich and Zbigniew Brzezinski, *Totalitarian Dictatorship and Autocracy* (New York: Praeger Publishers, 1962), p. 80.

most authors seem to be in agreement that: (a) totalitarianism usually emerges in industrial countries, or in those countries that are in a rapid process of development; (b) totalitarianism usually relies on a doctrine or ideology that tolerates no dissent; (c) totalitarianism aims at encompassing the entire citizenry, the means of communication, radio, television, etc., and subjecting them to the total and absolute control of the state and one single party; and, (d) in order to implement control and ensure social compliance, totalitarianism resorts to terror and police surveillance.[2]

A path-breaking inquiry into the phenomenon of totalitarianism was initiated by Hannah Arendt, the author who wrote a concise, well-documented, and comprehensive treatise on totalitarianism in the early 1950s. It is unquestionable that Arendt's theories still command respect both among liberal and conservative scholars, including those of the New Right.

Arendt contends that totalitarian movements started to proliferate as a reaction to the disintegration of the traditional social structures in most European countries in the aftermath of the First World War. The worst effect of this social disintegration triggered feelings of *uprootedness and superfluousness* among the masses, 'who for one reason or another have acquired the appetite for political organisation'.[3] In an effort to elucidate the psychology of the newly deracinated masses, Arendt argues that the new political climate became ripe for the gradual rise of the rule of 'mobocracy', within which subsequent totalitarian movements began to thrive.[4] She writes:

> The truth is that the masses grew out of the fragments of a highly atomised society whose competitive structure and concomitant loneliness of the individual had been held in check only through membership in a class.[5]

When these class ties and social structures burst apart, the uprooted masses, in search of social and psychological security, became amenable to ideologies or secular religions that provided a 'scientific' and

2   *Ibid.*, pp. 9-10.

3   Hannah Arendt, *The Origins of Totalitarianism* (New York: Meridian Books, 1958), p. 311.

4   *Ibid.*, pp. 305-316.

5   *Ibid.*, p. 317.

all-embracing explanation of all universal and existential problems. Arendt remarks that 'the totalitarian movements, each in its own way, have done their utmost to get rid of the party programs that specified concrete content and that they inherited from earlier non-totalitarian stages of development'.[6] The masses usually flock to totalitarian leaders and movements, continues Arendt, because of their irrepressible need for promises of political stability and social cohesion, which unpredictable party politics is not always able to secure.

Of particular concern for Arendt is the ominous marriage between the masses and the intellectual elite. Citing the names of Ernst Jünger, Louis-Ferdinand Céline, Vilfredo Pareto, Georges Sorel, and many other prominent anti-democratic thinkers and writers, Arendt argues that without the 'temporary alliance of the clerks' with the mob, the totalitarian movements would have never had such a brilliant success.[7] In the 'treason of the clerks', Arendt incidentally sees the biggest crime of the intellectuals and a voluntary escape from freedom. Henceforth, in the name of new ideas that contained either pseudo-scientific Darwinism, Gobineau's and Lapouge's racialism, or scientific Marxism, the mob could identify itself with the elite and carry out its totalitarian delirium to its historical apotheosis. Thus, Hitler could justify Auschwitz in the name of the purportedly scientifically verifiable racial and intellectual superiority of the Aryans, in the same manner as the Bolsheviks justified their purges and camps in the name of scientific Marxism. For Arendt, all ideologies claim to be scientific and those individuals who have doubts about their veracity risk being rejected as the pariahs of the human race. 'Ideologies always assume', writes Arendt, 'that one idea is sufficient to explain everything in the development from the premise, and that therefore no experience can teach anything because everything is comprehended in this process of consistent logical deduction.'[8] In short, for Arendt, all ideologies contain traces of totalitarianism, although they become fully operational only within the context of the consolidation of mob rule. Ideology is to totalitarianism, argues Arendt, what water is to fish; if there is no ideology, totalitarian movements cannot thrive.

---

6   Ibid., p. 324.

7   Ibid., pp. 327-340.

8   Ibid., p. 470.

However, notes Arendt, in the long run, totalitarian ideology is bound to lead to total entropy — it first starts off devouring one category of people, and finally ends up devouring itself. Arendt argues that even if the Nazis had survived the war and remained in power, they would have extended their 'final solution' to other social categories, which would have finally resulted in their own self-destruction.[9]

In a visibly pessimistic tone, Arendt comes to the conclusion that an acute sense of social alienation, loneliness, and isolation is the first harbinger of the totalitarian phenomenon — a phenomenon unlikely to disappear from modern societies.[10]

It must be pointed out that Arendt's observations concerning mob rule were, earlier in this century, elaborated just as persuasively by Gustave Le Bon, José Ortega y Gasset, and to some extent Louis Rougier — in short those authors whom the New Right claims as its spiritual forefathers. As we proceed, we shall try to explain where the New Right agrees with Arendt's theories and where it thinks they appear deficient.

Another author who developed a distinct theory of totalitarianism is Jacob L. Talmon, who chronicles the roots of totalitarianism much earlier in history. Similar to Pareto and Gérard Walter, Talmon traces modern totalitarianisms to millennial utopias, religious and chiliastic beliefs, and their secular descendants that sprang up at the beginning of the Eighteenth century. In his book, *The Origins of Totalitarian Democracy*, Talmon writes that:

> Totalitarian democracy, far from being a phenomenon of recent growth, and outside the Western tradition, has its roots in the common stock of Eighteenth-century ideas. It branched out as a separate and identifiable trend in the course of the French Revolution and has had an unbroken continuity ever since.[11]

Totalitarianism, and particularly Communist totalitarianism, is the unfortunate backlash of the democratic theme that emerged in the era of the Enlightenment. Talmon observes that modern secular religions which spur totalitarianism became visible in Mably's and

9   *Ibid.*, pp. 392-419.

10 *Ibid.*, p. 478.

11 Jacob L. Talmon *The Origins of Totalitarian Democracy* (New York: Frederick A. Praeger Publishers, 1960), p. 249.

Condorcet's teachings, and especially Rousseau's theory of the General Will.[12] Talmon actually discerns the first totalitarian occurrences in the French Revolution and the Reign of Terror, notably when the Jacobins, such as Saint-Just and Babeuf, showed a similar 'totalitarian and messianic temperament', inherited from Rousseau.[13] For Talmon, Rousseau's sovereign is the externalised General Will that stands for the natural and harmonious order. He writes that 'in marrying this concept with the principle of popular sovereignty, and popular self-expression, Rousseau gave rise to totalitarian democracy'.[14] As Talmon further notes, 'This conception of sovereignty of the people was inspired not so much by the desire to give all men a voice and a share in government as by the belief that popular sovereignty would lead to complete social, political and economic equality'.[15]

Subsequently, one of those democratic themes which sprang up in the Eighteenth century developed into classical liberalism, whereas the other one merged into democratic or Communist totalitarianism. As Talmon notes, 'The Jacobin and Marxist conception of the Utopia in which history was destined to end were remarkably similar'.[16] Both were conceived as being perfectly in harmony with the interests of the people, although in order to enforce this harmony both had to resort to violence. For Talmon, totalitarian democracy in Communism becomes totalitarian against its own will. In the Soviet Union it developed not because it rejected the principles of the Enlightenment and human happiness — but precisely because it adopted too much of a perfectionist and 'impatient' attitude towards those principles:

> Totalitarian democracy early evolved into a pattern of coercion and centralisation not because it rejected the values of Eighteenth century liberal individualism, but because it had originally a too perfectionist attitude towards them. It made man the absolute point of reference.[17]

---

12 *Ibid.*, p. 8 and *passim*.

13 *Ibid.*, p. 39.

14 *Ibid.*, p. 43.

15 *Ibid.*, pp. 250-251.

16 *Ibid.*, p. 252.

17 *Ibid.*, p. 249.

It must be emphasised that Talmon's theory of totalitarianism has been utilised by many conservatives authors in depicting the political reality of Communist systems, although, as we shall shortly see, the New Right probes further beyond Rousseau's General Will and the French Revolution in order to uncover the roots of totalitarianism.

Before examining the New Right's own theory of totalitarianism, it is worth mentioning the name of Raymond Aron, a classical liberal author whose theories of totalitarianism are still used in analysing the crisis of modern society. For Aron, as for Carl J. Friedrich, totalitarianism is primarily the result of the bloated *political arena* (*le politique*), and the imposition of an ideological straitjacket by the police or the party in power. More than any other author, Aron sees in the overvaluation of the political, and the binding character of ideology, the main origins of totalitarianism. In other words, *strong* political beliefs and ideological fanaticism, spurred by one party rule, always bear the germs of totalitarianism:

> It can be seen that in the definition of totalitarianism either the monopoly of the party or the state control of economic life or the ideological terror can be considered essential. The phenomenon is complete when all these elements are united and fully achieved.[18]

Similar to Talmon and Arendt, Aron makes a distinction between Nazi totalitarianism and Communist totalitarianism. For him, the first was intrinsically perverse since it was already embodied in its own ideology. By contrast, the latter became totalitarian by following, as Talmon also indicated, its own extreme perfectionist and utopian line. In the last analysis, totalitarianism for Aron is 'voluntary' in Nazism, but 'involuntary' in Communism. Aron observes that '[Soviet totalitarianism] in order to create an angel, creates a beast; for that of the Nazi undertaking: man should not try to resemble a beast of prey, because when he does so, he is only too successful'.[19]

Before we turn to the New Right's theory of totalitarianism, it is important to note that the preceding paragraphs are just a fraction of what has been written on the subject of totalitarianism. Moreover,

---

18 Raymond Aron, *Democracy and Totalitarianism* (New York: Frederick A. Praeger Publishers, 1969), p. 194.

19 *Ibid.*, p. 204.

none of the authors described lays the blame, as the New Right does, on Judaeo-Christianity as the main vehicle of totalitarianism.

A conservative author worth mentioning in our discussion of totalitarianism is Karl Popper, whose theories of totalitarianism are viewed favourably by the New Right. In contrast to the preceding authors, Popper discerns the traces of totalitarianism in Plato's utopian idealism. In his renowned book, *The Spell of Plato* (the first volume of his *The Open Society and Its Enemies*), Popper writes that 'Plato's political programme, far from being morally superior to totalitarianism, is fundamentally identical with it.'[20]

Popper's remarks about Plato, whom he considers to be an enemy of freedom and a herald of the total state, are very similar to Pareto's and Sorel's earlier critique of Plato's state, in which they both saw an embodiment of a utopian and chiliastic political ideal.[21] According to Popper, Plato was opposed to any social change within his rigidly hierarchical entity that was designed to last forever. The social stratification within Plato's state was an ethical as well as categorical imperative for the citizens that were to live in it. Popper writes:

> I wish to make it clear that I believe in the sincerity of Plato's totalitarianism. His demand for the unchallenged domination of one class over the rest was uncompromising, but his ideal was not the maximum exploitation of the working classes by the upper class; it was the stability of the whole.[22]

One cannot help noticing that Popper's book was first published shortly after the war and that his description of Plato's state is strangely reminiscent of the *real* organisational and political structure of Nazi Germany. Undoubtedly, most of the authors discussed here personally experienced the trauma of Nazism, and therefore it must not come as a surprise that their theories are much more critical of Nazi totalitarianism than of Communist totalitarianism.

Nonetheless, the merit of Popper, Arendt, Talmon, and other authors seems to be the awareness that there are different forms of

---

20 Karl Popper, *The Open Society and Its Enemies*, vol. 1: *The Spell of Plato* (London: Routledge and Kegan Paul, 1952), p. 87.

21 Cf. Georges Sorel, *Le procès de Socrate: examen critique des thèses socratiques* (Paris: Alcan, 1889).

22 Popper, *ibid.*, p. 108.

totalitarianisms, and that hasty assumptions regarding Francoism, Perónism, Italian Fascism, or Salazarism, as forms of totalitarianism, are not always correct.

The New Right on Totalitarianism

While not completely rejecting these theories of totalitarianism, the authors of the New Right significantly amend them by adding their own interpretations as well as those by some other conservative authors. Michael Walker, an English author of the New Right, writes that the liberal interpretation of totalitarianism must be treated with great caution. Although he agrees with the statement that fascist and Communist totalitarianism are 'extreme' and intolerant, it should not follow that liberalism must always remain immune to its own home-grown totalitarianism. Moreover, remarks Walker, liberal theorists have an historical advantage in giving 'objective' definitions of totalitarianism, given the fact that liberal countries were instrumental in defeating Nazism. In addition, their other ideological opponent (but also an ally during the war), the Soviet Union, shares an equally critical and hostile view in regard to Nazi totalitarianism as the victorious liberal countries themselves. Walker writes:

> The total defeat of National Socialism left liberalism as the only coherent political ideology in the world opposed to Marxism. Traditionally liberalism has always been hostile to established religions... For many liberal commentators 'totalitarian' and 'religious' mean much the same in the political context... The most despised religion for the liberal is always National Socialism and not Communism, because whereas Communism, in principle at least, claims to work for the emancipation of the individual, the National Socialist admits to no time in the future when the individual can ever become emancipated from the doctrines of racial imperatives. From these facts it comes that a liberal defends Communist 'intentions' but condemns the 'methods', whilst National Socialism and Fascism (seen as its ultra-conservative collaborator) are condemned out of court.[23]

---

23 Michael Walker, 'Against All Totalitarianisms', *The Scorpion*, no. 10, Autumn 1986, p. 4.

For Michael Walker and the authors of the New Right, totalitarianism cannot be solely judged by the methods it employs, such as police terror, camps, or gas chambers, because these methods do not explain the more profound reasons that gave birth to totalitarian aberrations. Far more important is whether a given system aims at embracing the totality of man's existence and the totality of truth, which, according to Walker, is a trait common not only to Nazism or Communism, but to modern liberalism as well. Walker continues:

> There exists in other words a *totalitarian liberalism*. If this expression appears to be an oxymoron, it goes to show how far we have been trained to dissociate liberalism from any whiff of totalitarianism. Our criteria for judging what is totalitarian (extreme ideas, concentration camps, secret police, the cult of masculinity, the veneration of the state) are, as though by chance, the criteria that nicely exclude all probable liberal methods of exercising power.[24]

In other words, Walker, like other theorists of the New Right, suggests, as observed in the preceding chapter, that liberalism becomes totalitarian at the moment when it subordinates every aspect of human life to one sphere of social activity, that is, *economics*. In their recent book *La soft-idéologie*, François-Bernard Huyghe and Pierre Barbès reiterate this point by arguing that as much as liberalism can pride itself on abandoning muscled politics or ideological fanaticism, it has nonetheless imposed its own 'religion' of the commodity fetishism and the 'soft ideology' of consumerism, spiced up with horrendous economic Darwinism.[25] The fact that liberal totalitarianism does not necessarily have to resort to violence in order to implement its ambitions has already been observed in previous chapters and does not need further elaboration. In liberal totalitarianism, as the New Right observes, social compliance is ensured through soft conditioning, voluntary apoliticism, and omnipresent 'hidden persuaders', as earlier predicted by Orwell and Aldous Huxley.

For our further discussion of totalitarianism, Claude Polin, a French conservative philosopher, is of great importance. Polin objects that liberals tend to search for the origins of totalitarianism in the traditional

---

24 *Ibid.*, p. 5.

25 François-Bernard Huyghe and Pierre Barbès, *La soft-idéologie* (Paris: Robert Laffont, 1987).

holistic and organic European societies, where popular beliefs, attachment to myths and national customs remain much stronger than in liberal Anglo-Saxon countries.[26] Polin's view was elaborated and upheld in greater detail by the French scholar Louis Dumont, who writes, in his piece 'The Totalitarian Disease', that the tradition of collectivism and holism in continental European societies is not necessarily conducive to totalitarianism; in fact 'organicism' and holism are the very opposite of totalitarianism.[27] For Dumont, totalitarianism basically occurs when these holistic structures are broken, and when unbridled egalitarianism and individualism, developed earlier within liberalism, can no longer be contained. He writes:

> I previously wrote that totalitarianism is a disease of modern society that 'results from *the attempt, in a society where individualism is deeply rooted and predominant, to subordinate it to the primacy of the society as a whole*' (Dumont 1977:12). I added that the violence of the movement is rooted in this contradiction and that it 'abides in the very promoters of the movement, torn apart as they are by conflicting forces'.[28]

Although Polin's and Dumont's observations regarding the *effects* of totalitarianism do not radically depart from Arendt's observations, these theories, nonetheless, lay the blame for the rise of totalitarianism on the unrestrained economism and disruptive individualism that are the prime factors in causing feelings of superfluousness and loneliness. As for the origins of individualistic and the economic elements of modern societies, Dumont traces them, like Sombart, Spann, and Rougier, to Judaeo-Christianity and its offshoot, Protestantism.[29] This explanation of totalitarianism is also adopted by the authors of the New Right.

Following Dumont, de Benoist attempts to uncover the roots of totalitarianism not in the exacerbation of the political, or traditional Machiavellian power politics, or for that matter in ideological ferocity. Instead, he sees the earliest origins of totalitarianism in the Bible

---

26 Claude Polin, 'La totalité totalitaire et la totalité organique', *Le totalitarisme* (Paris: PUF, 1982), pp. 11-12.

27 Louis Dumont, 'The Totalitarian Disease' in *Essays on Individualism* (Chicago: The University of Chicago Press, 1986), p. 158.

28 *Loc. cit.*

29 Louis Dumont, *From Mandeville to Marx: The Genesis and Triumph of Economic Ideology* (Chicago: The University of Chicago Press, 1986).

and the Judaic religious legacy. As we already observed in the previous chapters, for de Benoist the precondition for a non-totalitarian world is the return to religious polytheism and the abandonment of Judaeo-Christian eschatology. For him, Biblical monotheism is by definition a religion of totality, which excludes all opposing 'truths' and all different value judgments. It follows, according to de Benoist, that all countries that are attached to the Biblical message show a latent proto-totalitarian bent. He writes:

> Each egalitarian and universalist ideology is *necessarily* totalitarian, because it aims at *reducing* all social and spiritual reality to a single model. Thus, monotheism implies the idea that there is only one truth, one God, one type of man who could please God. The Bible places on the scene only one God (*Deut.* 6.4) who is also a 'jealous God' (*Deut.* 6.15). Jesus says: 'Those who are not with me are against me.' Henceforth, to be against God means to be for Evil. And against Evil everything is permitted: genocide, torture, Inquisition.
>
> It is only with Judaeo-Christianity that totalitarianism appears in history, at the moment when Yahweh makes the massacre of infidels his primary task (*Deut.* 13.9.); when he declares to his people: 'You are going to destroy all peoples which the Lord, your God, will deliver to you.' (*Deut.* 7.16).[30]

From the foregoing observations, as well as from our previous chapters, we could conclude that for the New Right, the secular results of Judaeo-Christianity were egalitarianism, economism and individualism, which in turn *merged* into 'soft' liberal totalitarianism, *continued* into Communist totalitarianism, and triggered a *defence* against them in the rise of Nazi totalitarianism. The theory of Nazi totalitarianism as a 'defence' against its Communist enemy was also elaborated by the German revisionist historian Ernst Nolte.[31]

---

30 Alain de Benoist, 'L'Eglise, L'Europe, le Sacré', in *Pour une renaissance culturelle*, p. 204.

31 Ernst Nolte in the interview, 'Hitler war auch ein europäisches Phänomen', *Die Welt*, 21 September 1987. Also a survey favourable to Nolte's theory on totalitarianism, Anne-Marie Roviello, 'Relativiser pour minimiser?' in *Esprit*, October 1987, pp. 56-69. On p. 58, Roviello cites Nolte's rhetorical question: 'Has not the Gulag archipelago preceded Auschwitz? Were not the class murders of the Bolsheviks the logical and factual antecedents to racial murders of the Nazis?'

Based on the theories of Claude Polin and Alexander Zinoviev, the authors of the New Right contend that totalitarianism takes shape in both Communist and liberal countries. Their major arguments are as follows:

Totalitarianism is an inevitable outcome of contemporary social and political atomisation, followed by the individualisation and rationalisation of economic production, which in turn breeds alienation and reciprocal social resentment.

Totalitarianism is not the despotism of a few but a despotism of all against all at every moment (*terreur totale de tous sur tous à tous les instants*). This form of tyranny developed in Communist countries, although it is already incipient in liberalism.

Totalitarian systems are not constructed from the top of society but from the *bottom* of society. It is a terror of a myriad of Communist *kolektivi*, or democratic 'checks and balances', whereby everybody controls everybody.

A totalitarian system is not the apogee of the omnipotent state but rather the beginning of a huge impersonal society. Finally, a totalitarian system is fully operational only when it replaces physical violence with an 'aseptic', bloodless and 'cool' totalitarian ideology, such as consumerism, the cult of money, and the end of the political — goals actively sought in both liberal and socialist democracies.

As de Benoist argues, 'hard' totalitarianism exists in the East, 'soft' totalitarianism thrives in the liberal West.[32] Since we have already observed the 'soft liberal totalitarianism', we shall now focus on the modes of its transition into Communist totalitarianism.

From Liberalism to Communist Totalitarianism

In order to elucidate how the New Right observes the transition from liberalism into Communist totalitarianism, we must again focus on Claude Polin and his two major works, *L'esprit totalitaire* and *Le totalitarisme*. Although Polin cannot be haphazardly put into the category of the New Right, and despite the fact that he declares himself a 'classical liberal' in the manner of Alexis de Tocqueville, together with

---

32 Alain de Benoist, 'L'ennemi principal', *op. cit.*

the Russian author Alexander Zinoviev, Polin is one of the frequent sources of reference for the authors of the New Right.

Polin singles out *economism, egalitarianism,* and *universalism* as the three major components of totalitarianism. As we already noted, these elements are held by Spann, Sombart, and to some extent Schumpeter as decisive elements for the possible disintegration of liberalism.

Polin argues that the liberal 'good conscience' *vis-à-vis* socialist opponents increasingly necessitates that political power and economic benefits be conferred to more and more people ('welfare state', *l'état providence*). In a system that is based predominantly on economic exchange and the incessant search for pleasure, the notion of liberty is gradually bound to give way to unrestrained egoism and feelings of narcissism, inasmuch as each individual in liberal society gradually comes to believe that '[his] liberty is no longer the conquest of himself, but the conquest of the world'.[33] The modern man in liberalism, argues Polin, becomes a victim of his 'desire to desire, desire of desire', constantly in search of more material acquisitions, and increasingly blaming others if he is unable to attain them.[34] As we already observed, economic appetites and hyper-individualism may eventually prompt the masses of uprooted people to feel more and more alienated from their original social contract and eventually induce them to view liberty primarily as something associated with economic and monetary success. For Polin, the modern liberal society resembles a latter-day Sisyphus who, instead of the worthless stone, has imposed on himself the task of carrying the burden of the golden rock to the pinnacle of society in an effort to create the semblance of perfect justice and equal opportunity for everybody. Since this 'equality in affluence' is ultimately inaccessible, the only true avenue that becomes accessible is a society of 'equality in poverty' in which everybody will have an *equal* share in power and where nobody will have more power than his fellow citizen. Such a form of totalitarianism is made possible by the very fact that in democracy, not one party or ideology controls the masses, but everybody controls everybody. Polin notes:

> This logic causes this [liberal] power, which I first wanted to be limited, to become involved in all details of my life — all the more freely

---

33 Claude Polin, *Le libéralisme: espoir ou péril?* (Paris: La Table ronde, 1984), p. 211.
34 *Ibid.*, p. 213.

as I intended it to be sovereign. This logic requires that in order to be protected against people in whom I have no confidence, that I wish this sovereign power to be total. This is no longer a tyranny of a people's representative, or that of a majority that the popular sovereignty has introduced, but the tyranny of all against all at all moments.[35]

Polin further contends that the signs of totalitarian systems are best noticeable if a system assumes some universalist credo. The search for an *ideal man,* or as he puts it *l'homme générique,* may explain why a totalitarian system must constantly 'keep going' and spread out a universal vision of the world across the entire globe. Polin discerns in the quest for this inaccessible *paradigmatic* ideal man (a 'perfect proletarian' or *bon sauvage*) the trait of a society that is itself never able to become perfect. He notes:

> The perfect man can never be one's neighbour, he must necessarily be a remote, vague and abstract being. There is no known example of such a man and nobody knows whether a single act on earth has been accomplished by virtue alone. The perfect man finds his ideal representation in the asymptotic idea of humanity, generally viewed as arriving in the future.[36]

Universal human rights and general philanthropy, continues Polin, are principles which are henceforth upheld as categorical imperatives. Should one question those principles, one can be viewed as an outsider of humanity and therefore put outside humanity (cf. Schmitt). Polin notes that modern man's ideal of 'tenderness for humanity is also his ability to destroy humanity.... When one fights for humanity, one fights against enemies of humanity'.[37]

Polin, like Dumont, asserts that in rationalised and atomised societies in which individualism reigns supreme, the abstract conceptualisation of universal humanity is much more predominant than in close-knit societies where social moralising stops at the confines of

---

35   *Ibid.,* pp. 308-309.

36   Claude Polin, *L'esprit totalitaire* (Paris: Éditions Sirey, 1977), p. 131. Polin is a professor at the University of Sorbonne, and a former student of Raymond Aron. His theses echo those of the New Right, such as in his contention that materialism, individualism and economism breed egoism, which in turn results in 'total war of all against all'.

37   Polin, *op. cit.,* p. 132.

one's own nation or a tribe. Polin lays the blame for the disintegration of old holistic structures on a modern economic rationalisation of labour in contemporary society, whose anonymous citizens think it is much easier to relate to the ideal of a distant and inaccessible 'perfect' man. He continues:

> Undifferentiated man is *par excellence* a quantitative man; a man who accidentally differs from his neighbours by the quantity of economic goods in his possession; a man subject to statistics; a man who spontaneously reacts in accordance with statistics.[38]

Therefore, a 'proto'-totalitarian society will never be at peace with itself as long as it does not impose its vision everywhere — and this is precisely the first sign of the totalitarian temptation. The idea of the American 'global democracy' automatically comes to mind. In elucidating this point, Polin makes a significant distinction between Nazi and Communist totalitarianism, noting that 'totalitarianisms are internationalist by essence and nationalist by accident'.[39] As we already noted, this is the thesis that the New Right, along with some conservative historians, overwhelmingly supports.

Another salient trait of totalitarianism that Claude Polin and the authors of the New Right enumerate is its apparent love of modernity and hatred of history. The sense of history is generally viewed as a symbol of the 'dark ages' that hinder the implementation of future revolutionary achievements. This point was also substantiated by the neo-conservative Alain Besançon, a former student of Raymond Aron, whose views on Communist totalitarianism frequently parallel those of the New Right. In his book, *La falsification du Bien*, which deals with the description of Soviet 'pseudo-reality', Besançon writes:

> A man without memory is of absolute plasticity. He is recreated at all moments. He cannot look behind himself, nor can he feel a continuity within himself, nor can he preserve his own identity.[40]

Similar views are held by Michel Maffesoli, an author who contends that totalitarian systems, before they become fully operational, are

---

38 Polin, *op. cit.*, p. 111.

39 Polin, *op. cit.*, p. 113

40 Alain Besançon, *La falsification du Bien* (Paris: Commentaire/Julliard, 1985), p. 183.

bound to enter into a mode of overestimating the linear becoming of the past; time is no longer experienced in its mobility or as an evocation of memory for ancient myths or the continuity of human existence. In his book, *La violence totalitaire*, Maffesoli writes:

> We enter now the reign of finality propitious to political eschatology, which is the outcome of Christianity and its profane forms, liberalism and Marxism.[41]

When totalitarianism emerges, writes Maffesoli, it can be understood either as a Communist logical conclusion of a liberal odyssey, or, as Nolte argued, a violent and panic-stricken (Nazi) reaction to it. In other words, totalitarianism manifests itself either in a form of rabid nationalism or as a merging into Communist egalitarianism. On both counts, liberalism will be attacked: on the one hand for not running its full egalitarian course, on the other, for destroying traditional social ties and provoking social anomie that now needs a strong integrating force. Maffesoli writes:

> Totalitarianism, in our opinion, is the logical reaction to the process of atomisation, to the loss of organic solidarity; it is a panic-stricken response of an economic organisation to an individualism, deemed indispensable at the beginning — but which also carries with it the elements of anarchy and disintegration that can no longer be controlled.[42]

For the authors discussed above, the Industrial Revolution and the introduction of technology were instrumental in speeding up the rise of totalitarianism. Considered now to be an apolitical field of endeavour (cf. Schmitt), technology in totalitarianism becomes a subject of almost religious veneration, held as the best means of resolving all social contradictions. Maffesoli elucidates this point when he writes that 'all irrational or non-logical aspects within attitudes, thoughts and behaviours must be removed as primitive and unworthy of an evolved society.'[43] In practice this means that industrialisation and technology become the pivots of totalitarian structures.

---

41 Michel Maffesoli, *La violence totalitaire* (Paris: PUF, 1979), pp. 228-229.

42 *Ibid.*, p. 231.

43 *Ibid.*, p. 260.

These quotations are reminiscent of de Benoist's and Spann's earlier observations, since both thinkers argued that liberalism makes Communism acceptable by distilling an ideology of *technomorphic* conditioning, which in the long run renders people oblivious to liberty, and, beyond that, makes them ready to accept Communist totalitarianism on the grounds of their irresistible craving for equality and security.[44]

In conclusion we can observe that despite some differences among the authors that have been discussed, none of them asserts that contemporary liberalism needs to be replaced violently, i.e., by a popular socialist revolution or by a possible invasion from some Communist country. They all agree, however, that the technomorphic ideology underlying both Communist and liberal systems increasingly narrows the gap between their apparently different economic visions of the future leading, so to speak, to ideological *osmosis*. The managers of both camps, writes Maffesoli, are primarily preoccupied with the optimum utilisation of technology aimed at more rationalised economic productivity. 'The sole difference', writes Maffesoli, 'which remains between the East and the West is the colour of the star which adorns their national flag'.[45] This statement is strangely reminiscent of Martin Heidegger's earlier views:

> From a metaphysical point of view, Russia and America are the same; the same dreary technological frenzy, the same unrestricted organisation of the average man.[46]

As an irony of history, as Maffesoli further remarks, 'The individual who once served as a justification for destroying the community is now, in his turn, himself negated in a constricting system with which he cannot come to terms any longer'.[47] The egalitarian notion of individualism, accompanied by faith in technological progress which now takes on the characteristics of a new religion, creates in turn a great deal of volatility in human relationships and brings about appetites that are never able to be satisfied. Based on the ideas that are alleged to

---

44 Alain de Benoist, 'L'ennemi prinicipal', *Éléments*, April-May 1982, *op. cit.*

45 Maffesoli, *op. cit.*, p. 267.

46 Martin Heidegger, *Introduction to Metaphysics* (Delhi: Motilal Banarsidass, 1999), p. 37.

47 Maffesoli, *op. cit.*, p. 285.

be the best and the last in the history of mankind, a new system cannot tolerate opposing views any longer.

The perfection of totalitarianism, or, rather, the absolute form of democracy, seems to be completed in Communist countries. Unlike Nazism, writes Alexander Zinoviev, Communism is indeed a popular system, a system of absolute social consensus, imposed not from above, but spawned from the egalitarian and popular demands from the majority of the people. For Zinoviev, the paradoxical nature of contemporary Communism lies in the fact that *nobody believes in the Communist credo,* including the party potentates themselves, yet everybody behaves as if Communism is the ultimate truth. Thus, the system is provided with hitherto unseen social and political stability. Given that Zinoviev's theories of 'non-belief' in Communism, as well as his description of Communist 'pseudo-reality', have gained a considerable popularity among European conservatives, and particularly the authors of the New Right, it is now necessary to examine them in more detail.

V

HOMO SOVIETICUS: COMMUNISM AS EGALITARIAN ENTROPY

'Communism is not a temporary historical zig-zag. It is an epoch.'
—Alexander Zinoviev, *The Reality of Communism*[1]

The author Alexander Zinoviev, whose analyses are reminiscent of Pareto and de Benoist, writes that it is impossible to study Communism without the rigorous employment of an appropriate methodology, training in logic, and the construction of an entirely new conceptual approach.[2] He asserts that Western experts on Commu-

---

1   Alexander Zinoviev, *The Reality of Communism* (London: Victor Gollancz, 1984), p. 259.

2   Alexander Zinoviev is not related to Grigory Zinoviev (real name Ovshi Aronovich), head of the Third International, and a victim of Stalin's purge in 1936. Alexander Zinoviev is an ethnic Russian, a former member of the Soviet Academy of Sciences, and until his expulsion from the Soviet Union in 1976, a world-known authority on logic. It is worth noting here a book by Alexander Yanov, *The Russian New Right* (Berkeley: University of California, 1978), in which the author speaks about the revival of Russian Christian Orthodoxy and pan-Slavism among both Russian Communists (*sic*) and Russian émigrés. The European New Right, which commented on this book, points out that Soviet dissidents cannot be viewed as a homogeneous bloc; there is a considerable rift between Soviet dissidents of Russian and Ukrainian origins, and those of Jewish origin. Yanov attacks the Russian New Right for its alleged anti-Semitism. In contrast, Russian nationalist dissidents complained of being underrepresented in some Western-sponsored news agencies and institutions, such as Radio Free Europe and The Voice of America. See the Appendix, pp. 165-185. In his novels and sociological treatises, Zinoviev warned about the Western perception of Soviet dissidents as being unanimous concerning the possible alternatives to Soviet Communism. See for example his

nism are seriously mistaken in using social analyses and a conceptual framework appropriate for studying social phenomena in the West, but inappropriate for the analysis of Communist systems in the East. He writes:

> A camel cannot exist if one superimposes upon it the criteria of a hippopotamus. The opinion of those in the West who consider the Soviet society to be unstable, and who hope for its imminent disintegration from within (although they mistake their desires for realities), is in part due to the fact that they superimpose upon the phenomenon of Soviet society the criteria of Western societies, which are alien to Soviet society.[3]

Zinoviev's main thesis is that an average man living in a Communist system — whom he calls *Homo sovieticus* — behaves and responds to social stimuli in the same manner as his Western counterpart responds to the stimuli of his own social landscape. Communist systems are objective and positive systems in which the immense majority of citizens behave, live, and act in accordance with the logic of *social entropy*. Social entropy, however, is by no means a sign of the system's terminal illness. Quite the contrary; it is a sign that the system may have regressed to a social level that permits its citizenry to more effectively cope with such elemental threats as wars, economic chaos, famines, and cataclysms. In short, Communism is a system in which social devolution has enabled the masses to develop defensive mechanisms of political self-protection and indefinite biological survival. Using an example from biology that recalls Darwin's and Lorenz's theories, Zinoviev notes that less-developed species show signs of better biological and social adaptability to their habitat than those with intricate economic and social demands. He writes:

> A social system whose organisation is dominated by entropic principles possesses a high level of stability. Communist society is indeed such a type of association of millions of people in a common whole in

piece, 'Nous ne sommes pas tous des dissidents', in *Le Figaro*, 15 July 1985. Also a piece by François Maistre, 'Le panslavisme a la vie dure', in *Éléments*, Spring 1986, pp. 30-38.

3   Alexander Sinowjew, *Die Diktatur der Logik* (Munich and Zurich: Piper, 1985), p. 148. The phoneme 'z' corresponds to the German 's'. Both 'Sinowjew' and 'Zinoviev' will be used interchangeably.

which the more active and influential citizens strive for a more secure survival within their own social structure, for a more comfortable course of life, and for a favourable position for success.[4]

Communism, according to Zinoviev, means not only adherence to the Communist party or the governing elite; Communism means first and foremost a peculiar *mental attitude,* a social behaviour, whose historical realisation has been made possible by primordial egalitarian *impulses* congenial to all human beings. Throughout history, those impulses have been held in check by cultural endeavours and civilisational constraints. With the advent of mass democracy, the resistance to these impulses has become much more difficult. Here is how Zinoviev sees Communism:

> Civilisation is effort; communality is taking the line of least resistance. Communism is the unruly conduct of nature's elemental forces; civilisation sets them rational bounds....
>
> It is for this reason that it is the greatest mistake to think that Communism deceives the masses or uses force on them. As the flower and crowning glory of communality, Communism represents a type of society which is nearest and dearest to the masses no matter how dreadful the potential consequences for them might be.[5]

Zinoviev, who is often quoted by de Benoist, Besançon, and Polin, rejects the widespread belief that Communist power is vested among party officials and army officers or the *nomenklatura.*[6] He asserts that Communist power is truly egalitarian because this power is shared by millions of public servants, workers, and ordinary people scattered in their basic *working units* that operate as pillars of the society. Also crucial to the stability of Communist systems is the fact that the Party and the people are closely blended into one whole so that, as Zinoviev observes, the Soviet saying '"the Party and the people are one and the

---

4   *Ibid.,* p. 145.

5   Alexander Zinoviev, *The Reality of Communism,* p. 28.

6   The *nomenklatura* was a small group of Communist Party-appointed administrators who held key leadership positions in various departments of the Soviet Union and in Soviet-occupied Eastern Europe. Some critics of Communism, such as Leon Trotsky and Milovan Djilas, referred to its existence as the sign of the rise of a new aristocracy.-Ed.

same" is not just a propagandistic password".[7] The cleavage between the people and the Party, as liberal theorists assume, does not exist, because the Party rank and file are blended with the people itself. To therefore speculate about a hypothetical line of division between the Party and the people, writes Zinoviev in his usual sarcastic manner, amounts to comparing 'how a disembowelled and carved-out animal, destined for gastronomic purposes, differs from its original and biological whole'.[8]

It is a truism, continues Zinoviev, that in Communist countries, the incomes of workers are three to four times lower than in capitalist democracies. However, if one considers that, on the average, a worker in a Communist state puts three to four times less time into his work (for which he usually never gets reprimanded, let alone loses his job), it appears that his earnings often exceed those of a worker in a capitalist democracy. In order to explain the fascinating stability of Communist systems, Zinoviev writes:

> Let us assume that we have measured the magnitude of remuneration and the magnitude of the efforts expended to receive that remuneration. The quotient from the division of the first magnitude by the second gives the degree of remuneration, while the converse is the degree of exploitation. According to my observations and measurements (greatly simplified and approximate) the degree of remuneration of the most active and productive segments of the population in Communist society has a tendency to grow, while the degree of its exploitation diminishes. Moreover, the degree of remuneration is here higher than for corresponding people in Western countries; and the degree of exploitation is lower. This is the basic advantage that Communism has over Western society and the reason for its attraction for millions of people on this planet.[9]

Zinoviev dismisses the liberal reductionist perception of economic growth, based on the premises that the validity or efficiency of a country is best revealed by high economic output or the workers' standard of living. He observes that 'the economy in the Soviet Union continues to thrive, regardless of the smart analyses and prognoses of Western

---

7   Alexander Sinowjew, *Die Macht des Unglaubens: Anmerkungen zur Sowjet-Ideologie* (Munich and Zurich: Piper, 1986), p. 24.

8   *Ibid.*, p. 25.

9   Alexander Zinoviev, *The Reality of Communism*, pp. 103-104, and *passim*.

experts, and is in fact in the process of becoming stronger.[10] To speculate, therefore, whether capitalist economics is more efficient than Communist economics is pure nonsense, because such speculation does not take into account the long-term benefits that the Communist economy may yield in the future:

> In addition it is not yet known, when one observes a society in its entirety, where the social efficiency of labour is superior; in the West or in the Soviet Union. It is not to be excluded that in this aspect the Soviet Union has come ahead. The results will be only known in several centuries.[11]

Zinoviev points out that in addition to a guaranteed wage, a Communist worker enjoys full economic security and social predictability, which liberal societies are not able to afford if they wish to remain competitive. And as to the eternal idea of liberty, it also remains debatable whether the majority of people prefer liberty to security. He asserts that no matter how impoverished Communist systems may appear, or may become, they will always guarantee a modicum of security even for the most destitute citizen. For Zinoviev, *security* and *stability*, the traits which Polin and de Benoist also consider crucial elements of totalitarianism, are the two main factors that account for Communist appeal, even among those who may ordinarily define themselves as 'anti-Communists'. In short, Zinoviev observes that, despite universal disenchantment with Marxism, the legacy of the Gulag, Stalin's purges, and recurrent repression, Communism, as the most successful form of egalitarianism, has lost nothing of its universal popularity. Communism will continue to flourish precisely because it successfully projects the universal demand for security and predictability, which liberalism has only theoretically introduced, but never implemented. For Claude Polin, the very economic inefficiency of communism paradoxically 'provides much more chances for success to a much larger number of individuals than a system founded on competition and the rewarding of talents'.[12] Communism is basically a system that completely exonerates each individual from all social effort and social responsibility,

---

10 Sinowjew, *Die Diktatur der Logik*, p. 64.

11 *Ibid.*, p. 65.

12 Claude Polin, *Le totalitarisme* (Paris: PUF, 1982), p. 89.

and its stagnation only reinforces what de Benoist calls 'facile laziness' among citizens.[13]

For Zinoviev, Communist democracy essentially operates according to the laws of dispersed *communalism* and the total decentralisation of power into a myriad of workers' collectives. Collectives, as the first and foremost linchpins of Communism, carry out legal, coercive, but also remunerative measures on behalf of and against their members. In such a system it is virtually impossible to contemplate a successful coup or a riot because Communist power, according to Zinoviev, is not located in one centre but in a multitude of networks and cells which exist at every level of society. Should somebody be successful in destroying one centre of power, automatically new centres of power will emerge. The notion of 'democratic centralism', considered by many liberal observers as just another verbal gimmick of the Communist meta-language, is also a genuine reflection of an egalitarian democracy in which power derives from the people and not from the Party. Zinoviev notes:

> Even if you wipe out half of the population, the first thing that will be restored in the remaining half will be the system of power and administration. There, power is not organised to serve the population: the population is organised as material required for the functioning of power.[14]

The syndrome of Communist pathology has been further explored by Besançon, who argues that the functioning of Communism will be difficult to understand as long as efforts are not made to decipher the significance of the Communist *meta-language*. Thus, in his book *The Soviet Syndrome*, Besançon writes that 'having been based upon pseudo-reality, the regime as a result escapes history. Consequently it cannot be corrupted, for corruption is down to earth. The regime resides within the sphere of the unchanging'.[15] Moreover, the Communist linguistic manipulation of public discourse can lend itself as a perfect weapon against all those political opponents who hope to

---

13 Alain de Benoist, 'L'énigme soviétique dans le miroir de l'Occident', *Nouvelle École*, no. 38, Summer 1982, pp. 109-129.

14 Alexander Zinoviev, *Homo Sovieticus* (London: Victor Gollancz, 1985), p. 80.

15 Alain Besançon, *The Soviet Syndrome*, Foreword by Raymond Aron (New York: Harcourt Brace Jovanovich, 1976), p. 35.

change the system from within. According to the official ideological denomination, dissidents do not fall within the categories of 'martyrs' or 'freedom fighters' — terms usually assigned to them by Western well-wishers, yet terms which are meaningless in official Communist vocabulary. Not only for the party elite, but for the overwhelming majority of people, dissidents are primarily the enemies of democracy. At any rate, as Polin, Zinoviev, and de Benoist argue, the number of dissidents is constantly dwindling, while the number of their detractors is growing to astounding proportions. Thus, in a tone similar to Zinoviev, Sophie Ormières writes:

> [T]here are no oppressors and oppressed in the Soviet Union as in a classical dictatorship. Everybody is both a victim and a henchman from top down to the bottom of the social ladder. There is no mass of people oppressed by individuals; there are individuals oppressed by the masses.[16]

For the masses of Communist citizens, long accustomed to a system avoiding all social tensions, the very word 'dissident' creates a feeling of insecurity and unpredictability. Consequently, argues Marc Ferro in his piece, 'Y a-t-il "trop de démocratie" en URSS?', before dissidents turn into targets of official ostracism and legal prosecution, everybody, including their family members, will go to great lengths to disavow them. Finally, given the omnipotent and controlling character of the collectives, their dissident activity is impossible to hide forever. It is only when things get out of hand, i.e., when the collectives are no longer capable of bringing somebody to 'his senses', that the police step in. Hence this phenomenon of *self-surveillance*, which is the main feature of Communist stability. Marc Ferro, similar to Besançon, writes that the capacity of each citizen in Communism to self-censor himself has been brought to its ultimate paroxysm: 'The regime has moved from polymorphous power to institutional polymorphism'.[17]

Besançon, for his part, points to linguistic inflation and the political codification of ordinary language. He writes that 'from Vietnam to Weimar, from Havana to Yemen, one finds the same leader, the

---

16 Sophie Ormières, 'Dissidence et dictature de masse en Union Soviétique', *Esprit*, October 1986, p. 45.

17 Marc Ferro, 'Y a-t-il "trop de démocratie" en URSS?', *Annales ESC*, July-August 1985, p. 820.

same language, the same newspapers, the same forms of social behaviour. The mimesis reaches all the way to the international Communist movement.[18]

For Besançon, *heteroglossia*, or variations within a single linguistic code, is a mortal enemy of Communism, because its use directly challenges the uniformity of Communist meta-language, as well as the uniformity of Communist ideology. He writes:

> In the Communist world the malediction of Babel has been removed because the multiplicity of languages has been surpassed by the uniformity of style, whereby individual throats renounce the impulse to utter all sounds except those which will soon be known as 'wooden language'.[19]

In conclusion, one could argue that the complexity of the Communist enigma appears even bigger when one reviews the complexity of the work being done by existing experts on Communism and in particular on totalitarianism. De Benoist writes that the proliferation of countless 'experts' on the Soviet Union indicates that their true expertise is not the analysis of the Soviet Union, but rather in how to refute each other's expertise on the Soviet Union. The unanimous contention of Zinoviev, de Benoist, and Polin is that the lasting vulnerability of liberal systems *vis-à-vis* Communism lies in their own unresolved attitude towards the notion of egalitarianism and economism. Should liberalism be truly interested in containing Communism, it must firstly re-examine its own ideological premises. For de Benoist, criticising Communism is useless unless one examines the causes of its proliferation. What causes Communism? Why does Communism appear along with rapid urbanisation and industrialisation? Why cannot the purportedly democratic liberalism come to terms with its ideological opponents? In short, argues de Benoist, one must critically examine the dynamics of all *egalitarian* and *economic* beliefs and doctrines before one starts criticising the Gulags and psychiatric hospitals.[20]

---

18 Alain Besançon, *The Soviet Syndrome*, pp. 66-67.

19 Alain Besançon, *Les origines intellectuelles du léninisme* (Paris: Calmann-Lévy, 1977), p. 292. (Translated as *The Intellectual Origins of Leninism* [Oxford: Basil Blackwell, 1981] -Ed.)

20 Alain de Benoist, 'L'énigme soviétique', *op. cit.* Compare with Mikhail Heller and Aleksandr Nekrich, *Utopia in Power* (New York: Summit Books, 1986).

For his part, Zinoviev adamantly refuses the notion that the Communist Soviet Union is an empire in decline, beset by ethnic conflicts, or on the verge of economic collapse. The decline in Soviet prestige is accompanied by an increase in *real* Soviet influence. As he writes in his book *Homo Sovieticus*, 'prestige decreases in one sector, influence increases in another'.[21]

In his usual paradoxical way, Zinoviev rejects the notion that Communism is threatened by economic mismanagement, popular dissatisfaction, or an inability to compete with liberalism. Quite the contrary: Communism is at its best when it faces economic difficulties, famines or long queues. It is a system designed for the simple life and economic frugality. Affluence in Communism only creates rising economic expectations and the danger of political upheavals.[22]

For contemporary readers, Zinoviev's theses may often appear far-fetched. In an age of *glasnost* and the unravelling of Communist institutions all over Eastern Europe, one is tempted to believe that Communism is reversible. But if one reverses this assumption, *glasnost* may also be seen as a turning point for Communism, that is, as a sign of the system's consolidation that now allows all sorts of experiments with liberal gadgetry. In his book *Katastroika*, Zinoviev writes:

> The basic masses, beginning with the rank and file and ending with the official class at every level, will do everything they possibly can to limit the Gorbachevite reforms...
>   These masses have more chances to succeed than the reformers...
> A mature Communist society is by preference conservative.[23]

One could conclude that it is no accident that the spread of Communist totalitarianism goes hand in hand with urbanisation, industrialisation, and rising individualism. The ensuing alienation and anomie in liberal systems must ultimately be 'transcended' by shallow sentimental appeals to 'telescopic philanthropy' and the 'brotherhood of humanity'. In turn, this logic of false universalism requires that all people are eventually moulded into a single and uniform whole where everybody can control everybody else in a perfect system of *perfect*

21 Alexander Zinoviev, *Homo Sovieticus*, p. 129.

22 Alexander Sinowjew, *Die Macht des Unglaubens*, pp. 126-133.

23 Alexander Zinoviev, *Katastroika: Legend and Reality of Gorbachevism* (London: Claridge Press, 1990), p. 68.

checks and balances. For the New Right, whether such a new system will bear the tag of 'Communism' or 'liberalism' is of little importance. In many instances we can observe that 'soft totalitarianism' in the West is much more dangerous than totalitarianism in the East.

For Konrad Lorenz, the liberal 'religion' of consumerism and the destruction of organic society has caused what he calls 'genetic decay' (*genetischer Verfall*) and 'social entropy'—briefly, those phenomena that Zinoviev outlines as prime causes of Communist proliferation. For Lorenz and Arnold Gehlen, the liberal 'effortless' society, despite its material advantages, appears to be in a process of devolution, insofar as it impedes man's biological and cultural evolution. Worse yet, it is a society whose obsession with permanent peace and economic growth makes it vulnerable to tomorrow's conquerors. Thus, much earlier than Zinoviev, Lorenz wrote:

> The effects of luxury, produced by the vicious circle of supply-and-demand escalation, will sooner or later be the ruin of the Western world, particularly the United States. Eventually Western peoples will no longer be able to cope with the less pampered and more healthy people of the East.[24]

In conclusion, we can state that these pessimistic views are largely shared by the authors of the New Right. To them it appears that there is no escape, either from liberalism or from Communism, except by returning to an organic society. How this will be possible, and with what means this can be achieved, will probably depend more on the real course of events in liberal and former Communist societies and less on the theories adopted and elaborated by the New Right.

---

24 Konrad Lorenz, *Civilized Man's Eight Deadly Sins* (London: Methuen, 1974), p. 30.

CONCLUSION

In this book we have outlined some major characteristics of the European New Right: its genesis, its contemporary influence, and the debate that it has initiated among the Left-wing and Right-wing intelligentsia in Europe. Great similarities have been observed between the authors of the New Right and some earlier thinkers such as Nietzsche, Spengler, and Schmitt. Our conclusion is that the New Right has been able to restore some credibility to the conservative intellectual heritage and also significantly damage the Leftist cultural hegemony in Europe.

On the other hand it is undeniable that the New Right's own ideological positions will continue to be a subject of controversy and could possibly create a further rift in the European conservative scene. Its theories and ideas about paganism will likely continue to antagonise many sympathetic conservatives who are firmly persuaded that Christianity provides the best bulwark against Communism and against the growing anomie of liberal societies. As we have observed, despite the remarkable erudition of its authors and sympathisers, the New Right's public claim that the Judaeo-Christian legacy is directly responsible for the rise of modern totalitarianism is not likely to generate broader conservative support, and will continue to irritate intellectuals on both side of the ideological spectrum. Incidentally, the New Right still has to demonstrate how it will counter the criticism that a departure from Christianity, and a possible return to paganism, may also have unpalatable political consequences, as shown by recent European history. After all, if one accepts the thesis that monotheistic religions have traditionally been repressive throughout history, one must admit that paganism has also been repressive at times. One need only read certain works of the Classical Age in order to become convinced of the magnitude of pagan violence in Antiquity. Thus far, the New Right has not examined the scope of religious and political intolerance in ancient Greece in greater detail, nor the murderous wars and persecutions of the Roman Empire, as well as the social and political implications of 'paganism' in Nazi Germany.

Furthermore, there are reasons to agree with those authors who argue that the success of Christianity is primarily due to the Christian idea of piety and compassion, which paganism, with its intense striving towards self-overcoming and elitism, has never implemented to the same extent. Louis Rougier, despite his anti-Christian sentiments, concedes that the Christian proclamation of neighbourly love and universal brotherhood has instilled in the minds of the deprived and the dispossessed worldwide a certain sense of self-confidence and dignity, unparalleled by any other religion.

Although one could agree with the New Right that Christian and Marxist 'anthropologies' have inaugurated the practice of religious and social exclusion, one cannot help thinking that paganism presupposes the idea of exclusion as well. Have not the Nietzschean glorification of the 'pagan' will to power, Pareto's political relativism, and Schmitt's political realism, in short the ideas advocated by the New Right, often been interpreted as a justification for social and racial exclusion? The examples of these recent exclusions are still fresh in the European collective memory and need not be repeated here. According to the evidence, it is not far-fetched to argue that the reason why Christianity and Marxism are still attractive lies in the capacity of these two chiliastic beliefs to provide *principles of hope,* as well as a promise of secular or spiritual salvation. That this hope has often turned into a demonstrable nightmare, as the New Right correctly argues, does not change anything in its historical attractiveness. In contrast, with its complicated demands on human perfectibility, its tragic sense of life, and its constant exigency toward boundless Prometheanism, paganism, at least as Alain de Benoist sees it, is not likely to generate a massive following among the modern masses in search of spiritual hope or simply a better life. This may be one of the reasons why both Christianity and Marxism still continue to exert considerable influence in spite of their serious historical failures.

Despite some of its shortcomings, one must admit that the European New Right has made a groundbreaking effort in probing the roots of the modern crisis. By reviving the teachings of many conservative authors, by bringing into its own body of thought various critical ideas concerning liberalism and Communism, we are probably in a better position today to assess the problems that have been plaguing our tumultuous centuries. Thanks to Zinoviev, Polin, and Rougier, our still meagre understanding of totalitarianism can today be significantly improved. Polin, for instance, has brought to our attention the fact that liberal societies leave much to be desired, and every critical conservative observer cannot help asking: what kind of democracy does the liberal system claim to be, in view of the fact that the number of voters in liberal countries is rapidly dwindling? Is the loss of interest in politics a harbinger of social apathy, a retreat from reason, or an escape from freedom, which may herald the most horrendous form of totalitarianism yet? Undoubtedly, these and similar questions still remain unanswered, and they will certainly preoccupy the minds of political scientists in the years to come. The merit of the New Right has been to open a debate from a different sociological perspective and to warn us that totalitarianism need not necessarily appear under the sign of the swastika or the hammer and sickle. The New Right also warns us that the total departure from the political, the subordination of all aspects of life to the cult of money, and the 'soft ideology' of consumerism may lead to the worst possible totalitarianism to date. Regardless of how sympathetic one may feel toward liberalism or Communism, contemporary liberal and Communist societies are far from the ideal that they often strive to achieve, and the merit of the New Right is to draw our attention to their flaws.

Undoubtedly, some of the ideas examined in this book will always remain reminiscent of fascism to many contemporary liberal and socialist thinkers, and will have little support in the larger academic community, at least in the foreseeable future. Moreover, before the theories of the New Right can really catch on at the grassroots level, it remains to be seen how the handful of New Right authors and other conservatives will weather the ideological controversy that has surrounded their names and their ideas.

APPENDIXES

APPENDIX I:
MAJOR FIGURES OF THE
EUROPEAN NEW RIGHT

Some of the contemporary conservative authors cited or quoted in this book do not fall 'officially' under the category of the European New Right. Indeed, several of them are sceptical about the ideas expounded by some of the more outspoken members of the New Right.

Described below are the names and occupations of only those authors of the European New Right who have operated under the distinct name of the GRECE, Thule-Seminar, and Neue Kultur.

Alain de Benoist (b. 1943) is the chief intellectual figure and philosopher of the European New Right, and was one of the founders of GRECE in 1968. He is the editor of the journals *Nouvelle École* and *Krisis,* and is a contributor to *Éléments*. De Benoist has published many books dealing with philosophy, religion, politics, anthropology, and literature. His most important works include: *Vu de droite* (*View from the Right*), in 1977 (which received the Grand Prix de l'Essai from the Académie française); *On Being a Pagan* in 1979 (published in English in 2004); *The Problem of Democracy* in 1985 (published in English in 2011); and *Au-delà des droits de l'homme* (*Beyond Human Rights*) in 2004. His works have been translated into German, Dutch, Italian, Spanish, and English.

Guillaume Faye (b. 1949) is by profession a sociologist and political scientist. For many years he was one of the prominent members of

GRECE, but left in 1986 due to his growing dissatisfaction with the positions and strategy of the New Right. After working in French television and radio for a decade, he returned to the subject of politics in the late 1990s when he began to write essays and books independently of GRECE. His most famous recent works include *Archeofuturism* in 1998 (published in English in 2010) and *Pourquoi nous combattons* (*Why We Fight*) in 2001.

Julien Freund (1921-1993) was a student of Raymond Aron and Carl Schmitt. During the Second World War, he was a member of the French *Résistance* movement. He was imprisoned by the Vichy authorities during the Second World War. After the war he became a full-time professor of sociology at the University of Strasbourg. In 1980, out of protest against the French educational system and its methods of teaching political science, he decided to retire. Freund published important works such as *L'essence du politique* in 1965; *The Sociology of Max Weber* in 1968; *Pareto* in 1986; *La décadence* in 1984; and *Philosophie et sociologie* in 1985. He was also a contributor to New Right publications in both Germany and France.

Jean Haudry (b. 1934) is a former professor of linguistics, Latin, Sanskrit, and comparative grammar. Now retired, he was a professor of the comparative grammar of Indo-European languages at the École Pratique des Hautes Études. He was the founder and Chair of the Institut d'études Indo-Européennes at the University of Lyon until it was disbanded in 1998. He has published *L'emploi de cas en védique* in 1977 and *The Indo-Europeans* in 1992.

Sigrid Hunke (1913-1999) was a former disciple of Nicolai Hartmann, Martin Heidegger, and Eduard Spranger, and was an expert on the philosophy of religions. As a cultural attaché of the German government, she spent long periods of time in Arabic countries teaching at various Arabic universities. She was also an honorary member of the High Council for Islamic Matters (*Ehrenmitgliedschaft im Obersten Rat für islamische Angelegenheiten*) in Germany. Her published works include *Allahs Sonne über dem Abendland*, in 1960; *Europas andere Religion*, in 1969; *Der dialektische Unitarismus*, in 1982; *Das Reich is tot es lebe Europa*, in 1985. She was also a contributor to various New Right publications.

Pierre Krebs (b. 1948) is a major figure in the German chapter of the New Right and is also the leader of the Thule-Seminar. He holds diplomas in law, journalism, sociology, and political science. He published the books *Das unvergängliche Erbe*, in 1981, and *Die Strategie der kulturellen Revolution*, in 1985.

Giorgio Locchi (1923-1992) was a doctor in law, the foreign correspondent of *Il Tempo*, and a contributor to *La Destra* and *Elementi*. His published essays include '*Le mythe cosmogonique indo-européenne*', '*Richard Wagner et la Régéneration de l'Histoire*', and '*Wagner, Nietzsche e il nuovo mito*'. He was the co-author of *Das unvergängliche Erbe* with Pierre Krebs in 1981.

Robert Steuckers (b. 1956) was the founder of the Belgian branch of the New Right and is the editor of *Orientations* (Belgium), as well as being a contributor to *Nouvelle École*, *The Scorpion*, and *Éléments*. He is a certified translator and a specialist in geopolitics and the author of *Dossier géopolitique*, 1980. He maintains the extensive New Right sites *Euro-Synergies* at euro-synergies.hautetfort.com and *Vouloir* at vouloir.hautetfort.com.

Michael Walker is the chief figure of Neue Kultur in England. He is the editor of the journal *The Scorpion*. He has published numerous articles on literature and politics. He currently resides in Germany.

*

The following are some excerpts from the New Right (Neue Kultur) manifesto, published by the Thule-Seminar and translated from German into English by Tomislav Sunic:

Our concept of the world does not refer to one theorist, but instead to a given number of ideas, i.e., cognitions, which refer to specific heritages within common European values. We refer to the work of those theorists who have not handed down the dogmatic 'deciphering' of the world phenomenon: Friedrich Nietzsche, Karl Popper, Oswald Spengler, Ludwig Wittgenstein, Alexis Carrel, and Jacob von Uexküll, Konrad Lorenz, Arnold Gehlen, Hans Jürgen Eysenck... and Louis Rougier,

Vilfredo Pareto, and Helmut Schelsky, Georges Sorel and Max Weber, Ernst Jünger, Carl Schmitt, etc...

Our new school of thought sets its philosophical system of thought, as far as the domain of ethics is concerned, within the guidelines of the pre-Socratic thinkers, Stoics, Schopenhauer and Nietzsche...

Our school stresses the primacy of life over all inherited worldviews; the primacy of soul over spirit, the primacy of feelings over intellect, and finally of character over reason...

Hence, it follows that our school is unconditionally opposed to all systems of an absolutist character, given that these systems imply the idea of determinism, of a single truth or of a monotheism, in which we discern the roots of totalitarianism. Our new school shares the view that the common denominator for all these systems lies in universalism, i.e., in the teaching of egalitarianism, be it of Aristotelian, Thomist, Judaeo-Christian, or Marxist origin...

APPENDIX II:
MANIFESTO FOR A
EUROPEAN RENAISSANCE[1]

Alain de Benoist and Charles Champetier

Introduction

The French New Right was born in 1968. It is not a political move-ment, but a think-tank and school of thought. For more than thirty years — in books and journals, colloquia and conferences, semi-nars and summer schools, etc. — it has attempted to formulate a meta-political perspective.

Metapolitics is not politics by other means. It is neither a 'strat-egy' to impose intellectual hegemony, nor an attempt to discredit other possible attitudes or agendas. It rests solely on the premise that ideas play a fundamental role in collective consciousness and, more gen-erally, in human history. Through their works, Heraclitus, Aristotle, St. Augustine, St. Thomas Aquinas, René Descartes, Immanuel Kant, Adam Smith, and Karl Marx all triggered decisive revolutions, whose impact is still being felt today. History is a result of human will and action, but always within the framework of convictions, beliefs and

---

1   This essay was originally published in *Éléments* 94, February 1999, pp. 11-23, as 'Manifeste pour une renaissance européenne. À la découverte du GRECE, Son histoire, ses idées, son organisation'. This translation was published in *Telos* 115 (Spring 1999), pp. 117-144, under the title 'The French New Right in the Year 2000', and is by Martin Bendelow and Francis Greene. -Ed.

representations which provide meaning and direction. The goal of the French New Right is to contribute to the renewal of these sociohistorical representations.

Even more now, this metapolitical impulse is based on a reflection about the evolution of Western societies in view of the coming Twenty-first century. On the one hand, there is the growing impotence of political parties, unions, governments, classical forms of conquest and the exercise of political power, and, on the other, the rapid obsolescence of all antitheses (first and foremost, Left and Right) that have characterised modernity. Moreover, there is an unprecedented explosion of knowledge, which spreads with little regard for its consequences. In a world where closed entities have given way to interconnected networks with increasingly fuzzy reference points, metapolitical action attempts, beyond political divisions and through a new synthesis, to renew a transversal mode of thought and, ultimately, to study all areas of knowledge in order to propose a coherent worldview. Such has been the aim for over thirty years.

This manifesto summarises all of this. The first part ('Predicaments') provides a critical analysis of the present; the second part ('Foundations') outlines a view concerning man and the world. Both are inspired by a multidisciplinary approach that challenges most of today's intellectual antitheses. Tribalism and globalism, nationalism and internationalism, liberalism and Marxism, individualism and collectivism, progressivism and conservatism oppose each other with the same complacent logic of the excluded middle. For a century, these artificial oppositions have occluded what is most essential: the sheer size of a crisis that demands a radical renewal of modes of thought, decision and action. It is thus futile to seek this radical renewal in what has already been written. Yet, the French New Right has borrowed ideas from various theoretical sources. It has not hesitated to reappropriate what seems valuable in all currents of thought. This transverse approach has provoked the ire of the guardians of thought, concerned with freezing ideological orthodoxies in order to paralyse any new threatening synthesis.

From the very beginning, the French New Right has brought together people interested in participating in the development of a community. In France, as in other countries, it constitutes a community of work and reflection, whose members are not necessarily intellectuals, but all of whom are interested, in one way or another, in the battle of ideas. The third part of this manifesto ('Positions') takes positions on current issues, debates and the future of peoples and civilisation.

Predicaments

First and foremost, all critical thought attempts to put the age in which it develops in perspective. The present is a pivotal period — a turning point or an *interregnum*, characterised by a major crisis: the end of modernity.

1. What is Modernity?

Modernity designates the political and philosophical movement of the last three centuries of Western history. It is characterised primarily by five converging processes: *individualisation*, through the destruction of old forms of communal life; *massification*, through the adoption of standardised behaviour and lifestyles; *desacralisation*, through the displacement of the great religious narratives by a scientific interpretation of the world; *rationalisation*, through the domination of instrumental reason, the free market, and technical efficiency; and *universalisation*, through a planetary extension of a model of society postulated implicitly as the only rational possibility and thus as superior.

This movement has old roots. In most respects, it represents a secularisation of ideas and perspectives borrowed from Christian metaphysics, which spread into secular life following a rejection of any transcendent dimension. Actually, one finds in Christianity the seeds of the great mutations that gave birth to the secular ideologies of the first post-revolutionary era. Individualism was already present in the notion of individual salvation and of an intimate and privileged relation between an individual and God that surpasses any relation on Earth. Egalitarianism is rooted in the idea that redemption is equally available to all mankind, since all are endowed with an individual soul whose absolute value is shared by all humanity. Progressivism is born of the idea that history has an absolute beginning and a necessary end, and that it unfolds globally according to a divine plan. Finally, universalism is the natural expression of a religion that claims to manifest a revealed truth which, valid for all men, summons them to conversion. Modern political life itself is founded on secularised theological concepts. Reduced to an opinion among others, today Christianity has unwittingly become the victim of the movement it started. In the history of the West, it became the religion of the way out of religion.

The various concurrent and often contradictory philosophical schools of modernity agree on one issue: that there is a unique and universalisable solution for all social, moral and political problems. Humanity is understood to be the sum of rational individuals who, through self-interest, moral conviction, fellowship or even fear are called upon to realise their unity in history. In this perspective, the diversity of the world becomes an obstacle, and all that differentiates men is thought to be incidental or contingent, outmoded or even dangerous. To the extent that modernity is not only a body of ideas, but also a mode of action, it attempts by every available means to uproot individuals from their individual communities, to subject them to a universal mode of association. In practice, the most efficient means for doing this has been the marketplace.

2. The Crisis of Modernity
The imagery of modernity is dominated by desires of freedom and equality. These two cardinal values have been betrayed. Cut off from the communities which protected them, giving meaning and form to their existence, individuals are now subject to such an immense mechanism of domination and decision that their freedom remains purely formal. They endure the global power of the marketplace, techno-science, or communications without ever being able to influence their course. The promise of equality has failed on two counts: Communism has betrayed it by installing the most murderous totalitarian regimes in history; capitalism has trivialised it by legitimating the most odious social and economic inequalities in the name of equality. Modernity proclaims rights without in any way providing the means to exercise them. It exacerbates all needs and continually creates new ones, while reserving access to them to a small minority, which feeds the frustration and anger of all others. As for the ideology of progress, which responds to human expectations by nourishing the promise of an ever-improving world, it is in a deep crisis. The future appears unpredictable, no longer offering hope, and terrifying almost everyone. Each generation confronts a world different from the one its fathers knew. Combined with accelerated transformations of life-styles and living

contexts (*nomoi*),[2] this enduring newness predicated on discrediting the fathers and old experiences, produces not happiness but misery.

The 'end of ideologies' is an expression designating the historical exhaustion of the great mobilising narratives that became embodied in liberalism, socialism, Communism, nationalism, Fascism, and, finally, Nazism. The Twentieth century has sounded the death knell for most of these doctrines, whose concrete results were genocide, ethnic cleansing, and mass murder, total wars among nations and permanent rivalry among individuals, ecological disasters, social chaos, and the loss of all significant reference points. The destruction of the life-world for the benefit of instrumental reason, (economic) growth, and material development have resulted in an unprecedented impoverishment of the spirit, and the generalisation of anxiety related to living in an always uncertain present, in a world deprived both of the past and the future. Thus, modernity has given birth to the most empty civilisation mankind has ever known: the language of advertising has become the paradigm of all social discourse; the primacy of money has imposed the omnipresence of commodities; man has been transformed into an object of exchange in a context of mean hedonism; technology has ensnared the life-world in a network of rationalism — a world replete with delinquency, violence, and incivility, in which man is at war with himself and against all, i.e., an unreal world of drugs, virtual reality and media-hyped sports, in which the countryside is abandoned for unliveable suburbs and monstrous megalopolises, and where the solitary individual merges into an anonymous and hostile crowd, while traditional social, political, cultural or religious mediations become increasingly uncertain and undifferentiated.

This general crisis is a sign that modernity is reaching its end, precisely when the universalist utopia that established it is poised to become a reality under the form of liberal globalisation. The end of the Twentieth century marks both the end of modern times and the beginning of a postmodernity characterised by a series of new themes: preoccupation with ecology, concern for the quality of life, the role of 'tribes' and of 'networks', revival of communities, the politics of group identities, multiplication of intra- and supra-state conflicts, the return of social violence, the decline of established religions, growing

---

2 *Nomoi*, from the ancient Greek, refers to a system of rules enforced by an institution. -Ed.

opposition to social elitism, etc. Having nothing new to say, and observing the growing malaise of contemporary societies, the agents of the dominant ideology are reduced to the cliché-ridden discourse so common in the media in a world threatened by implosion — *implosion*, not explosion, because modernity will not be transcended with a *grand soir*[3] (a secular version of the Second Coming of Christ), but with the appearance of thousands of auroras, i.e., the birth of sovereign spaces liberated from the domination of the modern. Modernity will not be transcended by returning to the past, but by means of certain premodern values in a decisively postmodern dimension. It is only at the price of such a radical restructuring that anomie and contemporary nihilism will be exorcised.

3. Liberalism: The Main Enemy

Liberalism embodies the dominant ideology of modernity. It was the first to appear and will be the last to disappear. In the beginning, liberal thought contraposed an autonomous economy to the morality, politics and society in which it had been formerly embedded. Later, it turned commercial value into the essence of all communal life. The advent of the 'primacy of quantity' signalled this transition from market economics to market societies, i.e., the extension of the laws of commercial exchange, ruled by the 'invisible hand', to all spheres of existence. On the other hand, liberalism also engendered modern individualism, both from a false anthropology and from the descriptive as well as normative view based on a one-dimensional man drawing his 'inalienable rights' from his essentially asocial nature continually trying to maximise his best interest by eliminating any non-quantifiable consideration and any value unrelated to rational calculation.

This dual individualistic and economic impulse is accompanied by a Darwinian social vision which, in the final analysis, reduces social life to a generalised competition, to a new version of a 'war of all against all' to select the 'best'. Aside from the fact that 'pure and perfect' competition is a myth, since there are always power relations, it says absolutely nothing about the value of what is chosen: what is better or worse. Evolution selects those most apt to survive. But man is not

---

3   French: 'big night', as in when a significant event happens, such as a large celebration. -Ed.

satisfied with mere survival: he orders his life in a hierarchy of values about which liberals claim to remain neutral.

In the Twentieth century, the iniquitous character of liberal domination generated a legitimate reaction: the appearance of the socialist movement. Under the influence of Marxism, however, this movement became misdirected. Yet, despite their mutual hostility, liberalism and Marxism basically belong to the same universe and are both the heirs of Enlightenment thought: they share the same individualism, even the same universal egalitarianism, the same rationalism, the same primacy of economics, the same stress on the emancipatory value of labour, the same faith in progress, the same idea of an end of history. In almost all respects, liberalism has only realised more effectively certain objectives it shares with Marxism: the eradication of collective identities and traditional cultures, the disenchantment of the world, and the universalisation of the system of production.

The ravages of the market have also triggered the rise and growth of the welfare state. Throughout history, the market and the state have appeared on an equal footing, the latter seeking to subject inter-communal, non-market exchange, which is intangible, to the law of money, and to turn homogeneous economic space into a tool of its power. The dissolution of communal bonds, spurred by the commercialisation of social life, has necessitated the progressive strengthening of the welfare state, since it is entrusted with the redistribution necessary to mitigate the failures of traditional solidarity. Far from hindering liberalism, these statist interventions have allowed it to prosper by avoiding a social explosion, thus generating the security and stability indispensable to exchange. In return, the welfare state, which is nothing but an abstract, anonymous and opaque redistributive structure, has generalised irresponsibility, transforming the members of society into nothing more than recipients of public assistance, who no longer seek to overthrow the liberal system, but only to prolong the indefinite extension of rights with no *quid pro quo*.

Finally, liberalism denies the specificity of politics, which always implies arbitrariness of decisions and plurality of goals. From this viewpoint, the term 'liberal politics' appears to be a contradiction in terms. Seeking to form social bonds on the basis of a theory of rational choice that reduces citizenship to utility, it ends up with an ideal 'scientific' management of global society by technical experts. The liberal state, all too often synonymous with a republic of judges, is committed to the parallel goals of abstaining from proposing a model of the good life while seeking to neutralise conflicts inherent in the diversity of social life by pursuing policies aimed at determining, by purely juridical procedures, what is just rather than what is good. The public sphere dissolves into the private, while representative democracy is reduced to a market in which supply becomes increasingly limited (concentration of programs and convergence of policies) and demand less and less motivated (abstention).

In the age of globalisation, liberalism no longer presents itself as an ideology, but as a global system of production and reproduction of men and commodities, supplemented by the hypermodernism of human rights. In its economic, political and moral forms, liberalism represents the central bloc of the ideas of a modernity that is finished. Thus, it is the main obstacle to anything seeking to go beyond it.

Foundations

'Know thyself', said the oracle of Delphi. The key to any representation of the world, to any political, moral or philosophical engagement is, first of all, an anthropology, whereby activities are carried out through certain practical orders, which represent the essence of peoples' relations among themselves and with the world: politics, economics, technology, and ethics.

1. Man: An Aspect of Life
Modernity has denied any human nature (the theory of the *tabula rasa*) or it has related it back to abstract attributes disconnected from the real world and lived experience. As a consequence of this radical rupture, the ideal of a 'new man', infinitely malleable through the brutal and progressive transformation of his environment, has emerged. In the Twentieth century, this utopia has resulted in totalitarianism and the concentration camps. In the liberal world, it has translated into the superstitious belief in an all-powerful environment, which has generated deceptions, in particular in the educational sphere: in a society structured by abstract rationality, cognitive ability is the main determinant of social status.

Man is first and foremost an animal. He exists as such in the order of living beings, which is measured in hundreds of millions of years. If one compares the history of organic life to one day (twenty-four hours), the human species appeared only in the last thirty seconds. The process of humanisation has unfolded over umpteen thousands of generations. To the extent that life is generated above all through the transmission of information contained in genetic material, man is not born like a blank page: every single individual already bears the general characteristics of the species, to which are added specific hereditary predispositions to certain particular aptitudes and modes of behaviour. The individual does not decide this inheritance, which limits his autonomy and his plasticity, but also allows him to resist political and social conditioning.

But man is not just an animal: what is specifically human in him — consciousness of his own consciousness, abstract thought, syntactic language, the capacity for symbolism, the aptitude for objective observation and value judgment — does not contradict his nature, but extends it by conferring on him a supplementary and unique identity. To deny man's biological determinants or to reduce them by relegating his specific traits to zoology is absurd. The hereditary part of humanity forms only the basis of social and historical life: human instincts are not programmed in their object, i.e., man always has the freedom to make choices, moral as well as political, which naturally are limited only by death. Man is an heir, but he can dispose of his heritage. He can construct himself historically and culturally on the basis of the presuppositions of his biological constitution, which are his human limitations. What lies beyond these limitations may be called God, the cosmos, nothingness, or Being. The question of 'why' no longer makes sense, because what is beyond human limitations is by definition unthinkable.

Thus, the New Right proposes a vision of a well-balanced individual, taking into account both inborn, personal abilities and the social environment. It rejects ideologies that emphasise only one of these factors, be it biological, economic, or mechanical.

2. Man: A Rooted, Imperilled, and Open Being

By nature, man is neither good nor bad, but he is capable of being either one or the other. As an open and imperilled being, he is always able to go beyond himself or to debase himself. Man can keep this permanent threat at bay by constructing social and moral rules, as well as institutions and traditions, which provide a foundation for his existence and give his life meaning and references. Defined as the undifferentiated mass of individuals that constitutes it, humanity designates either a biological category (the species) or a philosophical category emanating from Western thought. From the socio-historical viewpoint, man as such does not exist, because his membership within humanity is always mediated by a particular cultural belonging. This observation does not stem from relativism. All men have in common their human nature, without which they would not be able to understand each other, but their common membership in the species always expresses itself in a single *context*. They share the same essential aspirations, which are always crystallised in different forms according to time and place.

In this sense, humanity is irreducibly plural: diversity is part of its very essence. Thus, human life is necessarily rooted in a given context, prior to the way individuals and groups see the world, even critically, and to the way they formulate their aspirations and goals. They do not exist in the real world other than as concretely rooted people. Biological differences are significant only in reference to social and cultural givens. As for differences between cultures, they are the effects neither of illusion nor of transitory, contingent or secondary characteristics. All cultures have their own 'centre of gravity' (Herder): different cultures provide different responses to essential questions. This is why all attempts to unify them end up destroying them. Man is rooted by nature in his culture. He is a singular being: he always locates himself at the interface of the universal (his species) and the particular (each culture, each epoch). Thus, the idea of an absolute, universal, and eternal law that ultimately determines moral, religious, or political choices appears unfounded. This idea is the basis of all totalitarianisms.

Human societies are both conflictual and cooperative, without being able to eliminate one to the benefit of the other. The ironic belief in the possibility of eliminating these antagonisms within a transparent and reconciled society has no more validity than the hypercompetitive (liberal, racist, or nationalist) vision that turns life into a perpetual war of individuals or groups. If aggressiveness is an essential part of the creativity and dynamism of life, evolution has also favoured in man the emergence of cooperative (altruistic) behaviours evident not only in the sphere of genetic kinship. On the other hand, great historical constructions have been possible only by establishing a harmony based on the recognition of the common good, the reciprocity of rights and duties, cooperation and sharing. Neither peaceful nor belligerent, neither good nor bad, neither beautiful nor ugly, human existence unfolds in a tragic tension between these poles of attraction and repulsion.

3. Society: A Body of Communities

Human existence is inseparable from the communities and social groups in which it reveals itself. The idea of a primitive 'state of nature' in which autonomous individuals might have coexisted is pure fiction: society is not the result of a contract between men trying to maximise their best interests, but rather of a spontaneous association whose most ancient form is undoubtedly the extended family.

The communities within which society is grounded are constituted by a complex net of intermediary bodies situated among individuals, groups of individuals, and humanity. Some are inherited (native), others are chosen (cooperative). The social bond, whose autonomy the classical Right parties have never recognised, and which should not be confused with 'civil society', is defined, first and foremost, as a model for individual actions, not as the global effect of these actions. It rests on shared consent and is prior to this model. Membership in the collective does not destroy individual identity; rather, it is the basis for it. When one leaves one's original community, it is generally to join another one. Native or cooperative communities are all based on reciprocity. Communities are constituted and maintain themselves on the basis of who belongs to them. Membership is all that is required. There is a vertical reciprocity of rights and duties, contributions and distributions, obedience and assistance, and a horizontal reciprocity of gifts, fraternity, friendship, and love. The richness of social life is proportional to the diversity of the members: this diversity is constantly threatened either by shortcomings (conformity, lack of differentiation) or excesses (secession, atomisation).

The holistic conception, where the whole exceeds the sum of its parts and possesses qualities none of its individual parts have, has been defeated by modern universalism and individualism, which have associated community with the ideas of submission to hierarchy, entanglement, or parochialism. This universalism and individualism have been deployed in two ways: the contract (politics) and the market (economics). But, in reality, modernity has not liberated man from his original familial belonging or from local, tribal, corporative or religious attachments. It has only submitted him to other constraints, which are harsher, because they are further away, more impersonal, and more demanding: a mechanistic, abstract, and homogeneous subjugation has replaced multiform organic modes. In becoming more solitary, man also has become more vulnerable and more destitute. He has become disconnected from meaning, because he can no longer identify himself with a model, and because there is no longer any way for him to understand his place in the social whole. Individualism has resulted in disaffiliation, separation, deinstitutionalisation (thus, the family no longer socialises), and the appropriation of the social bond by statist bureaucracies. In the final analysis, the great project of modern emancipation has resulted only in generalised alienation. Because modern societies tend to bring together individuals who experience each other as strangers, no longer having any mutual confidence, they cannot envision a social relation not subject to a 'neutral' regulatory authority. The pure forms are exchange (a market system of the rule of the strongest) and submission (the totalitarian system of obedience to the all-powerful state). The mixed form that now prevails is a proliferation of abstract juridical rules that gradually intersect every area of existence, whereby relations with others are permanently controlled in order to ward off the threat of implosion. Only a return to communities and to a politics of human dimensions can remedy exclusion or dissolution of the social bond, its reification, and its juridification.

4. Politics: An Essence and an Art

Politics is consistent with the fact that the goals of social life are always multiple. Its essence and its laws cannot be reduced to economics, ethics, aesthetics, metaphysics, or the sacred. It both acknowledges and distinguishes between such notions as public and private, command and obedience, deliberation and decision, citizen and foreigner, friend and enemy. If there is morality in politics, since authority aims at a common good and is inspired by the collectivity's values and customs, this does not mean that an individual morality is politically applicable. Regimes which refuse to recognise the essence of politics, which deny the plurality of goals or favour depoliticisation, are by definition 'unpolitical'.

Modern thought has developed the illusion of politics as 'neutral', reducing power to managerial efficiency, to the mechanical application of juridical, technical or economic norms: the 'government of men' ought to be modelled on the 'administration of things'. The public sphere, however, always affirms a particular vision of the 'good life'. This idea of the 'good' precedes the idea of the 'just' — not the other way around.

Domestically, the first aim of all political action is civil peace: internally, security and harmony between all members of society; externally, protection from foreign danger. Compared with this aim, the choice between values such as liberty, equality, unity, diversity and solidarity is arbitrary: it is not self-evident, but is a matter of the end result. Diversity of worldviews is one of the conditions for the emergence of politics. Because it recognises the pluralism of aspirations and projects, democracy seeks to facilitate peaceful confrontations at all levels of public life; it is an eminently political form of government. If the individual considers himself to be part of a community, then he will behave as a citizen in a democracy, which is the only form of government that offers him participation in public discussions and decisions, as well as the ability to make something of himself and to excel through education. Politics is not a science, given over to reason or technology, but an art, calling for prudence before everything else. It always implies uncertainty, a plurality of choices, a decision about goals. The art of governing provides the power to arbitrate between various possibilities, along with the capacity for constraint. Power is never merely a *means* that has value only as a function of the goals it is supposed to serve.

According to Jean Bodin, heir of the French jurists of the Middle Ages (the *légistes*), the source of independence and liberty resides in the prince's unlimited sovereignty, modelled after papal absolutist power. This is the concept of a 'political theology' based on the idea of a supreme political organ — a 'Leviathan' (Hobbes) — charged with controlling body, spirit and soul. It inspired the unified and centralised absolutist nation-state, which tolerated neither local power nor the sharing of law with neighbouring territorial powers. It was developed through administrative and judicial unification, the elimination of intermediary bodies (denounced as 'feudal'), and the gradual eradication of all local cultures. Eventually, it became absolutist monarchy, revolutionary Jacobinism, and, finally, modern totalitarianism. But it also led to a 'republic without citizens', in which there is nothing left between atomised civil society and the managerial state. To this model of political society, the French New Right contraposes the legacy of Althusius,[4] where the source of independence and liberty resides in autonomy, and the state defines itself first and foremost as a federation of organised communities and multiple allegiances.

In this view, which has inspired both imperial and federal constructions, the existence of a delegation of sovereign powers never results in the people losing their ability to make or abrogate laws. In their variously organised collectivities, the people (or 'states') are the ultimate repository of sovereignty. The rulers are above each citizen individually, but they are always subordinate to the general will expressed by the body of citizens. The principle of subsidiarity rules at all levels.

The liberty of a collectivity is not antithetical to shared sovereignty. Ultimately, politics is not reduced to the level of the state: the public person is defined as a complex of groups, families and associations, of local, regional, national or supranational collectivities. Politics does not deny this organic continuity, but takes its support from it. Political unity proceeds from a recognised diversity, i.e., it must admit that there is something 'opaque' in the social fabric: the perfect 'transparency' of society is a utopia that does not encourage democratic communication; on the contrary, it favours totalitarian surveillance.

5. Economics: Beyond the Marketplace

As far as one goes back into the history of human societies, certain rules have presided over the production, circulation and consummation of the goods necessary to the survival of individuals and groups. For all that, and contrary to the presuppositions of liberalism and Marxism, the economy has never formed the infrastructure of society: economic over-determination ('economism') is the exception, not the rule. Moreover, numerous myths associated with the curses of labour (Prometheus, rape of the Mother-Earth), money (Croesus, Gullveig, Tarpeia), and abundance (Pandora) reveal that early on the economy

---

4 Johannes Althusius (1563-1638) was a political philosopher who is credited with having formulated the idea of federalism, by which autonomous groups which retain local authority are bound together with others to form a common whole, with only some powers delegated to the central authority. His ideas were also crucial to the idea of subsidiarity in politics. An essay by de Benoist on Althusius, entitled 'The First Federalist', was published in *Telos* 118, Winter 2000. -Ed.

was perceived as the 'damned part' of all society, as an activity that threatened to destroy all harmony. The economy was thus devalued, not because it was not useful, but for the simple reason that it was only that. What is more, one was rich because one was powerful, and not the reverse, power being thus matched by a duty to share and to protect those under one's care. The 'fetishism of commodities' as a peculiarity of modern capitalism was clearly recognised as a danger: production of abundance of different goods arouses envy, the mimetic desire, which in turn generates disorder and violence.

In all pre-modern societies, the economic was embedded and con-textualised within other orders of human activity (Karl Polanyi).[5] The idea that economic exchange from barter to the modern market always has been regulated by the confrontation of supply and demand, by the consequent emergence of an equivalent abstract (money) and of objective values (use values, exchange values, utility, etc.) is a fairy-tale invented by liberalism. The market is not an ideal model whose abstraction allows universalisation. Before being a mechanism, it is an institution, and this institution can be abstracted neither from its history nor from the cultures that have generated it.

The three great forms of the circulation of goods are reciprocity (mutual gift-giving, equal or joint sharing), redistribution (centralisation and distribution by a single authority), and exchange. They do not represent stages of development, but have more or less always coexisted. Modern society is characterised by a hypertrophy of free market exchange, leading from an economy *with* a market, to a market society. The liberal economy has translated the ideology of progress into a religion of growth: the 'ever more' of consumption is supposed to lead humanity to happiness. While it is undeniable that modern economic development has satisfied certain primary needs of a much larger number of people than previously possible, it is not any less true that the artificial growth of needs through the seductive strategies of the system of objects (advertising) necessarily ends in an impasse. In a world of finite resources, subject to the principle of entropy, a certain slowing of growth prefigures humanity's inevitable horizon.

---

5   Karl Polanyi (1886-1964) was an Austrian sociologist who saw the rise of the mod-
    ern nation-state as the inevitable result of the development of the market econo-
    my, as argued in his book *The Great Transformation*. -Ed.

Given the breadth of transformations it has brought about, the commodification of the world from the Sixteenth to the Twentieth century has been one of the most important phenomena in human history. Decommodification will be one of the main phenomena in the Twenty-first century. Thus, it is necessary to return to the origins of the economy (*oikos-nomos*),[6] to the general laws of the human habitat in the world, which include those of ecological balance, human passion, respect for the harmony and beauty of nature, and, in a more general way, all the non-quantifiable elements that economic science has arbitrarily excluded from its calculations. All economic life implies the mediation of a large range of cultural institutions and juridical means. Today, the economy must be recontextualised within life, society, politics and ethics.

6. Ethics: The Construction of Oneself

The fundamental categories of ethics are universal: the distinctions between noble and ignoble, good and bad, admirable and despicable, just and unjust can be found everywhere. On the other hand, the designation and evaluation of behaviours relevant to each of these categories varies with epochs and societies. The French New Right rejects all purely moral views of the world, but it recognises that no culture can avoid distinguishing between the ethical values of various attitudes and behaviours. Morality is indispensable to this open being that is man; it is an anthropological consequence of his freedom. In articulating general rules necessary for the survival of any society, moral codes become attached to customs (*mores*), and cannot be dissociated completely from the context in which they are practiced. But they cannot be seen only in terms of subjectivity. Thus, the adage 'my country, right or wrong' does not mean that my country is always right, but that it remains my country even when it is wrong. This implies that I might eventually prove it wrong, which would mean that I subscribe to a norm beyond my belonging to it.

Since the Greeks, ethics for Europeans have designated virtues whose practice forms the basis of the 'good life': generosity over avarice, honour over shame, courage over cowardice, justice over injustice, temperance over excess, duty over irresponsibility, rectitude over

---

6   Greek: 'household economics', the term from which the word 'economics' is derived. -Ed.

guile, unselfishness over greed, etc. The good citizen is one who always tries to strive for excellence in each of these virtues (Aristotle). This will to excellence does not in any way exclude the existence of several modes of life (contemplative, active, productive, etc.), each arising from different moral codes, and each finding their place in the city's hierarchy. For example, European tradition, expressed in the ancient tripartite model, made wisdom prevail over force, and force over wealth. Modernity has supplanted traditional ethics, at once aristocratic and popular, by two kinds of bourgeois moral codes: the utilitarian (Bentham), based on the materialist calculation of pleasure and pain (what is good is what increases pleasure for the greatest number); and the deontological morality (Kant), based on a unitary conception of the just, toward which all individuals must strive in accord with a universal moral law. This last approach supports the ideology of human rights, which is at once a minimal moral code and a strategic weapon of Western ethnocentrism. This ideology is a contradiction in terms. All men have rights, but they would not know how to be entitled to them as isolated beings; a right expresses a relation of equity, which implies the social. Thus, no right is conceivable outside a specific context in which to define it, outside a society to recognise it and to define the duties which represent the counterpart to it, and the means of constraint sufficient to apply it. As for fundamental liberties, they are not decreed, but they must be conquered and guaranteed. The fact that Europeans have imposed by force a right to autonomy does not in any way imply that all the peoples of the planet must be held responsible for guaranteeing rights in the same way.

Against the 'moral order', which confuses the social with the moral norm, ultimately Europeans must sustain the plurality of forms of social life, and think together about order and its opposite, Apollo and Dionysius. One can only avoid the relativism and nihilism of the 'last man' (Nietzsche), who today reveals himself against the background of practical materialism, by restoring some meaning, i.e., by retrieving some shared values, and by assuming some concrete certainties that have been tried and defended by self-conscious communities.

7. Technology: The Mobilisation of the World

Technology has been around from the very beginning; the absence of specific natural defences, the deprogramming of instincts, and the development of cognitive capacities have proceeded apace with the

transformation of the environment. But technology has long been regulated by non-technological imperatives: by the necessary harmony of
man, city and cosmos, as well as by respect for nature as the home of
Being, submission of Promethean power, Olympian wisdom, repudia-
tion of *hubris*, concern for quality rather than productivity, etc.

The technological explosion of modernity is explained by the disappearance of ethical, symbolic or religious codes. It finds its distant
roots in the Biblical imperative: 'replenish the earth, and subdue it'
(*Genesis*), which two millennia later Descartes revived when he urged
man to 'make himself the master and owner of nature'. The dual theo-
centric split between the uncreated being and the created world is thus
metamorphosed into a dual anthropocentric split between subject and
object, the second unreservedly subjugated by the first. Modernity also
has subjected science (the contemplative) to the technological (the
operative), giving birth to an integrated 'techno-science', whose only
reason for being is accelerating ever more the transformation of the
world. In the Twentieth century, there have been more upheavals than
during the previous 15,000 years. For the first time in human history,
each new generation is obliged to integrate itself into a world that the
preceding one has not experienced.

Technology develops essentially as an autonomous system: every
new discovery is immediately absorbed into the global power of the
operative, which makes it more complex and reinforces it. Recent
developments in information technology (cybernetics and comput-
ers) are accelerating this systemic integration at a prodigious rate, the
Internet being the most well-known. This network has neither a centre of decision-making nor one of entry and exit, but it maintains and
constantly expands the interaction of millions of terminals connected
to it.

Technology is not neutral; it obeys a number of values that guide
its course: operability, efficiency, and performance. Its axiom is simple:
everything that is possible can and will be realised effectively, the general belief being that additional technology will be able to rectify the
defects of existing technology. Politics, the moral code, and law intervene *only afterwards* to judge the desirable or undesirable effects of
innovation. The cumulative nature of techno-scientific development,
which experiences periods of stagnation but not regression, has long
supported the ideology of progress by demonstrating the growth of the
powers of man over nature, and by reducing risks and uncertainties.

Thus, technology has given humanity new means of existence, but at the same time it has led to a loss of the reason for living, since the future seems to depend only on the indefinite extension of the rational mastering of the world. The resulting impoverishment is more and increasingly perceived as the disappearance of an authentically human life on earth. Having explored the infinitely small and then the infinitely large, techno-science now is tackling man himself, at once the subject and the object of his own manipulations (cloning, artificial procreation, genetic fingerprinting, etc.). Man is becoming the simple extension of the tools he has created, adopting a technomorphic mentality that increases his vulnerability.

Technophobia and technophilia are equally unacceptable. Knowledge and its application are not to blame, but innovation is not desirable simply because of its novelty. Against scientific reductionism, arrogant positivism and obtuse obscurantism, technological development should follow from social, ethical and political choices, as well as anticipations (the principle of prudence), and should be reintegrated within the context of a vision of the world as *pluriversum*[7] and continuum.

8. *The World:* A Pluriversum

Diversity is inherent in the very movement of life, which flourishes as it becomes more complex. The plurality and variety of races, ethnic groups, languages, customs, even religions has characterised the development of humanity since the very beginning. Consequently, two attitudes are possible. For one, this biocultural diversity is a burden, and one must always and everywhere reduce men to what they have in common, a process which cannot avoid generating a series of perverse effects. For the other, this diversity is to be welcomed, and should be maintained and cultivated. The French New Right is profoundly opposed to the suppression of differences. It believes that a good system is one that transmits at least as much diversity as it has received. The true wealth of the world is first and foremost the diversity of its cultures and peoples.

---

7   As opposed to a *universum*, which denotes something that is present everywhere, a *pluriversum* was defined by Julien Freund as a 'plurality of particular and independent collectivities or of divergent interpretations of the same universal idea' ('Schmitt's Political Thought', *Telos* 102, Winter 1995, p. 11). -Ed.

The West's conversion to universalism has been the main cause of its subsequent attempt to *convert* the rest of the world: in the past, to its religion (the Crusades); yesterday, to its political principles (colonialism); and today, to its economic and social model (development) or its moral principles (human rights). Undertaken under the aegis of missionaries, armies, and merchants, the Westernisation of the planet has represented an imperialist movement fed by the desire to erase all otherness by imposing on the world a supposedly superior model invariably presented as 'progress'. Homogenising universalism is only the projection and the mask of an ethnocentrism extended over the whole planet.

Westernisation and globalisation have modified the way the world is perceived. Primitive tribes called themselves 'men', implying that they considered themselves their species' only representatives. A Greek and a Chinese, a Russian and an Inca could live in the same epoch without being conscious of each other's existence. Those times are past. Given the West's pretense to make the world over in its own image, the current age is a new one in which ethnic, historical, linguistic or cultural differences coexist fully aware of their identity and the otherness that reflects it. For the first time in history, the world is a *pluriversum*, a multipolar order in which great cultural groups find themselves confronting one another in a shared global temporality, i.e., in a zero hour. Yet, modernisation is gradually becoming disconnected from Westernisation: new civilisations are gradually acquiring modern means of power and knowledge without renouncing their historical and cultural heritage for the benefit of Western ideologies and values.

The idea of an 'end of history', characterised by the global triumph of market rationality by generalising the lifestyle and political forms of the liberal West, is obviously false. On the contrary, a new 'Nomos of the Earth'[8] is emerging — a new organisation of international relations. Antiquity and the Middle Ages saw an unequal development of the great autarchic civilisations. The Renaissance and the Classical Age were marked by the emergence and consolidation of nation-states in competition for the mastery, first of Europe, then of the world. The Twentieth century witnessed the development of a bipolar world in

---

8   'The *nomos* of the Earth' was a term coined by Carl Schmitt to describe the expansion of European ideas of government throughout the world, and the subsequent construction of an international system based on them. He also authored a book by this title. -Ed.

which liberalism and Marxism confronted each other, the maritime American power and the continental Soviet power. The Twenty-first century will be characterised by the development of a multipolar world of emerging civilisations: European, North American, South American, Arabic-Muslim, Chinese, Indian, Japanese, etc. These civilisations will not supplant the ancient local, tribal, provincial or national roots, but will be constituted as the ultimate collective form with which individuals are able to identify in addition to their common humanity. They will probably be called upon to collaborate in certain areas to defend humanity's common interests, notably with respect to ecology. In a multipolar world, power is defined as the ability to resist the influence of others rather than to impose one's own. The main enemy of this pluriverse will be any civilisation pretending to be universal and regarding itself entrusted with a redeeming mission ('Manifest Destiny') to impose its model on all others.

9. The Cosmos: A Continuum

The French New Right adheres to a unitary worldview, the matter and form of which only constitute variations on the same theme. The world is at once a unity and a multiplicity, integrating different levels of the visible and the invisible, different perceptions of time and space, different laws of organisation of its constituent elements. Microcosm and macrocosm interpenetrate and interact with one another. Thus, the French New Right rejects the absolute distinction between created and uncreated being, as well as the idea that this world is only the reflection of another world. The cosmos (*phusis*) is the place where Being manifests itself, the place where the truth (*aletheia*) of mutual belonging in this cosmos reveals itself. *Panta rhei* (Heraclitus): the opening to all is in everything.

Man finds and gives sense to his life only by adhering to what is greater than himself, what transcends the limits of his constitution. The French New Right fully recognises this anthropological constant, which manifests itself in all religions. It believes the return of the sacred will be accomplished by returning to some founding myths, and by the disappearance of false dichotomies: subject and object, body and thought, soul and spirit, essence and existence, rationality and sensibility, myth and logic, nature and supernatural, etc.

The disenchantment of the world translates into the closure of the modern spirit, which is incapable of projecting itself above and beyond its materialism and constituent anthropocentrism. Today's epoch has transferred the ancient divine attributes to the human subject (the metaphysics of subjectivity), thereby transforming the world into an object, i.e., into an agglomeration of means at the unlimited disposal of its ends. This ideal of reducing the world to utilitarian reason has been coupled with a linear concept of history endowed with a beginning (state of nature, paradise on earth, golden age, primitive communism, etc.) and an equally necessary end (a classless society, the reign of God, the ultimate stage of progress, entry into an era of pure rationality, transparent and conciliatory).

For the French New Right past, present, and future are not distinct moments of a directional and vectored history, but permanent dimensions of all lived moments. The past as well as the future always remain present in all their actuality. This presence — a fundamental category of time — is opposed to absence: forgetfulness of origins and occlusion of the horizon. This view of the world already found expression in European Antiquity, both in cosmological histories and in pre-Socratic thought. The 'paganism' of the French New Right articulates nothing more than sympathy for this ancient conception of the world, always alive in hearts and minds precisely because it does not belong to yesterday, but is eternal. Confronted with the *ersatz* sectarianism of fallen religions, as well as with certain neo-pagan parodies from the times of confusion, the French New Right is imbued with a very long memory: it maintains a relation to the beginning that harbours a sense of what is coming.

Positions

1. Against Indifferentiation and Uprooting; For Clear and Strong Identities

The unprecedented menace of homogenisation which looms over the entire world leads to the pathological identities: bloody irredentisms, convulsive and chauvinistic nationalism, savage tribalisations, etc. Responsibility for these deplorable attitudes stems primarily from globalisation (political, economic, technological, and financial), which produced these attitudes in the first place. By denying individuals the right to locate themselves within a collective and historical identity, by imposing a uniform mode of representation, the Western system has given birth to unhealthy forms of self-affirmation. Fear of the 'Same' has replaced fear of the 'Other'. In France, this situation is aggravated by a crisis of the State which, for two centuries, has been the main symbolic social producer. Thus, the current weakening of the state has produced a greater void in France than in other Western nations.

The question of identity will assume even greater importance in the decades ahead. In undermining social systems that used to ascribe individuals their place in a clearly understood social order, modernity has actually encouraged questioning identity and has stirred up a desire for reliance and recognition in the public scene. But modernity has not been able to satisfy this need for identity. 'Worldwide tourism' is merely a pathetic alternative to withdrawing into one's own shell.

In regard to universalist utopias and the withering of traditional identities, the French New Right affirms the primacy of differences, which are neither transitory features leading to some higher form of unity, nor incidental aspects of private life. Rather, these differences are the very substance of social life. They can be native (ethnic, linguistic), but also political. Citizenship implies belonging, allegiance and participation in public life at different levels. Thus, one can be, at one and the same time, a citizen of one's neighbourhood, city, region, nation, and of Europe, according to the nature of power devolved to each of these levels of sovereignty. By contrast, one cannot be a citizen of the world, for the 'world' is not a political category. Wanting to be a citizen of the world is to link citizenship to an abstraction drawn from the vocabulary of the Liberal New Class.

The French New Right upholds the cause of peoples, because the right to difference is a principle which has significance only in terms of its generality. One is only justified in defending one's difference from others if one is also able to defend the difference of others. This means, then, that the right to difference cannot be used to exclude others who are different. The French New Right upholds equally ethnic groups, languages, and regional cultures under the threat of extinction, as well as native religions. The French New Right supports peoples struggling against Western imperialism.

2. Against Racism; For the Right to Difference

The term racism cannot be defined as a preference for endogamy, which arises from freedom of choice of individuals and of peoples.

The Jewish people, for instance, owe their survival to their rejection of mixed marriages. Confronted with positions that are often simplistic, propagandist, or moralising, it is necessary to come back to the real meaning of words: racism is a theory which postulates that there are qualitative inequalities between the races, such that, on the whole, one can distinguish races as either 'superior' or 'inferior'; that an individual's value is deduced entirely from the race to which he belongs; or, that race constitutes the central determining factor in human history. These three postulates may be held together or separately. All three are false. If existing races vary from one another as regards this or that statistically isolated criterion, there is no absolute qualitative difference among them. Nor is there a global paradigm outside mankind that would permit creating a racial hierarchy. Finally, it is evident that an individual receives his worth from those qualities which are his own. Racism is not a disease of the mind, generated by prejudice or 'pre-modern' superstition. (Such an explanation is a liberal fable suggesting irrationality as the source of all social ills.) Rather, racism is an erroneous doctrine, one rooted in time, which finds its source in scientific positivism, according to which one can 'scientifically' measure with absolute certainty the value of human societies, and in social evolutionism, which tends to describe the history of humanity as a single, unified history, divided into 'stages' corresponding to various states of progress. (Thus certain peoples are seen as temporarily or permanently more 'advanced' than others.)

In contrast to racism, there is a universalist and a differentialist anti-racism. The former leads to the same conclusions as does the racism it denounces. As opposed to differences as is racism, universalist anti-racism only acknowledges in peoples their common belonging to a particular species and it tends to consider their specific identities as transitory or of secondary importance. By reducing the 'Other' to the 'Same' through a strictly assimilationist perspective, universalist anti-racism is, by definition, incapable of recognising or respecting otherness for what it is. Differentialist anti-racism, to which the New Right subscribes holds that the irreducible plurality of the human species constitutes a veritable treasure. Differentialist anti-racism makes every effort to restore an affirmative meaning to 'the universal', not in opposition to 'difference', but by starting from the recognition of 'difference'. For the New Right, the struggle against racism is not won by negating the concept of races, nor by the desire to blend all races into an undifferentiated whole. Rather, the struggle against racism is waged by the refusal of both exclusion and assimilation: neither apartheid nor the melting pot; rather, acceptance of the other as Other through a dialogic perspective of mutual enrichment.

3. Against Immigration; For Cooperation

By reason of its rapid growth and its massive proportions, immigration such as one sees today in Europe constitutes an undeniably negative phenomenon. Essentially, it represents a mode of forced uprooting the cause of which is, first of all, economic — spontaneous or organised movements from poor and overpopulated countries to countries which are rich. But the cause is also symbolic — the attraction of Western civilisation and the concomitant depreciation of indigenous cultures in light of the growing consumer-oriented way of life. The responsibility for current immigration lies primarily, not with the immigrants, but with the industrialised nations which have reduced man to the level of merchandise that can be relocated anywhere. Immigration is not desirable for the immigrants, who are forced to abandon their native country for another where they are received as back-ups for economic needs. Nor is immigration beneficial for the host population receiving the immigrants, who are confronted, against their will, with sometimes brutal modifications in their human and urban environments. It is obvious that the problems of the Third World countries will not be resolved by major population shifts. Thus the New Right favours policies restrictive of immigration, coupled with increased cooperation with Third World countries where organic interdependence and traditional ways of life still survive, in order to overcome imbalances resulting from globalisation.

As regards the immigrant populations which reside today in France, it would be illusory to expect their departure *en masse*. The Jacobin nation-state has always upheld a model of assimilation in which only the individual is absorbed into a citizenship which is purely abstract. The state holds no interest in the collective identities nor in the cultural differences of these individuals. This model becomes less and less credible in view of the following factors: the sheer number of immigrants, the cultural differences which sometimes separate them from the population receiving them, and especially the profound crises which affect all the channels of traditional integration (parties, unions, religions, schools, the army, etc.). The New Right believes that ethnocultural identity should no longer be relegated to the private domain, but should be acknowledged and recognised in the public sphere. The New Right proposes, then, a communitarian model which would spare individuals from being cut off from their cultural roots and which would permit them to keep alive the structures of their collective cultural lives. They should be able to observe necessary general and common laws without abandoning the culture which is their very own. This communitarian politic could, in the long run, lead to a disassociation of citizenship from nationality.

4. Against Sexism; For the Recognition of Gender

The distinction of the sexes is the first and most fundamental of natural differences, for the human race only insures its continuation through this distinction. Being sexual from the very outset, humanity is not one, but rather two. Beyond mere biology, difference inscribes itself in *gender* — masculine and feminine. These determine, in social life, two different ways of perceiving the Other and the world, and they constitute, for individuals, their mode of sexual destiny. The existence of a feminine and masculine nature is evident. However, this does not preclude the fact that individuals of each sex may diverge from these categories due to genetic factors or socio-cultural choices. Nonetheless, in general, a large number of values and attitudes fall into feminine and masculine categories: cooperation and competition, mediation and repression, seduction and domination, empathy and detachment, concrete and abstract, affective and managerial, persuasion and aggression, synthetic intuition and analytic intellection, etc. The modern concept of abstract individuals, detached from their sexual identity, stemming from an 'indifferentialist' ideology which neutralises sexual differences, is just as prejudicial against women as traditional sexism which, for centuries, considered women as incomplete men. This is a twisted form of male domination, which in the past had excluded women from the arena of public life, and admits them today— on the condition that they divest themselves of their femininity.

Some universalist feminists claim that masculine and feminine genders stem from a social construct ('One is not born a woman, one becomes a woman'). In this way, feminism falls into a male-centred trap as it adheres to 'universal' and abstract values which are, in the final analysis, masculine values. The New Right supports a differentialist feminism which, to the contrary, wants sexual difference to play a role in the public domain and upholds specifically feminine rights (the right to virginity, to maternity, to abortion). Against sexism and unisex utopianism, differentialist feminism recognises men as well as women by acknowledging the equal value of their distinct and unique natures.

5. Against the New Class; For Autonomy from the Bottom Up

In the process of globalisation, Western civilisation is promoting the worldwide domination of a ruling class whose only claim to legitimacy resides in its abstract manipulations (logico-symbolic) of the signs and values of the system already in place. Aspiring to uninterrupted growth of capital and to the permanent reign of social engineering, this New Class provides the manpower for the media, large national and multinational firms, and international organisations. This New Class produces and reproduces everywhere the same type of person: cold-blooded specialists, rationality detached from day-to-day realities. It also engenders abstract individualism, utilitarian beliefs, a superficial humanitarianism, indifference to history, an obvious lack of culture, isolation from the real world, the sacrifice of the real to the virtual, an inclination to corruption, nepotism and to buying votes. All of this fits in with the tactic of mergers and the globalisation of worldwide domination. The further that those in power distance themselves from the average citizen, the less they feel the need to justify their decisions. The more a society offers its citizens impersonal tasks to do, the less that society is open to workers of real quality; the less the private domain encroaches upon the public domain, the less are individual achievements recognised and acknowledged by the public; the more one is obliged to 'fulfil a function', the less one is able to 'play a role'. The New Class depersonalises the leadership of Western societies and even lessens their sense of responsibility.

Since the end of the Cold War and the collapse of the Soviet Bloc, the New Class finds itself again confronted with a whole series of conflicts (between capital and labour, equality and freedom, the public and the private) which it had attempted to avoid for over a half a century. Likewise, its ineffectiveness, its wastefulness, and its counter-productivity appear more and more evident. The system tends to close in upon itself, while the public feels indifferent toward or angry at a managerial elite which does not even speak the same language as they do. As regards every major social issue, the gulf widens between the rulers who repeat the usual technocratic discourse and those governed who experience, in their day-to-day lives, the consequences of all this. All the while the media draw attention away from the real world towards one of mere representation. At the highest levels of society, we find technocratic doubletalk, sanctimonious babble, and the comfort of capital yield; at the bottom of the social ladder, the pains of day-to-day life, an incessant search for meaning, and the desire for shared values.

Average citizens have nothing but scorn for the 'elite' and they are indifferent to the traditional political factions and agendas which have today become obsolete. Satisfying the people's (or populist) aspirations would entail giving more autonomy to structures at the lower end of the social ladder, giving them the opportunity to create or recreate specific *nomoi*. In order to create a more 'user-friendly' society, one would have to avoid the anonymity of the masses, the commodification of values, and the reification of social relations. Rather, local communities would have to make decisions by and for themselves in all those matters which concern them directly, and all members would have to participate at every stage of the deliberations and of the democratic decision-making. It is not the Welfare State that ought to decentralise in their favour. Rather, it is the local communities themselves that ought not cede to State power to intervene except in those matters for which they are not able or competent to make decisions.

6. Against Jacobinism; For a Federal Europe

The first Thirty Years War (1618-1648), concluded by the Treaty of Westphalia, marked the establishment of the nation-state as the dominant mode of political organisation. The second Thirty Years' War (1914-45) signalled, to the contrary, the start of the disintegration of the nation-state. Born out of absolute monarchy and revolutionary Jacobinism, the nation-state is now too big to manage little problems and too small to address big ones. In a globalised world, the future belongs to large cultures and civilisations capable of organising themselves into autonomous entities and of acquiring enough power to resist outside interference. Europe must organise itself into a federal structure, while recognising the autonomy of all the component elements and facilitating the cooperation of the constituent regions and of individual nations. European civilisation will remake itself, not by the negation, but by the recognition of historical cultures, thus permitting all inhabitants to rediscover their common origins. The principle of subsidiarity ought to be the keystone at every level. Authority at the lower levels should not be delegated to authorities at the upper levels except in those matters which escape the competence of the lower level.

As opposed to the centralising tradition, which confiscates all powers to establish a single level of control, as opposed to a bureaucratic and technocratic Europe, which relinquishes sovereignty without transferring it to a higher level; as opposed to a Europe which will only be a big market unified by free trade; as opposed to a 'Europe of Nations', a mere assemblage of national egos which cannot prevent future wars; as opposed to a 'European Nation' which is nothing more than a larger version of the Jacobin state; as opposed to all of the above, Europe (Western, Central, and Eastern) must reorganise itself from the bottom up, in close continental association with Russia. The existing states must federalise themselves from within, in order to better federalise with each other. Each level of the association should have its own role and its own dignity, not derived with approval from above, but based on the will and consent of all those who participate. The only decisions that would come from the summit of this structure would be those relating to all the peoples and federal communities: diplomatic matters, military affairs, big economic issues, fundamental legal questions, protection of the environment, etc. European integration is equally necessary in certain areas of research, industry, and new communications technology. A single currency ought to be managed by a central bank under the control of European political authority.

7. Against Depoliticisation; For the Strengthening of Democracy

Democracy did not first appear with the Revolutions of 1776 and 1789. Rather, it has constituted a constant tradition in Europe since the existence of the ancient Greek city and since the time of the ancient German 'freedoms'. Democracy is not synonymous with former 'popular democracies' of the East nor with liberal parliamentary democracy today so prevalent in Western countries. Nor does democracy refer to the political party system. Rather, it denotes a system whereby the people are sovereign. Democracy is not endless discussion and debate, but rather a popular decision in favour of the common good. The people may delegate their sovereignty to managers whom they appoint, but they may not relinquish that sovereignty. Majority rule, exercised through the vote, does not imply that truth necessarily proceeds from majority vote; this is only a technique to assure, as closely as possible, an agreement between the people and their leaders. Democracy is also the system best suited to take care of a society's pluralism: by peaceful resolution of conflicts in ideas and by maintaining a positive relationship between the majority and the minority, and by maintaining freedom of expression for minorities, because the minority could be tomorrow's majority.

In democracy, where the people are the subject of constituent power, the fundamental principle is that of political equality. This principle is quite distinct from that of the legal equality of all people, which can give birth to no form of government (equality of all human beings is an apolitical equality, because it lacks the corollary of any possible inequality). Democratic equality is not an anthropological principle (it tells us nothing about the nature of man); it does not claim that all men are *naturally* equal, but only that all citizens are *politically* equal, because they all belong to the same political body. It is, thus, a substantial equality, based upon belonging or membership. As with all political principles, it implies the possibility of a distinction, in this case between citizens and non-citizens. The essential idea of democracy is neither that of the individual nor of humanity, but rather the idea of a body of citizens politically united into a people. Democracy is the system which situates within the people the source of power's legitimacy and then attempts to achieve, as closely as possible, the common identity of the governors and the governed. The objective, existential difference between the one and other can never be a difference of quality. This common identity is the expression of the identity of the people which, through its representatives, has the opportunity to be politically present through its action and participation in public life. Non-voting and turning one's back on public issues rob democracy of its very meaning.

Today, democracy is threatened by a whole series of offshoots and aberrations: the crisis of representation; the interchangeability of political programs; lack of consultation with the people in cases of major decisions affecting their very lives; corruption and technocracy; the disqualification of political parties, many of which have become machines geared primarily toward their election to office and whose candidates are often chosen only on the basis of their ability to be elected; the dominance of lobbyists upholding their private interests over the common good, etc. Add to all this the fact that the modern model of politics is obsolete: political parties are almost all reformist, while most governments are more or less impotent. 'The seizure of power', or 'political takeover', in the Leninist sense of the term, now leads to nothing. In a world of networks, revolt may be possible, but not revolution.

Renewing the democratic spirit implies not settling for mere representative democracy, but seeking to also put into effect, at every level, a true participatory democracy ('that which affects all the people should be the business of all the people'). In order to achieve this, it will be necessary to stop regarding politics as exclusively a state matter. Each citizen must be involved in the pursuit of the common good. Each common good must be identified and upheld as such. The self-absorbed consumer and the passive spectator-citizen will only become involved by the development of a radically decentralised form of democracy, beginning from the bottom, thereby giving to each citizen a role in the choice and control of his destiny. The procedure of referendum could also be useful. To counteract the overwhelming power of money, the supreme authority in modern society, there must be imposed the widest separation possible between wealth and political power.

8. Against Productivism; For New Forms of Labor

Work (in French *travail*, from the Latin *tripalium*, an instrument of torture) has never occupied a central position in ancient or traditional societies, including those which never practiced slavery. Because it is born out of the constraints of necessity, work does not exercise our freedom, as does the work accomplished wherein an individual may see an expression of himself. It is modernity which, through its productivist goal of totally mobilising all resources, has made of work a value in itself, the principal mode of socialisation, and an illusory form of emancipation and of the autonomy of the individual ('freedom through work'). Functional, rational, and monetised, this is 'heteronomous' work that individuals perform most often by obligation than out of vocation, and this work holds meaning for them only in terms of buying power, which can be counted out and measured. Production serves to stimulate consumption, which is needed as a compensation for time put in working. Work has thus been gradually monetised, forcing individuals to work for others in order to pay those who work for them. The possibility of receiving certain services freely and then reciprocating in some way has totally disappeared in a world where nothing has any value, but everything has a price (i.e., a world in which anything that cannot be quantified in monetary terms is held as negligible or non-existent). In a salaried society, each one gives up his time, more often than not, in trying to earn a living.

Now, due to new technologies, we produce more and more goods and services with constantly fewer workers. In Europe, these gains in productivity result in unemployment and they destabilise some of society's very structures. Such productivity favours capital, which uses unemployment and the relocation of workers to weaken the negotiating power of salaried workers. Thus, today the individual worker is not so much exploited, than rendered more and more useless; exclusion replaces alienation in a world ever globally richer, but where the number of poor people constantly increases (so much for the classic theory of trickle-down economics). Even the possibility of returning to full employment would demand a complete break with productivism and the gradual end of an era where payment by salary is the principal means of integration into social life.

The reduction of the length of the work week is a secular given which makes obsolete the Biblical imperative, 'You will labour by the sweat of your brow'. Negotiated reductions in the length of the work week and the concomitant increase of new workers to share their work ought to be encouraged, as well as the possibility of flexible adjustments (annual leaves, sabbaticals, job training courses, etc.) for every type of 'heteronomous' job: to work less in order to work *better* and in order to have some time for oneself to live and enjoy life. In today's society, the attraction and promise of goods grow ever larger, but increasing also is the number of people whose buying power is stagnating or even diminishing. Thus, it is imperative to gradually disassociate work from income. The possibility must be explored of establishing a fixed minimum stipend or income for every citizen from birth until death and without asking anything in return.

9. Against the Ruthless Pursuit of Current Economic Policies; For an Economy at the Service of the People

Aristotle made a distinction between *economics*, which has as its goal the satisfaction of man's needs, and *chrematistics*, whose ultimate end is production, the earning and appropriation of money. Industrial capitalism has been gradually overtaken by a financial capitalism whose goal is to realise maximum returns in the short run, all to the detriment of the condition of national economies and of the long-term interest of the people. This metamorphosis was brought about by the easy availability of credit, widespread speculation, the issuance of unreliable bonds, widespread indebtedness of individuals, firms, and nations, the dominant role of international investors, mutual funds that seek to make speculative profits, etc. The ubiquity of capital allows the financial markets to control politics. Economies become uncertain and even precarious, while the immense world financial bubble bursts from time to time, sending shockwaves throughout the entire financial network.

Economic thought is, moreover, couched in mathematical formulas which claim to be scientific by excluding any factor that cannot be quantified. Thus, the macroeconomic indices (GDP, GNP, the growth rate, etc.) reveal nothing about the actual condition of a society: disasters, accidents, or epidemics are here counted as positive, since they stimulate economic activity.

Faced with arrogant wealth, which aims only at growing larger still by capitalising on the inequalities and sufferings that it itself engenders, it is imperative to restore the economy to the service of individuals and their quality of life. The first steps should include: instituting, at an international level, a tax on all financial transactions, to cancelling the debt of Third World countries, and drastically revising the entire system of economic development. Priority should be given to self-sufficiency and to the needs of internal, national and regional markets. There needs to be an end to the international system of the division of labour. Local economies must be freed from the dictates of the World Bank and the IMF. Environmental laws ought to be enacted on an international scale. A way has to be found out of the double impasse of ineffective governmental economies, on the one hand, and hypercompetitive market-oriented economies, on the other, by strengthening a third sector (partnerships, mutual societies, and cooperatives) as well as autonomous organisations of mutual aid based on shared responsibility, voluntary membership, and non-profit organisations.

10. Against Gigantism; For Local Communities

The tendency to over-expansion and concentration produces isolated individuals who are thus more vulnerable and defenceless. Widespread exclusion and social uncertainty are the logical consequences of this system, which has wiped out almost all possibilities of reciprocity and solidarity. Faced with traditional, vertical pyramids of domination that inspire no confidence, faced with bureaucracies that are reaching more and more rapidly their level of incompetence, we enter a world of all sorts of cooperative networks. The former tension between a homogeneous civil society and a monopolistic Welfare State has, little by little, been reduced by the existence today of a whole web of organisations supportive of deliberative and well-functioning communities which are forming at every level of social life: the family, the neighbourhood, the village, the city, the professions and in leisure pursuits. It is only at this local level that one can create a standard of living worthy of human beings, not a fragmented life, and free of the demanding imperatives of speed, mobility and return on investment. This standard of living would be supported by fundamental, shared values, directed at the common good. Solidarity must no longer be seen as the result of an anonymous equality (poorly) guaranteed by the Welfare State, but rather as the result of a reciprocity implemented from the bottom up by organic communities taking charge of such matters as insurance and equitable distribution. Only responsible individuals in responsible communities can establish a social justice which is not synonymous with welfare.

This return to the local community will, by its very nature, return their natural vocation to families to provide education, socialisation, and mutual support. This will, in turn, permit individuals to interiorise social rules and laws which, today, are simply imposed from above and outside. The revitalisation of local communities must also be accompanied by a renaissance of the popular traditions that modernity has largely caused to decline. Even worse, modernity has often tried to 'market' these cultural traditions for the benefit of tourists only ('folkloric' shows). Fostering social interaction and a sense of celebration, such traditions inculcate a sense of life's cycles and provide temporal landmarks. Emphasising rhythmic passing of the ages and of the seasons, great moments in life, and the stages of the passing year, they nourish symbolic imagination and they create a social bond. These traditions are never frozen in time, but are in a constant state of renewal.

11. Against Megalopolis; For Cities on a Human Scale
Urbanism has, for more than fifty years, surrendered to the aesthetic of the ugly: bedroom communities with no horizon; residential areas totally lacking soul; grimy suburbs serving as municipal dumping

grounds; endless malls which disfigure the approaches to every city; the proliferation of anonymous 'non-places' given over to visitors who are all in a hurry; downtown areas given over completely to business and stripped of their traditional form of social life (cafés, universities, theatres, cinemas, public parks, etc.); disparate styles of apartment buildings; run-down neighbourhoods, or on the opposite end of the spectrum, neighbourhoods constantly under surveillance by hidden cameras and monitored by citizen patrols; the population shift from rural areas and concomitant urban crowding. They no longer build homes for living in but rather for surviving in an urban environment spoiled by the law of maximum financial return on investment and cold practicality. However, a place is, first and foremost, a link: working, moving about, living are not separate functions, but complex acts encompassing the totality of social life.

The city needs to be rethought as the locus of all our potentialities and the labyrinth of our passions and actions, rather than as the cold, geometric expression of economic order. Architecture and urbanism are practiced in the context of a local history and a particular geography which they should reflect. This would entail the revitalisation of an urbanism rooted in and harmonious with the local community, the revival of regional styles, the development of villages and moderate-sized towns in a network centred upon regional capital cities. It would also imply the opening up of rural areas; the gradual dismantling of bedroom communities and areas that are now strictly used for commercial or business purposes; the elimination of now-ubiquitous advertising; as well as diversification of means of transportation: undoing the current tyranny of the private car, increasing transportation of goods by rail, and revitalising public transportation, taking into consideration ecological imperatives.

12. Against Unbridled Technology; For an Integral Ecology

In a finite world, there are limits to growth. Resources, like growth itself, eventually reach their limit. The rapid generalisation of Western levels of production and consumption throughout the whole world could lead, within several decades, to the depletion of most available resources and to a series of climatic and atmospheric disasters with unforeseen consequences for the human race. The disregard shown for nature, the exponential undermining of biodiversity, the alienation of man by the machine, the depletion of our food supplies, all prove that 'always more' is not synonymous with 'always better'. Various ecological groups have upheld this position, which rejects completely the ideology of unlimited progress. We need to become more aware of our responsibilities as regards the organic and inorganic worlds in which we all move about.

The 'mega-machine' knows only one law — maximum return on investments. This must be countered with the principle of responsibility, which demands that the present generation act in such a way that future generations live in a world which is no less beautiful, no less rich, and no less diverse than the world we know today. We must also affirm the importance of the concrete person over the acquisition of wealth, power, and goods (to be more instead of to have more). Sound ecology calls us to move beyond modern anthropocentrism toward the development of a consciousness of the mutual coexistence of mankind and the cosmos. This 'immanent transcendence' reveals nature as a partner and not as an adversary or object. This does not diminish the unique importance of mankind, but it does deny man his exclusive position that Christianity and classical humanism had assigned to him. Economic *hubris* and Promethean technology must be held in check by a sense of balance and harmony. A worldwide effort must be undertaken to establish binding norms and guidelines for the preservation of biodiversity. Man has obligations to the animal and vegetal world. In like manner, standards must be set worldwide for the reduction of pollution. Firms and corporations which pollute should be taxed in proportion to the damage done. A certain level of de-industrialisation in the field of food-processing might favour local production and consumption as well as diversification of food sources. Approaches sympathetic to the cyclical renewal of natural resources must be sustained in the Third World and given priority in 'developed' societies.

13. For Independence of Thought and a Return to the Discussion of Ideas

Incapable of renewing itself, powerless and disillusioned by the failure of its objectives, modern thought has slowly transformed itself into a form of 'thought police' whose purpose is to excommunicate all those who diverge in any way from the currently dominant ideological dogmas. Former revolutionaries have rallied around the *status quo* while carrying over a taste for purges and anathemas from their former lives. This new form of treachery relies upon the tyranny of public opinion, as fashioned by the media, and takes the form of cleansing hysteria, enervating mawkishness or selective indignation. Rather than trying to understand the approaching new century, they keep rehearsing outdated issues and recycling old arguments, which are nothing more than a means to exclude or to discredit opponents. The reduction of politics to the sound management of increasingly problematic growth excludes the possibility of radically changing society or even the possibility of an open discussion of the ultimate goals of collective action.

Democratic debate thus finds itself reduced to nothing. One no longer discusses, one denounces. One no longer reasons, one accuses. One no longer proves, one imposes. All thoughts, all writings suspected of 'deviation' or even of 'drifting' are represented as consciously or unconsciously sympathetic to ideologies that are held to be highly suspect. Incapable of developing their own ideas or even of refuting the ideas of others, these censors fight not only against stated opinions, but also against supposed intentions. This unprecedented decline of critical thought is still more aggravated in France by Parisian navel-gazing. Thus, we have come to forget the traditional rules of civilised debate. One also begins to forget that freedom of opinion, whose disappearance has largely been met with indifference, allows for no exceptions. Fearing free choice by the people and disdaining their aspirations, one prefers the ignorance of the masses.

The New Right advocates a return to critical thinking and strongly supports total freedom of expression. Faced with censorship, 'disposable' ideas and the futility of passing fads, the New Right insists, now more than ever, on the need for a true renewal of critical thinking. The New Right advocates a return to debating issues, freed from the old divisions and fixed positions which block new approaches to old problems as well as new syntheses. The New Right calls all free minds to join in a common front against the disciples of Trissotin, Tartuffe, and Torquemada.[9]

---

9   Trissotin is a character from the play *The Learned Ladies* by Molière who pretends to be a great scholar in order to become the tutor to a group of women, although his real intention is only to make money from them. Similarly, Tartuffe is a character in a French play of the same name by Molière, written in 1664. In it, Tartuffe is believed to be a man of great religious fervour by others, but he is, in fact, a hypocrite who manipulates others into giving him what he wants. Tomás de Torquemada (1420-1498) was the most infamous Grand Inquisitor of the Spanish Inquisition. -Ed.

BIBLIOGRAPHY

Books

Arendt, Hannah. *The Origins of Totalitarianism.* New York: Meridian Books, 1950.

Aron, Raymond. *Democracy and Totalitarianism.* New York: Frederick A. Praeger Publishers, 1969.

Besançon, Alain. *La falsification du Bien.* Paris: Commentaire/Julliard, 1985. (Translated as *The Falsification of the Good: Soloviev and Orwell.* London: Claridge Press, 1994.)

_____. *Les origines intellectuelles du léninisme.* Paris: Calmann-Lévy, 1977. (Translated as *The Intellectual Origins of Leninism.* Oxford: Basil Blackwell, 1981.)

_____. *The Soviet Syndrome.* New York: Harcourt Brace Jovanovich, 1976.

Brzezinski, Zbigniew, and Carl J. Friedrich. *Totalitarian Dictatorship and Autocracy.* New York: Praeger Publishers, 1962.

Buchholz, Fritz. *Gleichberechtigung in Staats- und Völkerrecht.* Bleicherode am Harz: Verlag Carl Nieft, 1937.

Chaunu, Pierre. *Histoire et foi.* Paris: France-Empire, 1980.

Cohn, Norman. *Millennial Dreams in Action.* New York: Schocken, 1970.

de Benoist, Alain. *Die entscheidenden Jahre.* Tübingen: Grabert Verlag, 1982.

_____. *Les Idées à l'endroit*. Paris: Libres-Hallier, 1979.

_____. *Europe, Tiers monde, même combat*. Paris: Robert Laffont, 1986.

_____. *On Being a Pagan*. Atlanta: Ultra, 2004.

Debray, Régis. *Les Empires contre l'Europe*. Paris: Gallimard, 1985.

de Maistre, Joseph. *Considerations on France*. Cambridge: Cambridge University Press, 2003.

Dumont, Louis. *Essays on Individualism*. Chicago: The University of Chicago Press, 1986.

_____. *From Mandeville to Marx: The Genesis and Triumph of Economic Ideology*. Chicago: The University of Chicago Press, 1977.

Eliade, Mircea. *Histoire des croyances et des idées religieuses*. Paris: Payot, 1976. (Translated as *A History of Religious Ideas*, 3 vols. Chicago: University of Chicago Press, 1978-1985.)

_____. *The Myth of the Eternal Return, or Cosmos and History*. Princeton: Princeton University Press, 1965.

Eysenck, Hans Jürgen. *The Inequality of Man*. London: Temple Smith, 1973.

Faye, Guillaume. *Contre l'économisme: Principes d'économie politique*. Paris: Le Labyrinthe, 1982.

_____. *Le système à tuer les peuples*. Paris: Copernic, 1981.

Feuerbach, Ludwig. *The Essence of Christianity*. New York: Harper, 1957.

Flew, Antony. *The Politics of Procrustes*. New York: Prometheus Books, 1981.

Forsthoff, Ernst. *Der Staat der Industriegesellschaft*. Munich: Beck Verlag, 1971.

Gramsci, Antonio. *The Modern Prince and Other Writings*. New York: International Publishers, 1959.

Grant, Madison. *The Passing of the Great Race*. New York: Scribner, 1916.

Günther, Hans F. K. *The Racial Elements of European History*. Sussex: Historical Review Press, 2007.

_____. *The Religious Attitudes of the Indo-Europeans*. Sussex: Historical Review Press, 2001.

Hauer, Wilhelm. *Deutscher Gottschau*. Stuttgart: Karl Gutbrod, 1934.

Heidegger, Martin. *Introduction to Metaphysics*. Delhi: Motilal Banarsidass, 1999.

Heller, Mikhail, and Aleksandr Nekrich. *Utopia In Power*. New York: Summit Books, 1986.

Hocquenghem, Guy. *Lettre ouverte à ceux qui sont passés du col Mao au Rotary*. Paris: Albin Michel, 1986.

Hunke, Sigrid. *La vraie religion de l'Europe*. Paris: Le Labyrinthe, 1985.

Huyghe, François-Bernard, and Pierre Barbès. *La soft-idéologie*. Paris: Robert Laffont, 1987.

Jellinek, Georg. *Die Erklärung der Menschen- und Bürgerrechte*. Leipzig: Duncker und Humblot Verlag, 1904.

Jünger, Ernst. *Strahlungen*. Tübingen: Heliopolis Verlag, 1955.

King, Desmond S. *The New Right*. Chicago: The Dorsey Press, 1987.

Koestler, Arthur. *Darkness at Noon*. New York: The Modern Library, 1941.

Le Bon, Gustave. *The Crowd*. New York: Viking Press, 1960.

_____. *Psychologie politique*. Paris: Les amis de Gustave Le Bon, 1984.

Locke, John. *On Civil Government*. London: J. M. Dent and Sons, 1924.

Lorenz, Konrad. *Civilized Man's Eight Deadly Sins*. New York: Harcourt Brace Jovanovich, 1973.

_____. *The Waning of Humaneness*. Boston: Little, Brown, 1983.

Maffesoli, Michel. *La violence totalitaire*. Paris: PUF, 1979.

Marx, Karl. *Critique of the Gotha Programme*. New York: International Publishers, 1938.

Michels, Robert. *Political Parties.* New York: Dover Publications, 1959.

Miller, David. *The New Polytheism.* New York: Harper and Row, 1974.

Milner, Murray. *The Illusion of Equality.* Washington and London: Jossey-Bass Publishers, 1972.

Mohler, Armin. *Vergangenheitsbewältigung, oder wie man den Krieg nochmals verliert.* Krefeld: Sinus Verlag, 1980.

_____. *Die konservative Revolution in Deutschland 1918-1932.* Darmstadt: Wissenschaftliche Buchgesellschaft, 1972.

Mosca, Gaetano. *The Ruling Class.* New York: McGraw-Hill, 1934.

Pareto, Vilfredo. *Les systèmes socialistes,* 2 vols. Paris: Marcel Giard, 1926.

_____. 'Danger of Socialism'. *The Other Pareto.* Edited by Placido Bucolo. New York: St. Martin's Press, 1980.

Petitfils, Jean-Christian. *La Droite en France de 1789 à nos jours.* Paris: PUF, 1973.

Polin, Claude. *L'esprit totalitaire.* Paris: Éditions Sirey, 1977.

_____. *Le totalitarisme.* Paris: PUF, 1982.

_____. *Libéralisme, espoir ou peril?* Paris: La Table ronde, 1984.

Popper, Karl. *The Open Society and Its Enemies,* vol. 1: *The Spell of Plato.* London: Routledge and Kegan Paul, 1952.

Pound, Ezra. *Impact: Essays on Ignorance and the Decline of American Civilization.* Chicago: Henry Regnery, 1960.

Rauschning, Hermann. *The Revolution of Nihilism.* New York: Alliance Book Corporation, 1939.

Rees, John. *Equality.* New York: Praeger Publishers, 1971.

Renan, Ernest. *Histoire générale des langues sémitiques.* Paris: Imprimerie Impériale, 1853.

Revel, Jean-François. *Comment les démocraties finissent.* Paris: Pluriel, 1983. (Translated into English as *How Democracies Perish.* Garden City: Doubleday, 1984.)

Rihs, Charles. *Les philosophes utopistes.* Paris: Marcel Rivière, 1970.

Rosenberg, Alfred. *The Myth of the Twentieth Century.* Sussex: Historical Review Press, 2004.

Rougier, Louis. *La mystique démocratique: ses origines, ses illusions.* Paris: Éditions Albatros, 1983.

_____. *Celse contre les chrétiens.* Paris: Copernic, 1977.

_____. *Du Paradis à l'utopie.* Paris: Copernic, 1977.

Russell, Bertrand. *Why I am Not a Christian.* New York: Simon and Schuster, 1963.

Scheler, Max. *Das Ressentiment im Aufbau der Moralen.* Leipzig: Verlag der weissen Bucher, 1915. (Translated into English as *Ressentiment.* New York: Free Press of Glencoe, 1961.)

Schmitt, Carl. *Ex Captivitate Salus: Erfahrungen der Zeit 1945-47.* Cologne: Greven Verlag, 1950.

_____. *Die politische Romantik.* Munich and Leipzig: Duncker und Humblot Verlag, 1925. (Translated into English as *Political Romanticism.* Cambridge: MIT Press, 1986.)

_____. *The Concept of the Political.* Chicago: The University of Chicago Press, 2007.

_____. *The Crisis of Parliamentary Democracy.* Cambridge: MIT Press, 1986.

Scholz, Heinrich. *Zum 'Untergang des Abendlandes'.* Berlin: Verlag von Reuther und Reichard, 1920.

Schumpeter, Joseph A. *Capitalism, Socialism and Democracy.* New York: Harper and Row, 1942.

Sombart, Werner. *The Jews and Modern Capitalism.* Glencoe, Illinois: Free Press, 1951.

_____. *The Quintessence of Capitalism.* New York: Howard Fertig, 1967.

Sorel, Georges. *Le procès de Socrate: examen des thèses socratiques.* Paris: Alcan, 1889.

_____. *Reflections on Violence.* Cambridge: Cambridge University Press, 2002.

Spann, Othmar. *Der wahre Staat.* Leipzig: Verlag von Quelle und Meyer, 1921.

Spengler, Oswald. *The Decline of the West,* 2 vols. New York: Alfred A. Knopf, 1962.

_____. *Selected Essays.* Chicago: Henry Regnery, 1967.

Steinfels, Peter. *The Neoconservatives.* New York: Simon and Schuster, 1979.

Sternhell, Zeev. *The Birth of Fascist Ideology.* Princeton: Princeton University Press, 1994.

_____. *La Droite révolutionnaire, 1885-1914.* Paris: Seuil, 1978.

Stoddard, Lothrop. *Lonely America.* New York: Doubleday, 1932.

Talmon, Jacob L. *The Origins of Totalitarian Democracy.* New York: Frederick Praeger Publishers, 1960.

Thomson, David. *Equality.* Cambridge: Cambridge University Press, 1949.

Tillich, Paul. *The Eternal Now.* New York: Charles Scribner's Sons, 1963.

Troeltsch, Ernst. *The Social Teaching of the Christian Churches.* New York: Harper, 1960.

Viereck, Peter. *Metapolitics: The Roots of the Nazi Mind.* New York: Capricorn Books, 1961.

Walter, Gérard. *Les origines du communisme.* Paris: Payot, 1931.

Yanov, Alexander. *The Russian New Right.* Berkeley: University of California Press, 1978.

Yockey, Francis Parker. *Imperium.* New York: The Truth Seeker, 1962.

Zinoviev, Alexander. *Homo Sovieticus.* London: Victor Gollancz, 1985.

_____. *Le Gorbatchevisme.* Lausanne: L'Age d'homme, 1987.

_____. *The Reality of Communism.* London: Victor Gollancz, 1984.

Sinowjew, Alexander. *Die Diktatur der Logik.* Munich and Zurich: Piper, 1985.

_____. *Die Macht des Unglaubens: Anmerkungen zur Sowjet-Ideologie.* Munich and Zurich: Piper, 1986.

Books Containing Several Authors and Articles

Bérard, Pierre. 'Ces cultures qu'on assassine', in *La cause des peuples.* Paris: Le Labyrinthe, 1982.

Bokser, Ben Zion. 'Democratic Aspirations in Talmudic Judaism', in *Judaism and Human Rights.* Edited by Milton Konvitz. New York: W. W. Norton, 1972.

de Benoist, Alain. 'Pour une déclaration du droit des peoples', in *La cause des peuples.* Paris: Le Labyrinthe, 1982.

_____. 'Gleichheitslehre, Weltanschauung und "Moral"', in *Das unvergängliche Erbe.* Edited by Pierre Krebs. Tübingen: Grabert Verlag, 1982.

_____. 'L'Eglise, l'Europe et le Sacré', in *Pour une renaissance culturelle.* Edited by Pierre Vial. Paris: Copernic, 1979.

de Benoist, Alain, and Thomas Molnar. *L'éclipse du sacré.* Paris: La Table ronde, 1986.

Eysenck, Hans Jürgen. 'Vererbung und Gesellschaftspolitik: die Ungleichheit der Menschen und ihre gesellschaftlichen Auswirkungen', in *Die Grundlagen des Spätmarxismus.* Stuttgart: Verlag Bonn Aktuell, 1977.

Friedrich, Carl J. 'A Brief Discourse on the Origin of Political Equality'. *Equality.* Edited by J. R. Pennock and J. W. Chapman. New York: Atherton Press, 1967.

Krebs, Pierre. 'Gedanken zu einer kulturellen Wiedergeburt', in *Das unvergängliche Erbe: Altenativen zum Prinzip der Gleichheit.* Edited by Pierre Krebs. Tübingen: Grabert Verlag, 1981.

Lakoff, Sanford. 'Christianity and Equality', in *Equality.* Edited by J. R. Pennock and J. W. Chapman. New York: Atherton Press, 1967.

Markale, Jean. 'Aujourd'hui l'esprit païen?', in *L'Europe païenne.* Paris: Seghers, 1980.

Mohler, Armin. 'Die nominalistische Wende: ein Credo', in *Das un-vergängliche Erbe*. Edited by Pierre Krebs. Tübingen: Grabert Verlag, 1981.

Rackman, Emanuel. 'Judaism and Equality', in *Equality*. Edited by J. R. Pennock and J. W. Chapman. New York: Atherton Press, 1967.

Schaar, John. 'Equality of Opportunity and Beyond', in *Equality*. Edited by J.R. Pennock and J.W. Chapman. New York: Atherton Press, 1967.

Tawney, Richard H. Excerpts from *Equality. The Idea of Equality: An Anthology*. Edited by George L. Abernethy. Richmond: John Knox Press, 1959.

Valla, Jean-Claude. 'Une communauté de travail et de pensée', in *Pour une renaissance culturelle*. Edited by Pierre Vial. Paris: Copernic, 1979.

Vial, Pierre. 'Nouvelle Droite ou Nouvelle Culture?' *Pour une renaissance culturelle*. Edited by Pierre Vial. Paris: Copernic, 1979.

_____. 'Servir la cause des peuples?' *La cause des peuples*. Paris: Le Labyrinthe, 1982.

Book Reviews

Faye, Guillaume. Review of *Lettre ouverte à ceux qui sont passés du col Mao au Rotary*, by Guy Hocquenghem. *Éléments*, Autumn 1986, pp. 54-56.

Gottfried, Paul. Review of *L'éclipse du sacré*, by Alain de Benoist and Thomas Molnar. *The World and I*, December 1986, pp. 450-453.

Interviews

Interview with Ernst Nolte. 'Hitler war auch ein europäisches Phä-nomen'. *Die Welt*, 21 September 1987.

Unsigned Articles

'Behavior and Heredity'. *American Psychologist*, July 1972, pp. 660-661.

'Darwinisme et société'. *Nouvelle École*, Summer 1982, pp. 11-13.

'Gewalt statt Argumente gegen das Thule-Seminar'. *Elemente*, January-March, 1987, pp. 44-45.

'L'économie organique'. *Pour une renaissance culturelle.* Edited by Pierre Vial. Paris: Copernic, 1979, pp. 54-66.

'Mais qu'est-ce donc la Nouvelle droite?'. *La Quinzaine littéraire*, November 15, 1979, pp. 8-9.

'Les habits neufs de la droite française'. *Le Nouvel Observateur*, 8 July 1979, pp. 33-38.

Journals and Periodicals

Auerbach, Jerol S. 'Liberalism and the Hebrew Prophets'. *Commentary*, August 1987, pp. 58-60.

Baechler, Jean. 'De quelques contradictions du libéralisme'. *Contrepoint*, May 1976, pp. 41-62.

Barnes, I. R. 'Creeping Racism and Anti-Semitism'. *Midstream*, February 1984, pp. 12-14.

Bloom, Alexander. 'Neoconservatives in the 1980s'. *The World and I*, October 1986, pp. 679-692.

de Benoist, Alain. 'L'énigme soviétique dans le miroir de l'Occident'. *Nouvelle École* Summer 1982, pp. 109-129.

_____. 'Intelligentsia: les jeux du cirque'. *Le Figaro Magazine*, May 1979, pp. 81-83.

_____. 'L'ennemi principal'. *Éléments*, April-May 1982, pp. 37-47.

_____. 'Ludwig Woltmann et le darwinisme, ou le socialisme prolet-aryen'. *Nouvelle École*, Summer 1982, pp. 87-98.

_____. 'Monothéisme-polythéisme: le grand débat'. *Le Figaro Magazine*, 28 April 1979, pp. 81-84.

_____. 'Terrorisme: le vrai probleme'. *Éléments*, Winter 1986, pp. 5-18.

_____. 'Un homme supérieure'. *Éléments*, Spring 1983, pp. 5-12.

Faye, Guillaume. 'La fin du bas de laine'. *Éléments*, Spring-Summer 1984, pp. 29-42.

_____. 'Pareto "doxanalyste"'. *Nouvelle École*, Summer 1981, pp. 73-80.

Ferro, Marc. 'Y-a-t-il "trop de démocratie" en URSS?'. *Annales ESC*, July-August 1985, pp. 811-825.

Freund, Julien. 'Die Lehre von Carl Schmitt und die Folgen'. *Elemente*, First Quarter 1986, pp. 21-23.

Gress, David. 'Conservatism in Europe and America'. *The World and I*, October 1986, pp. 665-678.

_____. 'Benoist: From the Right to the Left'. *The World and I*, May 1987, pp. 434-439.

Hewitson, Harold T. 'G.R.E.C.E. Right Side Up'. *The Scorpion*, Autumn 1986, pp. 20-28.

Kaplan, Roger. 'The Imaginary Third World and the Real United States'. *The World and I*, May 1987, pp. 443-446.

Locchi, Giorgio. 'L'histoire'. *Nouvelle École*, Autumn-Winter, 1975, pp. 183-190.

Molnar, Thomas. 'American Culture: A Possible Threat'. *The World and I*, May 1987, pp. 440-442.

_____. 'La tentation païenne'. *Contrepoint*, June 1981, pp. 47-55.

Nisbet, Robert. 'The Fatal Ambivalence'. *Encounter*, December 1976, pp. 10-21.

_____. 'The Pursuit of Equality'. *Public Interest*, Spring 1974, pp. 103-120.

Ormierès, Sophie. 'Dissidence et dictature de masse en Union Soviétique'. *Esprit*, October 1986, pp. 45-52.

Polin, Claude. 'Le libéralisme et l'état providence ou le double dépit amoureux'. *Contrepoint*, nos. 50-51, 1985, pp. 59-69.

Roviello, Anne-Marie. 'Relativiser pour minimiser'. *Esprit*, October 1987, pp. 56-69.

Walker, Michael. 'Against All Totalitarianisms'. *The Scorpion*, Autumn 1986, pp. 3-6.

_____. 'Spotlight on the French New Right'. *The Scorpion*, Autumn 1986, pp. 8-14.

Wunenburger, Jean-Jacques. 'Les droits de l'homme, du fondement philosophique à l'illusion idéologique'. *Contrepoint* (no. 50-51, 1985), pp. 99-109.

INDEX

Books published by Arktos:

The Problem of Democracy
by Alain de Benoist

The Jedi in the Lotus
by Steven J. Rosen

Archeofuturism
by Guillaume Faye

A Handbook of Traditional Living

Tradition & Revolution
by Troy Southgate

Can Life Prevail?
A Revolutionary Approach to the Environmental Crisis
by Pentti Linkola

Metaphysics of War:
Battle, Victory & Death in the World of Tradition
by Julius Evola

The Path of Cinnabar:
An Intellectual Autobiography
by Julius Evola

Journals published by Arktos:

The Initiate: Journal of Traditional Studies

The Initiate 2: Journal of Traditional Studies

Lightning Source UK Ltd.
Milton Keynes UK
UKOW04f2050130917
309151UK00002B/401/P